How the game was played

How the game was played

Essays in sports history

Wray Vamplew

*Emeritus Professor of Sports History, University of Stirling.
Visiting Professor, Manchester Metropolitan University.
Special Projects Editor, International Journal of the
History of Sport.*

EER
Edward Everett Root, Publishers, Brighton, 2016.

Edward Everett Root, Publishers, Co. Ltd.,
30 New Road, Brighton, Sussex, BN1 1BN, England.
www.eerpublishing.com

edwardeverettroot@yahoo.co.uk

Wray Vamplew
How the game was played.
Essays in sports history.

First published in England in 2016.

ISBN 9781911204299 Paperback.
ISBN 9781911204312 Hardback.
ISBN 9781911204893 ebook.

© Wray Vamplew 2016.

Wray Vamplew has asserted his right under the Copyright, Designs and Patents Act 1998 to be identified as the author of this work.

The cover illustration is taken from the cover of Edmund Routledge, The Handbook of Cricket (London, Routledge, Warne, & Routledge, 1862), a volume in the series Routledge's Sixpenny Handbooks. Courtesy of the John Spiers Collection of Victorian and Edwardian Fiction and Non-fiction.

All rights reserved. No part of this publication may be reproduced, stored in a retrieval system or transmitted, in any form or by any means, electronic, mechanical, photocopying, recording or otherwise, without the prior permission of the copyright owner.

Cover designed by Pageset Limited, High Wycombe, Buckinghamshire.
Printed and bound in England by Lightning Source, Milton Keynes, UK.

Contents of Collection

Introduction to Collection vii

PRACTISING SPORTS HISTORY

Analysing the Game: Evidence and Knowledge in Sports History [originally published in *East Asian Sports Thoughts* 2 (2011), 1–17]. 1

SPORTING CONDUCT

Sports Crowd Disorder in Britain 1870–1914: Causes and Controls [originally published in *Journal of Sport History*, 7.1 (1980), 5–20] 15

Bulimic Practices and Alcohol Consumption: Performance Enabling and Performance Enhancing Mechanisms in Nineteenth-Century British Sport [originally published in *Performance Enhancement and Health* (2012), 51–54]......... 37

'Remembering Us Year After Year': The Glasgow Charity Cup 1876–1966 [originally published in *Recorde* 1.2, (2008), 1–27]... 51

FIELD SPORTS

Sports Without Rules: Hunting, Shooting and Fishing in Edwardian Britain [originally published in *European Studies in Sport History* 2.1 (2009), 34–51] 77

Captains Courageous: the Gentleman Rider in British Horseracing 1866–1914 (with Joyce Kay) [originally published in *Sport in History* 26.3 (2006), 370–385] 97

HORSERACING

Reduced Horsepower: The Jockey Club and the Regulation of British Horseracing [originally published in *Journal of Entertainment Law* 2.3 (2003), 94–111] 115

A Modern Sport? 'From Ritual to Record' in British Horseracing (with Joyce Kay) [originally published in *Ludica* 9 (2003), 125–139] 137

GOLF

Women to the Fore: Accommodation and Resistance at the British Golf Club before 1914 (with Jane George and Joyce Kay) [originally published in *Sporting Traditions* 23.2 (2007), 79–98] 161

The Rough and the Fairway: Processes and Problems in Ryder Cup Team Selection 1927–2006 (with Joyce Kay) [originally published in *Polish Journal of Physical Culture and Tourism* 14.1 (2007), 27–35] 185

Child Work or Child Labour? The Caddie Question in Edwardian Golf [originally published in *Idrottsforum* (April 2008 online)] 203

SPORTING HERITAGE

Facts and Artefacts: Sports Museums and Sports Historians [originally published in *Journal of Sport History* 25.2 (1998), 268–282] 223

Taking a Gamble or a Racing Certainty: Sports Museums and Public Sports History [originally published in *Journal of Sport History* 31.2 (2004), 177–191] 245

Introduction to Collection

This collection draws on publications that cover my career as a sports historian, a career in which I have endeavoured to pioneer new areas of research, combine theoretical concepts with sound empirical data, and bring elements of economic analysis to bear on the sporting past. I have supplemented the original articles with references to additional work that I have done in the particular areas documented here.

Article One, based on a keynote address to the Taiwanese Sociology Association's 2010 Congress, summarises how I feel sports historians should approach their work. I emphasise that sports history is a broad church that can encompass varying approaches but that my personal preference is for a quantified one that is anchored in empiricism but which applies social science concepts and theories. For variations on this theme readers are directed to some of my other publications including one that is part of a debate on the use of evidence by historical sociologists.[1]

The next three articles relate to aspects of sporting conduct, the modern catchphrase for what the Victorians called fair play. Article Two was a pioneering effort in looking at crowd behaviour which, unlike many later works by both social historians and historical sociologists, focussed on several sports not just football. Along with two other pieces, one written as part of a tribute to one of my Ph.D. supervisors and the other in a compilation of social science writing on violence, and a chapter in my book on the origins of professional sport in Britain, it shows that the 'hooligan' problem among sports spectators existed before the First World War.[2] In later years I looked at Australian sport, both at crowd misbehaviour and player violence.[3] Additionally with Paul Dimeo, a Stirling colleague, I prepared a report for UKSport on contemporary efforts to disseminate the concepts of sportspersonship and fair play globally.[4] The results were disappointing in that we found that improvement by exhortation and osmosis was the overwhelming feature of most strategies. For the record I am a firm believer in original sin where sport is concerned. I do not think that there ever was such a thing as pure sport devoid of cheating and gamesmanship. Article Three brought together in a nineteenth-century context two research interests of mine, weight-watching jockeys and the use and abuse of alcohol by athletes. More on these, with material for the twentieth century, can be found elsewhere.[5] In contrast to some of the negative images generated above, Article Four considers a positive side of sport, the development of the Glasgow Charity Cup, a precursor of what today is termed corporate social responsibility. The success of this Scottish competition stimulated similar charitable ventures throughout British elite football. More generally, as shown in an article I wrote with Joyce Kay, another Stirling colleague, charity matches and tournaments provided an intermediate stage as football transitioned from friendlies to league organisation.[6]

Rules are central to the conduct of most sports and in an article in 2007 I attempted to bring some structure to an explanation of their development.[7] Article Five was a follow up to this in which I examined the field sports of hunting, shooting and fishing that apparently existed in the absence of any rules, relying instead on custom and convention. More on field sports can be found in an encyclopedia that I edited with two ex-colleagues from De Montfort University.[8] The hunting field, along with military service, was a major training ground for the steeplechase jockey. Article Six shows that in the late nineteenth century the amateur ride could sometimes compete successfully against the professional jockey, but also, with reference back to sporting conduct, the term 'gentleman rider' could be interpreted very flexibly. More on jockeys, both amateur and paid, can be found in another article of mine.[9]

My work in sports history began with *The Turf* published in 1976 and horseracing has featured extensively in my publications over the years.[10] Article Seven develops a chapter of *The Turf* by further exploring the role of the Jockey Club in British flatracing and argues that, contrary to conventional belief, the Club did not control racing from its inception. Article Eight, written with Joyce Kay, tested one of the overarching theories of sports history, the modernisation schema of Allen Guttmann, with reference to British horseracing. Our conclusion was that too little attention had been given to the roles of gambling, professionalization and commercialisation. We went on to write an *Encyclopedia of Horseracing* in which we eschewed the traditional format of lists of winners and descriptions of courses and included entries some previously neglected areas such as the link between racing and the arts, the church and alcohol. It looked at the social, economic and political forces that shaped the development of the sport and emphasised the historical duality of continuity and change.[11]

The other sport to which I have devoted substantial research time is golf. Traditionally this sport has been viewed as a male preserve with obstacles raised against female involvement, but Article Nine suggests that, although discrimination against women certainly existed, it was not absolute and indeed women had a significant role in the organisation, promotion and development of golf. A later article expands this review of discrimination from gender to class.[12] Until the advent of the Ryder Cup in 1927, which saw teams representing the PGAs of Britain and America playing against each other, golf at the professional level was essentially composed of tournaments for individual competitors. The Ryder Cup has since become one of the premier competitions on the golfing calendar, especially after 1979 when the British team was expanded to include players on the European PGA tour, a rare instance of Europeans combining into one sports team. Article Ten explores the politics of national identity within the context of this particular biennial event. Elsewhere I have written on the on the Ryder Cup and on professional golfers more generally.[13] Article Eleven looks at the lowest level of employment in Edwardian professional golf, the humble bag carrier, the caddy. It can be seen as a pioneering effort to examine the employment of children historically in sport. The work of the caddy, child and adult, can be set in the wider context of the development of the golf club itself.[14]

I have also written on another aspect of golf's history in an assessment of the role of the British Golf Museum at St Andrews in preserving that sport's heritage.[15] Sports historians can be guardians of a nation's sporting heritage, but sports museums are its public face. Article Twelve has become a standard citation in sports museum historiography. It argued that, whilst they could replicate the performance, drama, passion and emotion of sport, too often they concentrated on sport that was competitive, adult and male-dominated; that they concentrated on the nostalgia market, perpetuated myths, lacked historical objectivity and context, eschewed the controversial and had an obsession with winners and winning. Article Thirteen was a follow up to this written after being involved in a National Horseracing Museum exhibition on betting. Working behind the scenes persuaded me to modify some of my earlier views and understand why the restrictions placed on museum curators forced them to adopt certain policies and stances. Since then I have produced a comparison of four London sports museums at Twickenham, Lord's, Wimbledon and Chelsea.[16] As a final point I note that some aspects of heritage should be remembered but not preserved or replicated. Would those golfers who commemorate their sport by playing in heritage competitions using hickory clubs and gutta percha balls still want children as young as seven to carry their bags?

References

1. Wray Vamplew, 'Empiricist Versus Sociological History: Some Comments on the "Civilizing Process"', *Sport in History* 27.2 (2007), 161–171; Wray Vamplew, 'Sport History' in Joseph Maguire (ed.), *Handbook of Social Sciences and Sport* (Champaign IL: Human Kinetics, 2014), 9–34; Wray Vamplew, 'Some Thoughts on Methodology in Sports History: Addresses to the Delegates at the Sports Government and Governance in Asia Conference', *International Journal of the History of Sport* 32.8 (2015), 982–985.

2. Wray Vamplew, 'Ungentlemanly Conduct: The Control of Soccer Crowd Behaviour in England 1888–1914' in T.C. Smout (ed.), *The Search for Wealth and Stability* (London: Macmillan, 1979), 139–154; Wray Vamplew, 'Unsporting Behaviour: The Control of Football and Horseracing Crowds in England 1875–1914' in Jeffrey H. Goldstein (ed.), *Sports Violence* (New York: Springer Verlag, 1983), 21–31; Wray Vamplew, *Pay Up and Play the Game: Professional Sport in Britain 1875–1914* (Cambridge: Cambridge University Press, 1988), 266–277.

3. Wray Vamplew, *Violence in Australian Sport: Its Extent and Control* (Canberra: Australian Sports Commission, 1991); Wray Vamplew,

Introduction to Collection [xi

'Sports Crowd Disorder: An Australian Survey in John O'Hara (ed.), *Crowd Violence at Australian Sport* (Sydney: ASSH, 1992), 79–111; Wray Vamplew, 'Wogball: Ethnicity and Violence in Australian Soccer' in Richard Giulianotti and John Williams (eds.), *Games Without Frontiers: Football Identity and Modernity* (Aldershot: Arena, 1994), 207–224.

4. Wray Vamplew and Paul Dimeo, *Sporting Conduct Initiatives: An International Perspective* (London: UKSport, 2004).

5. Tony Collins and Wray Vamplew, *Mud, Sweat and Beers: A Cultural History of Sport and Alcohol* (Oxford: Berg, 2002); 'Sport and Alcohol: An Anomalous Alliance' in Stephen Stannard, Farah Palmer and Neil Hood (eds.), *Sport and Alcohol: Understanding the Mix* (Palmerston North: Massey University Press, 2005), 183–190; 'Alcohol and the Sportsperson: An Anomalous Alliance' in Paul Dimeo (ed.), *Sport, Drugs and Alcohol: A Critical History* (Abingdon: Routledge, 2006), 390–411.

6. Wray Vamplew and Joyce Kay,' Beyond Altruism: British Football and Charity 1877–1914', *Soccer and Society* 11.3 (2010), 181–197. An expanded and amended version of this is being published as Wray Vamplew, '"It is pleasing to know that football can be devoted to charitable purposes": British Football and Charity 1870–1918', *Sport in Society* 19.3 (2016) 356–377.

7. Wray Vamplew, 'Playing with the Rules: Influences on the Development of Regulation in Sport', *International Journal of the History of Sport* 24.7 (2007), 843–871.

8. Tony Collins, John Martin and Wray Vamplew (eds.), *Encyclopedia of British Traditional Rural Sports* (London: Routledge, 2005).

9. Wray Vamplew, 'Still Crazy After All Those Years: Continuity in a Changing Labour Market for Professional Jockeys, *Contemporary British History* 14.2 (2000), 115–145.

10. For a survey see Wray Vamplew, 'From Godolphin to Godolphin: The Turf Relaid', in Rebecca Cassidy (ed.) *The Cambridge Companion to Horseracing* (Cambridge: Cambridge University Press, 2013), 57–68.

11. Wray Vamplew and Joyce Kay, *The Encyclopedia of British Horseracing* (London: Routledge, 2005).

12. Wray Vamplew, 'Sharing Space: Inclusion, Exclusion and Accommodation at the British Golf Club Before 1914', *Sport and Social Issues*, 34.3 (2010), 359–375.

13. Richard Holt, Peter N. Lewis and Wray Vamplew, *The Professional Golfers Association 1901–2001: One Hundred Years of Service to Golf* (Droitwich: Grant Books, 2002); Wray Vamplew, 'Exploited Labour or Successful Workingmen: Golf Professionals and Professional Golfers

in Britain before 1914, *Economic History Review*, 61.1 (2008), 54–79.

14. Wray Vamplew, 'Concepts of Capital: An Approach Shot to the History of the British Golf Club Before 1914', *Journal of Sport History* 39.2 (2012), 299–231.

15. Wray Vamplew, 'Replacing the Divots: Guarding Britain's Golfing Heritage, in Jeffrey Hill, Kevin Moore and Jason Wood (eds.), *Sport, History and Heritage: An Investigation into the Public Representation of Sport*, Boydell and Brewer, Oxford, 2012), 147–160.

16. Wray Vamplew, 'Renamed, Refurbished and Reconstructionist: Comparisons and Contrasts in Four London Sports Museums, in Murray G. Phillips (ed.), *Representing the Sporting Past in Museums and Halls of Fame*, New York: Routledge, 2012), 130–140.

Analysing the Game: Evidence and Knowledge in Sports History

Introduction

No fully informed debate on sport can take place without reference to the historical dimension. If we want to know where we are going it is useful to know where we have been. In simple terms history provides the benchmarks for measuring progress or, conversely, the lack of it. We cannot properly study contemporary sport without a sense of history for the sporting past helped shape the sporting present and, by implication, the sporting future. All sports have some 'inheritance from the past' (Polley 2007: 12), be it rules, governing bodies, styles of play, competitions or equipment, none of which are totally reinvented every time you go out to play.

The role of the sports historian is to set straight the sporting record: not just the basic 'sportifacts' confirming who won what, where and by how many, but, more importantly, offering an explanation of why and when sport changed [and also why change sometimes did not occur] and how it has arrived at a particular situation.

In doing this sports historians often borrow concepts from other disciplines, especially when they are investigating a historical topic in the light of modern developments in social science theory. However history, including sports history, can lay claim to some key concepts that it has made its own, in particular the duality of *continuity* and *change* as well as *heritage*. Sports historians are interested in explaining why some sports of the pre-industrial period, folk football being a prime example, continue to be played into the twenty-first century (Hornby 2008) but that others such as stowball, pall mall and hawkey have disappeared from the scene (Collins, Martin and Vamplew

2005). They want to trace the process of how some sports changed in character and structure so that, whilst maintaining their basic theme, they have been accepted by a modern audience as with cricket's limited overs and Twenty20 versions. They also wish to explain the development of new sports, often associated with technological change such as the coming of bicycle racing, speedway and sky-diving, but also the long residuals associated with sport, the unholy trinity of sex, alcohol and gambling.

Heritage is another historical concept. It can cover a wide spectrum of visual and material culture including defunct and nostalgic sports sites, statues and other effigies, streets and stadia named after sporting celebrities, photographs and film, ephemera and memorabilia. Sports heritage has also become part of our speech in that sporting terminology has entered the vernacular as with 'throwing in the towel' from prize-fighting, the' rub of the green' from golf, and 'stickler for the rules' from early wrestling in which judges used sticks to assess if a competitor's shoulders were pinned to the floor.

Approaches and Methodology

Within methodology there are dichotomies between those who opt for quantification and those who prefer a qualitative approach; between those who seek information at the aggregate level (often the quantifiers) and those who look at the individual (mainly the non-statistical historians); between those who apply theory and theoretical concepts and those who are more empirically focussed; and between those who pose modern questions in an historical setting and those who try to understand what mattered to those in the past.

Statistics provide a quantified basis for historical assertions. Sport is full of statistics but to batting averages and record times should be added such things as the proportion of players from a particular ethic background or the gender balance of sports club membership. As elsewhere in the social sciences, argument by example is no substitute for the use of hard, quantified data: measurement can allow historians to be more precise in their answers (Cronin 2009). Even to postulate that a relationship is positive or negative is not enough; we need to know the strength of the relationship not just its direction. The great contribution of the quantifiers is to help determine what is typical. A biography of Harry Vardon, the Tiger Woods of his day, contributes to the understanding of a champion golfer troubled by tuberculosis and marital difficulties (Howell 1991). This is interesting but more useful as sports history if it is contextualised into asking if tuberculosis was an industrial disease of professional golfers and whether the marriage problems emanated from the time away from home making a living as an elite professional designing courses and playing in championships. Staying with golf, if you study 3,000 professional golfers you are able to say something about the average age at appointment and retirement, the length of career, the degree of mobility between clubs, and the modal level of earnings (Vamplew 2008a). Yet this strength might be seen as a weakness by researchers more concerned with the experience of the individual. In seeking to generalise, aggregation can marginalise those who do not fit the standard pattern, those who are statistical outliers.

In his seminal work Booth (2005) takes sports historians to task for a failure to engage more extensively with theory and criticises those who simply gather facts to tell a story. Yet Booth can be too harshly judgemental and appears unwilling to accept that approaches other than his own can still be useful. Although (very) few sports historians discuss theoretical issues, many implicitly do use theory, or more precisely, theoretical concepts, to help them frame questions. Booth (2010) acknowledges that theoretical frameworks such as modernisation, hegemony, feminism, discourse and textualism have been embraced in this way. Yet there is a worry that these concepts are being applied uncritically. The concept of the 'body' pervades a corpus of writing by sports historians but how many of them are clearly aware of the subtleties and complexities of Foucault's work on the knowledge-body-power trilogy? Booth plays down the possibility that the theory being applied could be erroneous. However, no theory is immutable. If the facts do not fit the theory then the historian should check the facts again and, if still convinced they are correct, then the theory should be modified. Historians must not only be prepared to use theory, they also must be prepared to adapt it. Until substantiated by evidence theories are just competing hypotheses. They might aid our understanding but they do not explain a situation completely. Empirical support is a necessary concomitant for accepting any hypothesis.

Generally sports historians have applied the theories of other disciplines to historical material rather than develop theories of their own. Two notable exceptions are the overarching theories to explain the development of sport put forward by Guttmann and Szymanski.

Guttmann (1978; 2004) postulated sports history's own version of 'modernisation' in which he argued that seven features of modernisation could be used to measure how near a sport at any time in its history was to being modern. He saw such modernisation as being a cultural expression of an increasingly scientific world. First modern sport was secular with no religious reasons for participation. Second, it should demonstrate equality: theoretically everyone should have an opportunity to compete and conditions of competition should be the same for all contestants. Third, it introduced the idea of specialisation: everyone who wanted to could join in folk football, a sport in which there were no sharply defined roles, but the emphasis on achievement in modern sport brought in specialisation both within a sport and between sports. Fourth came rationalisation, in particular the development of rules which in primitive societies were often considered 'divine instructions' – God-given rituals, not to be tampered with by mere humans; in contrast non-secular modern sports have been invented and have written rules. Even more rationalisation came via the development of coaching and sports science. His fifth feature was bureaucratisation. Almost every major modern sport has its national and international organisation which have developed extensive bureaucracies to establish universal rules for their sport and oversee their implementation. These were not required when there were no written rules. Sixth was quantification by which modern sports transform every athletic feat into statistics. Following on from quantification is his seventh point, the modern emphasis on records.

In the early eighteenth century a movement began in Britain which involved the formation of clubs for many purposes not least sports such as cricket, golf, pugilism and horseracing. They enabled people with a common purpose to come together, provided a basis for agreeing common rules and regulations, created a framework for competitive interaction, and secured a location for participation and sociability. Szymanski (2008a, 2008b) has argued that modern British sport emerged from these new forms of associativity which developed autonomously in Britain following the retreat of the state from the control of associative activities. This was in contrast, he contends, to the situation in countries such as France and Germany where club formation continued to require the explicit or implicit approval of the state. Here modern sports developed in ways consistent with, or even in the service of, the objectives of the state, most notably the need to maintain military preparedness.

To return to the point about theory not being immutable, although Guttmann's model has stood the test of time it has not done so in its entirety. There have been modifications which suggest that his model required more input on press publicity, commercialisation and professionalisation and a recent major criticism has been made of his use of Weberian concepts (Adelman 1986; Vamplew and Kay 2003; Tomlinson and Young 2010). Symanski's critics (Riess 2008; Krüger 2008; MacLean 2008; Nathaus 2009), acknowledge the ambition of the analysis but suggest missing elements and alternative causal factors. They argue that more evidence is required to support the hypothesis; that he should have looked further back in time for his European material; that he failed adequately to address the issue of class; and that he understated the role of commercialisation.

Sports historians can approach the content of their research in two main ways. Issues of current interest can be taken and it can be asked whether these applied in the past. Historians might consider body performance in Victorian sport, whether private ownership of sports clubs raised any problems in Edwardian sport, or how sport coped in the past with economic recession. Here there is a possibility of applied history with the past offering advice to the present. The other approach is to ask what sport meant and what aspects of sport mattered during the time period being studied. Hence what might be looked at is the Scottish Football Association's worries about disguised professionalism in the early 1890s or President Roosevelt's concern with violence in American college football. Here the past is being understood on its own terms. Nevertheless it can still be analysed using modern concepts or theories.

Evidence

Booth (2005: 210, 81) maintains that sport history generally remains 'very firmly anchored to a bedrock of empiricism' and criticises sports historians' 'slavish devotion to sources and evidence'. However unless there is some evidence from the past there can be no sports history. Nevertheless it should be acknowledged that there is a danger that a totally empirical approach can result in the building up of far too much detail so that no patterns or explanations can be advanced. This is sometimes the case with the enthusiastic, non-academic historian amassing facts about their favourite team or player, but even then it can provide information with which to test ideas and hypotheses. Many writers too may offer 'history by example' in which statements are illustrated by pertinent examples but the reader should query whether the examples are representative or the most interesting. Readers also need to be aware that some researchers might follow the concept of what could be termed 'reverse research' in which the search is solely for evidence that will justify pre-determined views.

History is an empirically-based, interpretive social science. What historians do is utilise evidence in such a way as to create 'cumulative plausibility' so that readers are increasingly convinced by the argument (Holt 2000: 50). History is thus dependent on evidence though it important for sports historians to interrogate their sources so as to assess their authenticity and validity. Historians should be aware that archives are sites of power that privilege some information above others. What evidence is collected and what is saved can be functions of power in past and present society. Hence subordinate groups – usually people who do not keep diaries, are not interviewed, and are too often nameless – do not always get their voice 'heard' in historical documents. A case in point is an inquiry by the Agenda Club (1912) into the welfare of golf caddies in Edwardian Britain which took evidence from golf club secretaries but not from a solitary caddie. Booth (2006: 97) has shown that all references to the alleged misconduct of Australian swimming icon Dawn Fraser during the Tokyo Olympics have been physically cut from the archives of the Australian Swimming Union. Similarly photographs can be doctored, newspapers can be beholden to the political views of their proprietor, oral testimony may be affected by false memory, and committee minutes can hide the intensity of a debate. Prior to television newspapers were 'the great instrument of popular communication' (Hill 2006a:121), and sports historians have placed great, perhaps undue, reliance on them as a source for reconstructing the history of sport by dint of match reports, details of AGMs, and interviews with players. However, Hill for one has stressed that the press should be seen as a text to be interpreted rather than as a factual source to be accepted. Indeed some aspects of reportage are on a par with inventing tradition: adding anecdotes, selecting facts and forwarding opinion can help sell newspapers but tarnish them as a reliable, straightforward source material. As sportswriter Koppett has pointed out journalists write tomorrow's news not history (Booth 2005: 90).

Historians should always ask three four questions of any primary source material. When was it produced? What was the authority of the person producing it? Why was it produced? And what is its code? It is important to know if a document was contemporary to the event being investigated or one produced some time later with the benefit of hindsight. It is important to know if the author of the material had some expert knowledge or insider information and whether they were carrying any value judgements in their cultural baggage. It is important to know whether there were any hidden agendas lying behind the overt reason for the production of a document. It is also important to know the terminology which is employed.

Sports have changed over time and a description of a game or sporting event today might be almost incomprehensible to spectators of yesteryear; and, of course, the reverse. Ideas and philosophies can also change over time. A case in point is the perceived relationship between sport and alcohol. Today it is recognised that alcohol depresses the nervous system, impairs both motor ability and judgement, reduces endurance, and, as a diuretic, can cause dehydration, none of which are conducive to sports performance. In the past, however, the drinking of alcohol, particularly ales and porters, was positively encouraged as a perceived aid to strength and stamina. In the 1880s adverts professing the fitness-aiding qualities of alcohol were common and even in the interwar years Bass advertised its beers as health and fitness promoting (Collins and Vamplew 2002) Then there are the changing definitions of what constituted an 'amateur' and what a 'professional'. These used to be social not economic concepts. In rowing, for example, 'Gentlemen' could row against each other for money prizes and remain amateur, but working men were automatically labelled non-amateur (Vamplew 2004: 185–187).

Is the person responsible for producing the material they any value judgements in their baggage? For example, on the drug debate are they an official, an athlete, a convicted athlete, a chemist, a doctor, a member of the public, a member of the IOC. Whatever their position it is likely that their standpoint is not a neutral one and researchers must be aware of this when assessing the value of their statements.

It is important to know if there were any hidden agenda lying behind the overt reason for the production of a document. In the 1890s the Americans set up a Baseball Commission to decide when the game had originated in America. It decided that it was invented by Abner Doubleday at Cooperstown in 1839. Three things should be noted. First it is rare that a game can be invented at a particular point in time by any one individual: most games have long antecedents. Second, it was convenient to use Doubleday's name as the originator as he was a Civil War hero with whom few would take issue. Finally, the Commission was a political one with the task of showing that baseball did not emerge (as it really did) out of rounders which suffered the dual disadvantage of being not only a girl's game but also a British one (Block 2005)!

Finally if you take on sports history research you need to know the code i.e. the language and terminology of the sport under review. Every sport has its own concepts and terms impenetrable except to the initiated. Who but a pigeon fancier would know that a 'race ring' is what is clipped to a bird's leg before an event or, to maintain an ornithological theme, how many outside golf appreciate that an 'albatross' is three shots under par in golf?

Traditionally sports historians, like other historians, have relied on written sources for their evidence, among them minute books, letters, diary entries, official reports, and especially newspaper columns. In recent years these have, however, been supplemented by new sources: oral and email interviews, visual sources such as photographs, film and art works; ethnographic ones where sports history is explored by site visits; and others where material culture is subjected to historical examination. Yet, as with more conventional sources, these need to be interrogated and interpreted.

Oral history can provide a personal perception of events and what they meant to particular people, but they can go back only as far as living memory. Moreover there are the dangers of false and selective memory, the random survival of those involved, and the danger of hindsight being employed. However, in producing material not available from other sources, oral recollection can give life to dry historical evidence.

Huggins (2008: 327) has appealed for a more effective exploitation of visual material by sports historians for 'to exclude the visual is to reject a key area of human [sporting] experience.' Photographs have often been used by sports historians to illustrate points they were making, but they can also become the focus of the research itself as in Osmond's (2010) socio-political interpretation of the iconic picture of the 1968 black power salute at the Mexico Olympics in which he gave due credence to the white Australian athlete, Peter Norman, who shared the podium with black Americans Tommie Smith and John Carlos. Osmond points out that the captioning, positioning and accompanying text all have an explanatory and/or interpretive role. Some versions omit the white runner altogether! Both film and photograph confirm the very existence of the past with film having the added dimension of movement, the body in action being a central feature of sport. Early documentary film from Edwardian Britain has allowed historians to see how sport was actually played and shown the overt composition of the crowd (Toulmin 2006); Huggins (2007) has looked at how interwar newsreels showed women's sport through the male gaze; and in the antipodes Headon (1999) has studied how Australian sport was presented in silent movies. But again the visual evidence, like all other forms, has to be interrogated. When researching their book on the relationship between sport and alcohol, Collins and Vamplew (2002: 6–7) found that not all inn signs apparently depicting sport actually had a sporting heritage. Many bears, bulls, falcons and greyhounds represented the coats-of-arms of the local nobility rather than animals of sport.

Some postmodernists have suggested that fiction could be a

valuable source as it was a cultural force that shaped how people understood the world around them (Hill 2006b). Yet sports historians have been reluctant to use such sources, viewing them as unreliable and subjective. Nevertheless novels, particularly those written within the period being studied, can cast light on the context within which sport took place (Johnes 2007b). Literary texts can add colour and give insights into matters on which conventional sources are opaque, in particular the role of sport in everyday life. They can also bring in the passion and emotion of sport, something lacking in most academic histories.

Occupying the middle ground between the fiction of the novel and overtly factual accounts are autobiographies which often contain fictive elements and as such, despite being 'probably the most substantial body of published material on the history of sport' (Taylor 2008: 470), have been regarded by most sports historians as an imperfect source of information. Nevertheless these self-narratives do purport to relate to real experiences and are not written in cultural isolation. Hence, at a minimum, they can provide atmosphere, but often they can act as vehicles of subjective identity and self-representation which enables the historian to give meaning to a sporting career. In aggregate the sum of the parts may also allow something to be said about the sporting culture in which the players operated.

Post-modern sports historians argue that all sources are biased, all of them distort or filter the truth (whatever that might be), and all of them need interpretation. Indeed Booth (2005: 30) believes that all 'facts are propositional statements about the nature of reality.' At its extreme post-modern sports history is almost a nihilistic rejection of a subject in which no information can be trusted. A more moderate version would suggest two lessons for all sports historians, both of which are already operated by the better practitioners. First they should continually interrogate the archive so as to assess their sources carefully and certainly defend any privileging of material (Johnes 2007a). Second they should accept that there are different versions of events depending from whose perspective the narrative is being constructed: historical perspective is contested terrain with a plurality of meanings.

Although historians deal in facts, quite often these facts turn out to be percentage likelihood, reasoned speculations, or even personal bias – sometimes consciously so, more often a subconscious product of their background. Evidence is an issue but so is the historian who, it is often forgotten, has a personal relationship with the subject which can be influenced by upbringing, education and politics. Here indeed is a danger of 'reverse research'. We need greater reflexivity within the discipline: 'an awareness that historians play creative roles in the production and presentation of history' Booth (2005: 211). Historians should be more open with their value judgements and acknowledge how subjectivity affects their approach and narrative.

Conclusion

Sports history is dependent upon information, but this cannot always be relied upon. Too often the subject has suffered from false information and omitted information as well as partial information and imperfect information.

Sports myths are a prime example of false information that develops as nostalgia clouds memory. Much of what appears to be historical evidence is actually recycled without being researched. It simply becomes accepted over time as the 'truth', but often it is no more than conventional wisdom which falls apart when subjected to serious historical research. What can also occur is the deliberate invention of tradition in which a false continuity with the past is claimed and evidence to the contrary ignored or wilfully misinterpreted. So there are so-called traditional sports created for commercial or nostalgic reasons or, the reverse, the attempt to invent a history as with the Baseball Commission. Or the attempt with rugby to invent the origins of the sport so as to separate it from working-class folk football (Collins 2005). Then there is history with omissions. Sports museums are 'the public face of sports history'(Vamplew 1998: 279) and these can be the best places to replicate the performance, drama, romance, passion and emotion of sport but unfortunately too often they have catered to the nostalgia market and, in doing so, perpetuated myths, lacked historical objectivity and subtlety of argument, failed to contextualise artefacts, eschewed the controversial, and had an obsession with winners and winning. Additionally there has been a concentration on sport that was competitive, adult and a male-dominated activity (Vamplew 1998). And then there are the 'official' histories, authorised or commissioned by a governing body or the like. Here the criticism is both of omission and commission: the funders are told what they want to hear and a spin is often put on controversial issues. Celtic F.C.'s approved histories, for example, make much of the club being founded in 1888 to raise money to feed poor Catholics in the east end of Glasgow, but they never mention that within a decade Celtic had become a limited liability company and no longer made charitable donations (Kay and Vamplew 2010). Finally we have the most common situation of imperfect or partial information with which this paper has been mainly concerned.

Sports history, correctly practised, is a counter to nostalgia, myth and invented tradition. It can be considered the sports memory of a nation: without sports history there is sporting amnesia. It can set straight the sporting record but also it can explain why some things changed and why continuities also occurred. History's great contribution to sports studies is the time dimension. It provides the benchmarks for measuring progress and change (or the lack of it). It can help us appreciate the difference between trend and fluctuation and realise that not everything seen as 'important' in sport need have a permanent influence or that everything in modern sport is new.

Of course sports historians offer only an interpretation of the past. Apart from 'sportifacts' there is no absolute truth in sport history. History written on the basis of archived material should not be classified as fiction, but the past that it reveals may not be the whole truth. Increasingly it has been recognised that we can have history from different perspectives, involving diverse interrogations and interpretations of the source material. Sports history is a contested terrain with different views of the same situation. And any findings should be made with caution rather than certainty, respecting the point that historical knowledge must always be provisional.

Reference List

Adelman, M.L. 1986 *A sporting time: New York City and the rise of modern athletics 1820–70*. Urbana: University of Illinois Press.

Agenda Club 1912. *The rough or the fairway: an enquiry by the agenda club into the problem of the golf caddie*. London: Heinemann.

Block, D. 2005. *Baseball before we knew it*. Lincoln: University of Nebraska Press.

Booth, D. 2005. *The field: truth and fiction in sport history.* Abingdon: Routledge.
Booth, D. 2006. Sites of truth or metaphors of power? Refiguring the archive. *Sport in History* 26: 91–109.
Booth, D. 2010. Theory. In *Routledge companion to sports history*, edited by Pope, S.W. and Nauright, J. Abingdon: Routledge.: 12–13.
Collins, T. 2005. Invented traditions. In *Encyclopedia of British traditional rural sports*, edited by Collins, T., Martin, J. and W. Vamplew, W. London: Routledge: 171–173.
Collins, T. and Vamplew, W. 2002. *Mud, sweat and beers.* Oxford: Berg.
Cronin, M. 2009. What went wrong with counting? Thinking about sport and class in Britain and Ireland. *Sport in History* 29, 392–404.
Guttmann, A. 1978. *From ritual to record.* New York: Columbia University Press.
Guttmann, A. 2004. *From ritual to record.* New York: Columbia University Press.
Headon, D. 1999. Significant silents: sporting Australia on film, 1896–1930. *Journal of Popular Culture* 33:115–127.
Hill, J. 2006a. Anecdotal evidence: sport, the newspaper press, and history. In Phillips, In *Deconstructing sport history*, edited by Phillips, M. Albany: State University of New York Press: 117–130.
Hill, J. 2006b. *Sport and the literary imagination.* Oxford: Peter Lang.
Hill, J. and Williams, J. 1996. *Sport and identity in the north of England.* Keele: Keele University Press.
Holt, R. 2000. The uses of history in comparative physical education. In *Old borders, new borders, no borders*, edited by J. Tollener, J and Renson, R. Oxford: Meyer and Meyer: 45–57.
Hornby, H. 2008. *Uppies and downies.* Swindon: English Heritage.
Howell, A. 1991. *Harry Vardon.* London: Stanley Paul.
Huggins, M. 2007. And now, something for the ladies: representations of women's sport in the newsreels between the wars. *Women's History Review* 16: 681–700.
Huggins, M. 2008. The sporting gaze: towards a visual turn in sports history – documenting art and sport. *Journal of Sport History* 35: 311–329.
Johnes, M. 2007a. Archives, truths and the historian at work: a reply to Douglas Booth's 'Refiguring the archive'. *Sport in History* 27: 127–135.
Johnes, M. 2007b. Texts, audiences, and postmodernism; the novel as a source in sports history. *Journal of Sport History* 34: 121–133.
Kay, J. and Vamplew, W. (2010). Beyond altruism: British football and

charity 1877–1914, *Soccer and Society* 11: 181–197.
Krüger, A. 2008. Which associativity? a German answer to Szymanski's theory of the evolution of modern sport. *Journal of Sport History* 35: 39–48.
MacLean, M. 2008. Evolving modern sport. *Journal of Sport History* 35: 49–55.
Malcolm, D. 2008. A response to Vamplew and some comments on the relationship between sports historians and sociologists of sport. *Sport in History*. 28: 259–279.
Nathaus, K. 2009. The role of associativity in the evolution of modern sport: a comment on Stefan Szymanski's theory. *Journal of Sport History* 36: 115–122.
Osmond, G. 2010. Photographs, materiality and sport history: Peter Norman and the 1968 Mexico City black power salute. *Journal of Sport History* 37: 119–137.
Polley, M. 2007. *Sports history: a practical guide*. Basingstoke: Palgrave.
Riess, S.A. 2008. Associativity and the evolution of modern sport. *Journal of Sport History* 35: 33–38.
Szymanski, S. 2008a. A theory of the evolution of modern sport. *Journal of Sport History* 35: 1–32.
Szymanski, S. 2008b. A theory of the evolution of modern sport: response to comments. *Journal of Sport History* 35: 57–64.
Taylor, M. 2008. From source to subject: sport, history and autobiography. *Journal of Sport History* 35: 469–491.
Tomlinson, A, and Young, C. 2010. Sport in history: challenging the *communis opinion*. *Journal of Sport History* 37: 5–17.
Toulmin, V. 2006. 'Vivid and realistic': Edwardian sport on film. *Sport in History* 26: 124–149.
Vamplew, W. 1998. Facts and artefacts: sports historians and sports museums. *Journal of Sport History* 25: 268–292.
Vamplew, W. 2004. *Pay up and play the game*. Cambridge: Cambridge University Press.
Vamplew, W. 2008a. Exploited labour or successful workingmen: golf professionals and professional golfers in Britain before 1914. *Economic History Review* 61: 54–79.
Vamplew, W. 2010. Sharing space: inclusion, exclusion and accommodation at the British golf club before 1914, *Sport and Social Issues*.
Vamplew, W. and Kay, J. 2003. A modern sport? 'from ritual to record' in British horseracing', *Ludica* 9:125–139.

Sports Crowd Disorder in Britain, 1870–1914: Causes and Controls[1]

Commercialized sport for the masses was mainly a product of the late nineteenth century, a time when entrepreneurs and other less profit motivated individuals responded to the stimulus of rising working class incomes by creating the enclosed racecourse and the gate-money soccer ground and by further developing the gate-money cricket ground.[2] Large crowds at sports events were nothing new: what was novel was that now large crowds were regularly being attracted. By the late nineteenth century '... it [was] no rare thing in the North and Midlands for twenty to thirty thousand people to pay money to witness a League match or important cup-tie'. At this time racecrowds of 10,000 to 15,000 were not unusual; double this could be expected at leading meetings; and perhaps 70,000 to 80,000 at a major Bank Holiday event. As for cricket, it could be commented in 1885 that a decade ago 'where hundreds dawdled up of an afternoon to see a big match ... now thousands arrive early on the ground to secure a good place.'[3]

Clearly, it was in the interests of the club committees and course executives to take steps to control crowd behaviour since spectator disorder could prove costly to a gate-money sports enterprise. First, there was the risk to property if the crowd got out of hand. By the early twentieth century, many of the proprietors had expended considerable sums on their grounds. The cricket and soccer grounds at Old Trafford well illustrate this point. At the turn of the century Lancashire County Cricket Club purchased their ground for nearly £25,000 and then spent several more thousands building stands and improving other facilities.[4] Virtually across the road, Manchester United Football Club's new stands cost almost £36,000.[5] Such investments

15

could not be left to the mercy of a rampaging crowd. Secondly, there was the risk to the gate-money itself. Potential spectators might be dissuaded from attending by the fear of disorder. After Glasgow Rangers' first game at Ibrox, the Scottish *Athletic Journal* commented on 'the very large number of better classes that turned out to see the game. It behoves the Rangers to do everything in their power to retain the patronage of these people, who mostly belong to the district, and they can only do so by rigidly keeping the rowdier portion of the crowd in order'.[6] Ultimately, of course, there was the threat that the sports' authorities would close the ground or suspend the license of the racecourse.

Section I of this paper shows that the sports promoters had reason to worry in that crowd riot and spectator violence were not uncommon, particularly at soccer matches and horse-racing. Section II suggests possible causes of the disorder; and the final sections assess the success of the promoters' efforts to control crowd behaviour.

I

April 17, 1909 was the day on which a soccer crowd lost its head. Glasgow Celtic, bidding for a third successive League and Cup double, were replaying the Scottish Cup Final at Hampden Park, against their traditional rivals, Glasgow Rangers. At full time in the replay the scores were level, and, due to a false press report, many fans expected extra time to be played. When it became apparent that this was not the case, the field was invaded by an estimated six thousand disgruntled spectators. A few policemen attempted to stem the flow but they were beaten savagely. Police reinforcements were able to prevent the mob from reaching the dressing rooms, but that was all they could accomplish. Rioters tore out the goalposts, ripped up the nets, and smashed down fencing. Bonfires were made out of the broken barricading and the uprooted goalposts were used as battering rams against the turnstile entrances which were also set on fire. The arrival of the fire brigade signalled further trouble and the firemen were attacked and their hoses slashed. Not till early evening, two and a half hours after the match ended, were the rioters forced out of the ground and the fires brought under control. Much of the stadium was damaged: five gates and payboxes with twenty two turnstiles had been destroyed, a substantial proportion of fencing had been smashed and burned, and a large part of the playing area had been scarred by fire and broken glass; in all some £1000 worth of damage. Casualties were heavy: fifty eight policemen and sixty others received hospital treatment; only by a miracle was no-one killed.[7]

Although this was the worst soccer crowd disturbance in the period studied, it was no isolated occurrence. The minute books of the Football Association, the Football League Management Committee, and the Scottish Football Association clearly confirm for the 1880s and 1890s the view of one football historian, based on a study of contemporary comments, that "riots, unruly behaviour, violence, assault and vandalism appear to have been a well-established, but not necessarily dominant pattern of crowd behaviour at football matches at least from the 1870s".[8] Indeed, the Scottish Football Association's *Annual Report* for 1898/99 described spectator rowdyism, along with rough play, as "the hydra-headed monster of football".[9]

In horse-racing, too, the crowds often got out of hand. Certainly before the 1880s physical disorder was a common occurrence at British race-meetings. At several metropolitan meetings disturbances became so bad that in 1879 these events were suppressed by Parliamentary legislation.[10] Provincial meetings also had their troubles, particularly when backers felt that they had not had a fair run for their money or when bookmakers welshed on winning bets. So common was this latter feature that the treatment of welshers became ritualised or institutionalised at some courses. At Catterick they would be tarred and feathered; at Northallerton they were horsewhipped; and at Stockton, Durham, and Wetherby they were thrown in the river.[11] At most meetings before the development of the enclosed course, the race committee would employ a few pugilists to protect the horses and other racing property, and a gateman or two to keep undesirables out of the stands. Additionally, at events such as Ascot which were part of the British social calendar, police would be in attendance to control the rough element should they threaten to disturb their social superiors.[12] Generally that was the limit to the control measures. No wonder J. H. Peart, right hand man of the famous trainer John Scott, commented favourably on Chantilly where "the arrangements on the racecourses are far beyond what they have in England. The roughs are kept in their proper place, and there was no hustle or confusion, and no fear of being robbed of your wallet."[13]

Cricket does not appear to have experienced the kind of crowd violence frequently observed at soccer matches or race-meetings. There were instances of field invasion as at the Middlesex versus Lancashire game of 1907 when the crowd, exasperated by a failure to let them know when play was to begin, even though their money had been taken at the gate, invaded the playing area and allegedly tore up the pitch.[14] Nevertheless, disorder at cricket matches was generally verbal rather than physical, such as the community whistling of the Dead March by the Surrey crowd when Australia's opening pair was making slow progress at the Oval in 1899, the jeering of so-called batsmen who seemed to prefer to use their pads, and the booing of bowlers who persisted in bowling negatively down the legside.[15]

II

Certainly there was a problem of crowd behaviour to be faced by the promoters of the gate-money sports. However, what they could do to solve it was not clear: even today the actual causes of sports crowd disorder are not fully understood or agreed upon.[16] Nevertheless, most modern studies do suggest that deeprooted structural strains and social tensions have an important role to play. Clearly, such a hypothesis has relevance to any explanation of the involvement of the working class in crowd disorder. Deprived of power and esteem at work, the working class sports fan can find a surrogate identity as a member of a larger group, as a partisan team supporter, basking in the reflected glory of a winning team or regarding defeat as an intolerable deprivation to an already deprived group. Alternatively, he may seek to control his fate by using his skill to select winning horses. Sport also allows the working man openly to challenge authority by barracking the referee, umpire, or racing official. Although he himself can rarely triumph over social and economic institutions, his team can defeat its opponents. Thus the personal psychological frustrations and tensions of the working man can be partially released by such group identification. The intense role of sport in such persons' lives, however, means that their reactions to sports events become highly emotional: thus the euphoria of winning or the despair of defeat can easily spill over into disorder, or anything which threatens their enjoyment of their sport can provoke a riot.

Conflict between rival fans also stems from the emotional attachment of supporters to their team. As was pointed out in the early 1890s, 'football in the North is something more than a game ... it awakes local patriotism to its highest pitch'.[17] The supporters' identification with their teams can be based on several factors, among them geographical attachment, or a common bond of religion, ethnic, or national background. Such identification is often strengthened by the local team providing a source of popular culture in the community. The supporters of that team become an identifiable sub-culture with their team songs and distinctive garb.[18] The team becomes their reference group, conferring a sense of pride and esteem. Where supporters have developed a strong sense of collective identity, then 'us' versus 'them' conflict situations can erupt into disorder with matches becoming symbolic struggles for supremacy between Protestant and Catholic, between one area of the city and another, between England and Scotland. Team, group, and personal status is at stake.

Applying this thesis of structural strains to the period being studied is not easy as we are not certain of the identity of those involved in disorder. Hard empirical data is practically non-existent: at the Hampden riot, for example, there was only one arrest. Contemporary media comment attributed most of the disorder to the working class, but there is the possibility of selective reportage. Moreover, we do know that some of the worst excesses in cricket undoubtedly did not stem from the working class. In the 1860s, an acrimonious clash at Lords between the supporters of Eton and Harrow forced the abandonment of play; and in 1896, at one of the society events of the year, the annual University fixture, the deliberate bowling of no-balls by Cambridge so as to avoid enforcing the follow-on led, in the words of a member of the Oxford side, to "a very hostile demonstration" with many members of the M.C.C., the ruling body of cricket, "losing all control over themselves." Other reports suggest that the Cambridge team was actually manhandled.[19]

At present, the historian cannot even be certain of the social composition of the sports crowd, let alone the sports rioters. Nevertheless, contemporary observations, lists of accident victims, and photographs have led to the suggestion that soccer was followed by the upper levels of manual workers, skilled tradesmen and foremen, and the lower levels of white collar workers, clerks and minor administrators, whereas horse-racing appealed to those on the lowest and the highest rungs of the socio-economic ladder.[20] The county cricket crowd was ranked above that of soccer by W. McGregor, even though, as a founder of the Football League, he was anxious to give soccer a respectable image.[21] Certainly, the timing of the games with Saturday the third day and a result possible before the working man could reach the ground, would lend support to this view. So, too, would the complaint of C.E.B. Russell that few boys at the Lads Clubs, an institution aimed at working class youths, had watched first class cricket but most had seen professional football, possibly because, whereas most soccer stadia were situated in working class areas, only two county cricket grounds, the Oval and Bramall Lane, were similarly located.[22]

If social tension and structural strains in society are conducive to sports crowd disorder, then, *ceteris paribus*, it might be expected that crowd behaviour would not have improved in the late nineteenth and early twentieth centuries. Indeed, it may have worsened as this period witnessed a growing awareness by many groups in society of their relative economic, social or political deprivation, and a growing militancy in their efforts to change the position. Among other occurrences, the suffragettes took to direct action to support their demands for women's rights, trade unionists went on strike more frequently and more violently, and socialism established itself in working class politics.[23]

There was nothing that individual sports promoters, club committees, or boards of directors could do to remedy social structural strains, even if they appreciated the situation. What they concentrated on were the symptoms rather than the disease, endeavouring to reduce or remove the apparent triggers to disorder. However, a recent social psychological study, which categorised sports crowd disorder according to the apparent major motivation of those involved, has shown that disorder can be sparked off by a variety of circumstances and thus several different control mechanisms may be required.[24] The work differentiates five categories of riot and disorder, known as the FORCE typology, a handy mnemonic for frustration, outlawry, remonstrance (protest), confrontation and expressive disorders, all of which can be identified in Victorian and Edwardian sports crowds.

The Hampden disorder of 1909 is a classic case of the *frustration* riot, an outburst which follows the blocking of the spectator's legitimate expectations regarding access to the game and the way it will be played and adjudicated. In this case many fans had expected extra time to be played, but officialdom decreed otherwise. Perceived injustice can also be a source of frustration, as when a bookmaker refuses to pay out winning punters, or when fans believe that an incompetent or biased official has cost their team or horse victory or that a jockey, player, or team has not tried its best.

Outlawry disorder occurs when groups of violence-prone spectators use sports events to act out their anti-social activities by attacking officials, fighting with rival fans, and destroying property. Such crowd violence is seen as the work of a delinquent or criminal element. It is difficult to pin-point historical examples particularly as this type of rioter no doubt would join in most other disturbances. A possible indication of their existence comes from a critic of those professional sports organised for betting purposes, who claimed that such sports attracted 'a varying but always large blackguard element,' 'a mob of loafers' and 'a base rabble,' and that 'disorder and attacks on the police are not things of rare occurrence among the rougher spectators.' Another critic of horse-racing crowds blamed the railways for 'facilitating the movement of bands of indolent roughs.' A further lead is the comment on soccer crowds that 'it all depends upon the measure of civilisation in your locality whether there is or is not a good deal of fighting after the match.'[25] Unfortunately, all these comments suffer from being labels applied by outside observers who can only indirectly perceive the motivations of the groups involved.

The third category of disorder is that of *remonstrance*. This occurs when a section of the crowd uses the sports event as an arena for the expression of political grievances. In the early twentieth century sports events were used as a means of political protest by the suffragettes. Sport was a bastion of male chauvinism and exclusiveness: thus, when the suffragettes turned to militant protest, sport was an obvious target. Throughout 1913 racecourses, bowling greens, soccer and cricket pitches, and golf courses had their turf torn up and their buildings set on fire. And it was at a sports event, the 1913 Derby, that the suffragettes found their martyr when Emily Davison threw herself under the King's horse and was killed, though this may have been a quest for publicity rather than feminist action directed at the attitudes of the racing authorities.[26]

Confrontation disorder can break out when spectators from rival religious, geographic, ethnic, or national groups come into conflict. Given the appropriate circumstances, smouldering resentment can easily spark into open hostility. Local derby games where regional supremacy is at stake are a prime setting for confrontation disturbances.

Finally, in an *expressive* riot the intense emotional arousal which accompanies victory or defeat, particularly if it is exciting or unexpected, triggers uninhibited behaviour. When Blackburn Olympic, essentially a working class team, beat the Old Etonians in the 1883 Cup Final to take the trophy to the North for the first time, their supporters reputedly went mad with excitement, particularly as the result had been snatched during extra time.[27]

What is apparent from the above categorization is that no single control measure could cope with all the triggers to disorder and that action which might be suitable for one situation could be inappropriate in another. To some extent, the sports promoters learned this lesson by trial and error and rules for crowd control took time to evolve, but by the end of the nineteenth century five major methods had been devised: improvements in the conduct of the sport, improvements in the organization of the sports event, segregation within the crowd, control of ancillary activities, and the use of control agents.

First, there were efforts to improve the conduct of the sport. In most cases, decisions in this regard were taken by the national controlling bodies and not always with the major aim of improving crowd behaviour. Nevertheless, with less overt malpractice to anger the crowd, the spectators' propensity to riot would clearly be reduced. In racing, the Jockey Club took steps to clean up the sport by introducing revocable licenses for trainers, jockeys, officials, and even for racecourses.[28] In soccer, the referee was given powers to send players off the field for serious misconduct and suspensions were introduced for such offenses. Little clean-up was required in cricket: indeed 'it's not cricket' as a cry against unfairness was soon to become part of the English language.[29]

In racing, the measures taken probably had an effect because, although there were instances of foul riding in a tight finish, most misconduct was permeditated and thus susceptible to a deterrent. In soccer, however, there was far more scope for heat-of-the-moment violence.[30] Moreover, the power given to referees could aggravate disorder because of the number of decisions which they had to make during the game, any one of which could spark off a riot; and, even though refereeing standards improved with the introduction of exams and supervisors, the partisan supporter would still cast doubts on the neutrality and efficiency of the match officials. Cricket umpires rarely seem to have been accused of bias, possibly because allegiance to a *county* cricket team was less strong than that to a *local* soccer club.[31] What could be dealt with in soccer, as in racing, was premeditated corruption and the ensuing policies of suspending players who even gambled on matches, let alone fixed them, led to an acknowledgement by a severe critic of the game that it seemed 'irreproachably straight.'[32] Cricket remained above suspicion: according to Wisden's *Almanac* of 1895, 'no whisper of matches being sold for money is ever heard ... no charge of cheating is brought against players.'[33]

Improved organization of the sports events did much to reduce the chances of frustration riots. A simple but effective improvement was to have races and matches start on time. Traditionally, race meetings had commenced in the morning, and the times of the afternoon races depended upon the quality of the luncheon partaken by the race committee. Even then, the method of starting races with a shout of 'no' or 'go' was apt to lead to false starts. The enclosed courses ran to a much stricter timetable, thanks to the employment of professional starters and, from the late 1890s, the use of the starting gate.[34] In soccer in the 1870s and 1880s, matches frequently had to be abandoned because darkness fell; but, with the coming of professionalism and the development of leagues, a balance was struck between starting late enough to allow fans to get from their work and early enough to allow the games to finish.[35] With cricket, the spectator's complaint was not so much starting time, but the delays which occurred between innings or between the fall of wickets. Generally, this did not lead to more than verbal abuse, but in the longer run failure to combat the problem led to a public dissatisfied with the resulting plethora of drawn games and preferring to spend their entrance money elsewhere.[36]

Segregation of the crowd, another method of crowd control, was first of all a matter of managing the physical environment by fencing off parts of the courses and grounds; and then it was a question of controlling entry to the various enclosures, stands, and terraces. This was achieved in several ways. One was differential pricing. By the late 1880s the more important soccer clubs had settled on a 6d admission to the ground and an extra 6d for the stand. With the investment in improved facilities from the 1890s stand prices were increased, though generally the 6d ground admission charge was retained. For example, when Manchester United opened its Old Trafford stadium in 1910, it was still only 6d to enter the ground but 1s, 1s 6d, and 2s for various sections of the covered stand and 5s for a reserved seat in the center stand.[37] In cricket, too, extra was paid to enter the various stands.[38] The same practice held also in racing. At York, for example, in the 1890s it cost 10s (5s for ladies) to enter the grandstand, 5s for the paddock, and 2s 6d for the second class enclosures.[39] Another method of segregation adopted in both racing and cricket was the reservation of particular areas for club members, entry to which was controlled by strict social vetting and high subscription costs. In soccer, club membership seems to have been more open socially, but, apart from committee members and their friends, viewing privileges were restricted to first claim on season tickets.

Both differential pricing and the formation of clubs were primarily economic policies, designed to increase returns by supplying different markets at different prices, but they did have the indirect effect of making it easier to contain any disorder to the areas in which it broke out, thus making the disturbance less offensive to those elsewhere and also possibly making it easier to put down the trouble.[40] Unfortunately it is also possible that in certain circumstances segregation may have encouraged disorder. Crowd density, a significant influence on spectator behaviour, may have been intensified in certain areas. Moreover, if segregation led to the grouping together of similarly-motivated, one-class spectators, then, as communication is easier when persons have pre-existing group ties, the dynamics of crowd disorder could spread faster.[41] The best policy regarding segregation was the absolute exclusion of undesirable spectators. Traditionally, at race meetings segregation had been a matter of keeping the 'riff-raff' out of the stands and other exclusive areas. With the development of the enclosed meeting, however, the lower elements of the racing world were not even allowed on the course. In soccer, too, the authorities insisted that clubs exclude known troublemakers. Policies of exclusion at all gate-money sports became easier with the adoption of the turnstile in the late nineteenth century.

Most sports promoters also took action to control the ancillary activities associated with their short, in particular drinking and gambling. Less gambling, or at least more stringently controlled gambling, could lead to fewer precipitating factors, and less alcohol might prevent some sections of the crowd from becoming uninhibited and possibly guard against false perception of events.

No doubt gambling losses and alcohol had contributed to many a crowd fracas at pre-enclosed race meetings, but before spectators began to pay at the gate, rentals from the gaming and drinking booths were vital to the prize-funds.[42] With the emergence of the gate-money course, the number of beer tents was reduced and gambling was restricted to betting on the races and the cardsharps, thimblemen, and even/odd table operators were no longer welcomed. In fact the racecourse executives chose to enforce laws which they had previously disregarded. Legislation of 1853 had made it illegal to monopolize a place for betting purposes and this was interpreted as outlawing gaming booths; and the Vagrancy Act Amendment Act of 1873, which made it illegal to use betting machines, was taken as ruling out roulette and even/odd tables.[43] However, racing faced a special problem in controlling its ancillary activities in that traditionally races had been associated with local holidays and people had come to race meetings in expectation of a carnival. The race promoters were faced with having to persuade the race crowd to accept a dampening of the traditional holiday atmosphere. Their solution was to change the nature of the racing along with that of the race meeting. Long-distance, staying events were increasingly replaced by sprints, handicaps, and two-year-old races, all of which had a degree of unpredictability sufficient to make for exciting racing and betting.[44]

Racing had a symbiotic relationship with gambling and could not afford to do without it. Gambling had no such importance for either soccer or cricket, but as the law stood in the late nineteenth century,[45] gambling was believed to be legal at any sports events at which gate-money had been charged, providing that the betting was on the event being staged. It thus seemed that the ground proprietors could do little to prevent gambling. Indeed, it was felt that the police could not eject bookmakers from the ground even if the promoters requested them to to so. Fortunately for the promoters, new interpretations of the law towards the turn of the century made it difficult for the bookmaker to set up business inside the grounds. The 1853 legislation regarding the monopolization of a place for betting purposes was deemed as preventing the bookmaker from standing on a box, under an umbrella, or using any colours or placards to draw attention to himself.[46] Cricket did not have much of a problem to contend with, but certainly in soccer enforcement of such an interpretation was seen as necessary because of crowd misconduct associated with betting. In the 1890s referees were being assaulted by losing gamblers, but then firm action by the clubs and football authorities, assisted by the police, appears to have reduced drastically the volume of betting taking place at the grounds.[47] In the immediate pre-war years, however, coupon betting developed and there was little the football promoters could do about it. Thus, it is possible that spectators had bet on the matches which they were watching and this could have had an adverse effect on their behaviour.

It is difficult to determine how much drinking went on at cricket and soccer matches. Certainly in the early twentieth century, it was claimed that 'really there is comparatively little drinking done at football matches,' but, as the claimant was the founder of the Football League and anxious to promote a respectable image for soccer, his views have to be treated with caution.[48] An impression gained from a reading of Lancashire County Cricket Club's minutes concerning catering arrangements suggests that bar facilities were provided primarily for the spectators in the more expensive parts of the ground. It certainly seems that drinking was an accepted part of sports spectatorship and thus, even though limited and controlled, a possible contributing factor to crowd disturbance.

A final method employed in all the sports was the use of control agents in the form of gatemen, stewards, and the police. Additionally, most soccer grounds allowed free admission to soldiers and sailors in uniform in the expectation that they would lend the police a hand if trouble broke out as in the 1890 FA Cup Final.[49] Gatemen at the enclosed race meetings improved in caliber once they became subject to Jockey Club licence, and the best of them would be employed at many meetings and, by travelling the racing circuits, would be able to familiarize themselves with defaulting bookmakers and itinerant troublemakers.[50] Gatemen at cricket, and especially at football, possibly found identification of potential bothercausers easier because of the more regular nature of their events. Law and order outside the grounds and courses was part of the normal duty of the police, but payment had to be made for their use inside. Initially, the number to be employed was left to the discretion of the ground committees and course executives, but certainly in the early twentieth century the relevant chief constable made the decision for soccer matches.[51] If insufficient police were used, there could be problems, as in the 1892 Scottish Cup Final when 150 foot police and four on horseback were unable to prevent an invasion of the field; however, the lesson was learned and thirty mounted police plus 200 on foot were able to cope at the replay.[52] The basic function of the control agents was to enforce compliance with the regulations and to deter miscreants, but they were also there to act to contain any trouble if it did break out. Although it is possible that the crowd could be provoked by the tactics or the demeanour of the control agents, only one reported incident has come to light, at Lancaster races in 1840, and this was political in nature.[53]

IV

The sports promoters and sports authorities could do little to rectify the societal, structural strains which may have underlain the outbursts of crowd disorder. Instead, they concentrated upon a combination of reformative and repressive methods designed either to remove the triggers to disorder or to restrict and contain any disturbances which did break out. These policies achieved some degree of success. Hutchinson's study of soccer crowds shows that by the early twentieth century, media mention of field invasions was less frequent.[54] There is other statistical evidence to support the implication of Hutchinson's view. In the period 1895–97, twenty-one clubs had their grounds closed by the Football Association and a further twenty-three clubs were cautioned because of the misbehaviour of fans, but in the years 1910–12 only four grounds were closed and only five cautions issued.[55] Quantified data on racing crowd behaviour are not available, but remarks of two knowledgeable racing writers enable a contrast to be drawn between some enclosed courses in the early twentieth century where "ruffianism [is] practically unknown" and the position "outside the enclosures [where] the unfortunate state of our racecourses is too notorious to need comment."[56]

In cricket, however, there were numerous allegations that crowd behaviour worsened.[57] There were almost as many reasons advanced to explain the change. Among them was the claim that "leagues and cups have been instituted for cricket as for football" and that the press were encouraging "the football element among the spectators at our cricket grounds."[58] Yet perhaps the main reason was that the wishes of the spectators were not being adequately considered. For one thing, no offical steps were taken over the increase in slow and negative play, and over the time-wasting which were rendering the game less entertaining.[59] It was also a question of poor facilities and amenities.[60] Cricket was bringing trouble on itself by taking the crowd's entrance fees and then not giving value for the money.[61]

Yet what the complaints isolated was verbal not physical aggression, and such barracking was commonplace and generally accepted as part of the game in both soccer and racing.[62] The attitudes of the cricket authorities are epitomized in the remarks of P.F. Warner, amateur England captain and staunch pillar of the M.C.C., that the spectator "should not, for instance, 'boo' or jeer at the players. The only time he has a right to act thus is when a player has been obviously guilty of an unsportsmanlike or ungentlemanly action. or is clearly not trying. Then I think he might justifiably express his disapproval in an obvious manner, though the better and more dignified course would be to leave the ground. Too often spectators, ignorant of the finer points of the game, cheer ironically, and even make rude remarks. These people should be dealt with firmly, and told that they will not be allowed to stay in the ground if they persist in their attitude, their sixpence being returned to them. It is contrary to the dignity of any cricket ground to allow the cricketers to be subjected to undeserved censure."

"The truth of it," Warner maintained, "is that the attitude of the public towards cricket has changed."[63] What he failed to add was that it was equally true that the attitude of the authorities had not changed. They refused to accept that the spectator was not content to pay his money and remain a passive observer. In reality, cricket had more to fear from spectators voting with their feet and not attending: and this is what they were beginning to do in the decade before the first world war.[64]

Why the cricket crowds never became as violent as those at race meetings and soccer matches is a matter for conjecture. Certainly, the absence or low level of gambling on cricket reduced one stimulus to disorder. Possibly another answer lies in the larger middle class element among cricket spectators for whom structural strains relating to social or economic tensions might be less than for working class football fans or turf gamblers. Or it might simply be a matter of the relatively drawn-out nature of cricket matches generally resulting in less tension among the crowd, particularly among one which usually was seated, thereby lessening body contact between spectators and also clearly demarcating personal territory, both factors which reduce the scope for offense to be taken.

V

Once sports promoters began to take steps to counteract crowd disorder, then the behaviour of gate-money sports crowds improved, in so far as riots, field invasions, and general spectator violence diminished. Actions taken to improve the conduct and organization of the sports events did much to remove the triggers to frustration, confrontation, and expressive disorders; the segregation of various sections of the crowd and the absolute exclusion of other spectators reduced the danger of confrontation and outlawry disorders; and the stricter controls on gambling and drinking and the deterrent effect of control agents lessened the possibility of all kinds of disturbance, save perhaps for remonstrance disorders. If trouble did break out, then the segregation of the crowd, the restricted avail ability of alcohol, and the presence of the police generally acted to weaken the contagion dynamics of disorder and to contain the disturbance.

Crowd disorder, however, could not be totally eliminated. Not all the triggers to disturbance could be removed. Little could be done, for example, about heat-of-the-moment violence on the field of play. Nor were the perceptions of the partisan spectator likely to be influenced by legislation or entreaties from the clubs, particularly when drinking and gambling remained an accompaniment of many sports events. It is also possible that some of the measures intended to solve the disorder may actually have aggravated the problem. Improved organization and less misconduct helped swell attendance figures, and crowd size and density can have a significant influence on spectator disorder. Segregation of the crowd, too, could have increased crowd density. Moreover, the social structural strains that are an important antecedent to disorder were still apparent. In fact, as mentioned above, the working man was increasingly becoming aware of his relative economic and social deprivation. Indeed, in the light of the working class's growing militancy in political and economic life, it might have been anticipated that sports crowd disorder would have worsened. That it did not is a measure of the efficiency of the control policies of the sports organisers.

References

1. I am indebted to the Football Association, the Football League, the Scottish Football Association, Lancashire County Cricket Club, the M.C.C. York Racing Committee, and Durham County Record Office for access to their records and libraries, and to John Hutchinson for permission to use data from his unpublished work on the Heart of Midlothian FC. I also thank Flinders University for assistance towards the research costs of the paper which is part of an on-going project on the economic and social history of sport in Britain. Professor Leon Mann, Dr. R. J. Holton, and the referees of this journal made helpful

comments on an earlier version of the paper.
2. W. Vamplew, *The Turf* (London: Allen Lane, 1976), p. 41; J. Walvin, *The People's Game* (London: Allen Lane, 1975), pp. 50–68; R. Bowen, *Cricket* (London: Eyre & Spottiswoods, 1970). pp. 116–119; 139–140; 145.
3. W. J. Oakley & M. Shearman in M. Shearman, *Football* (London: 1895), p. 166; C. Richardson, *The English Turf* (London: 1901), p. 123; Lord Harris, 'Cricket,' *Contemporary Review*, 48(1885), 125.
4. *Minutes of Lancashire C.C.C.*, passim.
5. *Report of the Football Association Committee on Manchester United F.C.*, 30 September, 1910.
6. *Scottish Athletic Journal*, 23 august, 1887.
7. *Glasgow Herald*, 19 April, 1909; *Minutes of Scottish Football Association*, 19 April, 7 June, 1909.
8. J. Hutchinson, 'Some Aspects of Football Crowds Before 1914,' in Society for the Study of Labour History Conference Papers on *The Working Class and Leisure* (mimeo, University of Sussex, 1974), paper 13, p. 11.
9. English examples of soccer crowd disorder can be found in the author's 'Ungentlemanly Conduct: The Control of Soccer Crowd Behaviour in England, 1888–1914,' in T. C. Smout, ed., *The Search For Wealth and Stability* (London: Macmillan, 1979) pp. 139–154.
10. 'Modern Horse Racing,' *Edinburgh Review*, 151 (1880), 412; 'Turf Ethics in 1868,' *Broadway* (1868). 379–380; *Hansard*, 3rd series, 237,29 January, 1878; 240, 13 June 1878; 243, 14 February, 1879; E. Spencer, *The Great Game* (London: 1900), pp. 223–226.
11. L. H. Curzon, *A Mirror of the Turf* (London: 1892), p. 328; J. Fairfax-Blakeborough. *The Analysis of the Turf* (London: 1927), p. 271.
12. C. W. Searle, *The Origins and Development of Sunninghill and Ascot* (London: 1937). p. 82; D. Laird. *Royal Ascot* (London: Hodder & Stroughton. 1976), p. 93.
13. Letter to John Bowes, 7 June 1870. *Racing and Personal Correspondence of John Bowes*. D/St Box 162. Durham County Record Office.
14. *Scores of Lancashire C.C.C.*, 22–24 July, 1907.
15. Home Gordon, 'The Champagne of Cricket,' *Badminton Magazine*, 27 (1908). 176; Home Gordon. 'The Past Cricket Season,' *Badminton Magazine*, 25 (1907), 413; Home Gordon, 'Cricket and Crowds.' *Badminton Magazine*, 29 (1909), 199; R. W. W., 'Illustrated Interviews—W. G. Grace,' *Strand Magazine*, 10 (1895).
16. See, for example, R. Ingham et al., *Football Hooliganism* (London:

Inter-Action. 1978); P. Marsh et al., *The Rules of Disorder* (London: Routledge & Kegan Paul, 1978); Sports Council. *Public Disorder and Sporting Events* (London: Sports Council, 1978); M. D. Smith, "Sport and Collective Violence' in D. W. Ball & J. W. Loy, *Sport and Social Order: Contributions to the Sociology of Sport* (Reading. Mass: Addison Wesley. 1975).

17. 'Football Notes,' *Tinsley's Magazine*, XLVI (1890/91), 65.

18. These were in existence by the 1880s. See, e.g., *Scottish Athletic Journal.* 15 February. 5 April. 2 August. 1887.

19. P. F. Warner, *Lords 1787–1945* (London: White Lion, 1974 ed.), pp. 54–55, 113; W. J. Ford. 'Thoughts on Spectators,' *Badminton Magazine*, 8 (1899), 529; B. Dobbs, *Edwardians at Play* (London: Pelham. 1973). p. 139.

20. Hutchinson, pp. 7–9; Vamplew, pp. 131–137.

21. 'Characteristics of the Crowd' in B. O. Corbett et al., *Football* (London: 1907). p. 19.

22. P. F. Warner, 'The End of the Cricket Season,' *Badminton Magazine*, 35 (1912). 397; S. Meacham. *A Life Apart* (London: Thames & Hudson, 1977), p. 167; W. G. Mandle, 'Games People Played: Cricket and Football in England and Victoria in the late Nineteenth Century,' *Historical Studies*, 15 (1973). 515.

23. See S. Meacham, 'The Sense of an Impending Clash: English Working Class Unrest Before the First World War,' *American Historical Review*, 77 (1972), 1343–64; J. Lovell, *British Trade Unions, 1874–1933* (London: Macmillan, 1977); G. Dangerfield, *The Strange Death of Liberal England* (New York: Capricorn. 1963), D. Kynaston, *King Labour: The British Working Class 1850–1914* (London: George Allen & Unwin, 1976).

24. L. Mann & P. Pearce, 'Social Psychology of the Sports Spectator,' in D. Glencross, *Psychology and Sport* (Sydney: McGraw Hill, 1979). Unfortunately limitations of time and other resources have not allowed any attempt to assess the relative occurrence of the various types of disorder categorized by Mann & Pearce. For the same reasons the relative efficacy of the various control measures could not be discussed in quantitative terms.

25. 'Rioting at Lillie Bridge,' *Saturday Review*, 64 (1887), 409; 'Turf Ethics,' 379–80; C. Edwardes, 'The New Football Mania,' *The Nineteenth Century*, 32 (1892), 622.

26. Dobbs, p. 178; Vamplew, p. 128. I am informed by Sandra Holton, Ph.D. student at Stirling University, that there was a background to the

deliberate choice of the King's horse in that the suffragettes had been trying to win over the King but had not succeeded.

27. G. Green, *The Official History of the FA Cup* (London: Naldrett Press, 1949), p. 34.

28. Vamplew, pp. 94–6.

29. As a comment on unfair play within cricket the phrase was established by the 1860s (Bowen, p. 112). It became accepted in its wider context by the very early 1900s. E.H. Partridge, *A Dictionary of Catch Phrases* (London: Routledge and Kegan Paul, 1977), p. 125.

30. That foul play is difficult to control by punitive measures is suggested by the SFA figures for players suspended for violent conduct. Despite a firm policy of meting out punishment to offenders the number of sendings off for such misconduct increased from 0.47 per club in 1895/6–1899/1900 to 0.88 in the period 1905/6–1909/10. (Calculated from data in *Scottish Football Association Annual Reports*).

31. One writer in the early 1880s maintained that in England 'we want to see good cricket, and are not overwhelmed with mortification when we lose, or puffed up with pride when we win,' though he did allow that at the University match 'local patriotism is interested.' ('Cricket Fifty Years Ago,' *Saturday Review*, 53 (1882), 524). However, the 1880s and 1890s, and early 1900s witnessed the formation of several competitive cricket leagues in the Midlands and the North of England in which apparently winning mattered much more than in county cricket. Whether this affected the behaviour of the crowd is difficult to say, though Roy Genders' history of the leagues does not mention any crowd disorder. (*League Cricket in England*, London. Werner Laurie: 1952).

32. Edwardes, 623.

33. *Wisden's Cricketers' Almanac* (London, 1895). p. lxvii.

34. Vamplew. pp. 117–8.

35. *Minutes of the Football League Management Committee.* 11 November. 1896.

36. Home Gordon, Cricket Now-And-Then, p. 291; H. G. Hutchinson, 'The Parlous Condition of Cricket.' *National Review*, 35 (1900), 790; 'Test Match Cricket of 1912.' *Blackwood's Magazine.* 192 (1912). 857.

37. P. M. Young, *A History of British Football* (London: Sportsmans Book Club. 1969). p. 164.

38. *Minutes of Lancashire Country Cricket Club*, 10 May, 1878, 24 April, 1899; *Accounts of Marylebone Cricket Club*, passim.

39. *York Racing Committee* Records—Collection of Racecards.

34] *How the Game was Played*

40. 'Lord Cadogan on the Turf,' *Saturday Review*, 59 (1885). 79.
41. Smith, p. 313.
42. It is significant that complaints about the behaviour of the race crowd at Darlington in the 1840s stressed 'the great rioting and drunkenness *in the booths* on the racecourse.' William Clayton to John Bowes. 10 December 1846. *Racing and Personal Correspondence of John Bowes*, D/St Box 162. Durham CRO.
43. Vamplew. pp. 140–1.
44. Vamplew. p. 141.
45. For a discussion of the law and gambling see Vamplew, pp. 199–212 and D. M. Downes et al., *Gambling, Work and Leisure* (London: Routledge & Kegan Paul, 1976). pp. 29–43. See also, R. McKibben, 'Working-Class Gambling in Britain 1880–1939,' *Past and Present* No. 82 (1979). 147–178.
46. Vamplew, pp. 207–8.
47. G. O. Smith, 'Football', *Pall Mall Magazine*, 13 (1897). 370–371; E. Needham. *Association Footbull* (London, 1901), p. 7; *Select Committee on Betting*, 1901 V, q 376,2906.
48. McGregor, pp. 23–4.
49. Green, p. 30.
50. Vamplew, p. 140.
51. *Minutes of Scottish Football Association*, 27 February, 1912.
52. *Scottish Football Association Annual Report*, 1891/92.
53. R. B. Storch, "The Plague of Blue Locusts: Police Reform and Popular Resistance in Northern England, 1840–57,' *International Review of Social History*, 20 (1975), 77–78.
54. Hutchinson, p. 14.
55. Calculated from the Minutes of the Football Association Council and Emergency Committee. However, it is possible that Scottish football fans did not confrom to this pattern. Figures of clubs being cautioned by the Scottish Football Association for crowd misbehaviour increased from an average of 5 or 6 in seasons 1903/41908/9 to an average of 19 in the three pre-war seasons (calculated from *Scottish Football Association Annual Reports*). No aggregate earlier figures are available. This increase may be partially a statistical illusion in that it reflects a firmer line taken by the Scottish Football Association and the latter years include suspensions issued by the Scottish Junior Football Association which unfortunately cannot be isolated from the aggregate figures. In addition, it would seem that the Scottish Football Association was not penalizing clubs solely for invasion and assaults

but for 'objectionable practices by spectators [such as] the blowing of whistles, the prevalence of obscene language, and the use of ratchets and bells' (*Scottish Football Association Minutes*, 26 October, 1910). The author is currently investigating other differences between Scottish and English soccer in the hope of throwing light on this phenomenon.
56. R. Ord, 'Horseracing in the North of England,' *Badminton Magazine*, 14 (1903), 174; H. Graves, 'A Philosophy of Sport,' *Contemporary Review*, 78 (1900), 888.
57. See, e.g., E. Ensor, 'The Football Madness,' *Contemporary Review*, 74 (1898), 757; Ford, 527; Home Gordon, 'The Past Cricket Season,' *Badminton Magazine*, 21 (1905), 437; Home Gordon, 'Cricket and Crowds,' *Badminton Magazine*, 29 (1909) 198.
58. E. H. D. Sewell, 'Has Public Interest in First Class Cricket Declined?,' *Badminton Magazine*, 37 (1913). 193; Ensor, 75.
59. P. Trevor, 'The Future of Cricket,' *Fortnightly Review*. 80 (1906). 532–533; Home Gordon. 'The Coming Cricket Season,' *Badminton Magazine*, 30 (1910); 'Cricket Prospects.' *Saturday Review*. 12 May. 1900.
60. H. S. Altham, 'Then and Now—Cricket,: *Badminton Magazine*. 36 (1913). see also Warner 'The End of the Cricket Season,' *Badminton Magazine*, 35 (1912). 397–398.
61. See, e.g., 'Test Match Cricket of 1912,' *Blackwoods Magazine*. 192 (1912). 854.
62. Although the Scottish Football Association objected to this behaviour (see note 55). the Football Association Committee which visited the Stockport County ground in 1911. following its closure for crowd violence in 1910, found nothing to censure in the fact that 'there was shouting and strong remarks and improper language used by some of the spectators towards visiting players.' (Minutes of *Football Association Emergency Committee* 25 September—15 November, 1911).
63. Warner, 'The End of the Cricket Season,' 396–7.
64. Trevor, 532–3; Home Gordon, 'What is Wrong with Cricket'?,' *Fortnightly Review*. 93 (1913). 1183–7: Home Gordon. 'Is first Class Cricket Losing its Popularity?.' *Badminton Magazine*. 21 (1905). 328–334.

Bulimic Practices and Alcohol Consumption: Performance Enabling and Performance Enhancing Mechanisms in Nineteenth-Century British Sport

Abstract

Search of contemporary documents and secondary literature based on primary source material has revealed that nineteenth-century British jockeys faced health problems because of wasting forced on them by the low weights assigned to the horses that they rode, a situation aggravated by an over supply of riders in a highly competitive labour market. A second investigation using similar materials showed that nineteenth-century British sportsmen more generally were advised to drink alcohol to aid their performance, particularly in events requiring stamina. A third line of enquiry involving biographies and the press suggests that weight-watching and alcohol consumption still influence the careers of modern sportsmen.
Keywords: alcohol, weight, Britain, horseracing, football.
Acknowledgements: Financial assistance was provided by the Leverhulme and Carnegie Trusts. There were no ethical issues.

Introduction

In the 1886 Cambridgeshire, a major British horserace, *St Mirin* was beaten a neck by *Sailor Prince*. Jockey, Fred Archer, rider of the second-placed horse, blamed himself for the defeat as his mount carried a pound overweight. While riding in

Ireland Archer had received a telegram from the Duchess of Montrose, owner of *St Mirin*, stating that 'my horse runs in the Cambridgeshire. I count on you to ride it'. Archer needed little persuasion. He had been champion jockey for thirteen consecutive seasons but had never won a Cambridgeshire. He had been racing in Ireland at 9 stones 4 lbs but, so keen was he to break this drought, that he undertook to ride at 8 stones 6 lbs, a reduction of 12 lbs in less than a week. He attempted to achieve this by not eating at all on three days, counteracting the intake at other times by doses of a purgative, especially devised for him by Dr. J.R. Wright, a Newmarket physician, and, when not riding, making use of the Turkish bath attached to his Falmouth House residence. This left him so weak that when riding on Wednesday 3 November at Brighton, eight days after the Cambridgeshire defeat, he contracted a chill, which he aggravated by insisting on fulfilling his engagement at Lewes the following day. He left that course in an extremely weakened state and was diagnosed on the morning of Monday 8 November as suffering from typhoid fever. The date was the second anniversary of his wife's death in childbirth. That afternoon his sister, who was taking care of him, heard a noise in his bedroom and found Archer armed with a revolver. She attempted to disarm him but he placed the muzzle in his mouth and fired. He died a victim of illness, depression, and wasting (Welcome, 1990).

Thomas Hicks, an English-born athlete representing the United States, won the marathon at the St Louis Olympic Games of 1904 running in a searing temperature of 30 degrees centigrade. At the nineteen mile mark he faltered on the hilly course and his coach fed him 1/60th grain of sulphate of strychnine as a stimulant (within a raw egg to disguise the taste). Although a poison, the drug can stimulate the central nervous system if given in small doses. Another mile on the procedure was repeated but accompanied by a glass of brandy; this to a dehydrated runner who lost ten pounds during the race! He continued, finishing at walking pace and collapsing over the line, but a mile ahead of the second-placed athlete (Lucas, 1905).

The tragedy resulting from Archer's wasting and the apparent success of Hicks' drug-taking illustrate the health risks that sportsmen were prepared to take to ensure that they could perform at the top level. This article will further explore, in a

British context, weight-loss mechanisms and the use of alcohol as performance-enabling and performance-enhancing practices for sportsmen in the nineteenth century.

Weight-Watching Jockeys

There is no such individual as a fat professional jockey: the artificial weights imposed on the sport see to that. In the nineteenth century the minimum weight was sometimes set as a 'feather', nominally around four stones (25.5 kilos). Some would actually ride at less than this and make up the weight with lead. When little Kitchener won the Chester Cup in 1844 his actual body weight was alleged to be only 2 stones 12 pounds (Kent, 1892)! In 1860 Lord Redesdale proposed that Parliament legislate a minimum weight of seven stones for all horse races. His motive was to preserve the quality of the British thoroughbred which he feared was being undermined by them needing less stamina to carry smaller riders (Hansard, 1860). For much of the eighteenth century nine stones seems to have been a minimum in racing for thoroughbreds (Middleton, 2000). Redesdale withdrew his bill when the Jockey Club agreed to set a minimum of 5 stones 7 lbs, raised to six stones by the end of the century but not to seven stones till the 1920s. There were two schools of thought on the minimum weight, each championed by a reputable trainer. William Day wanted a seven stone minimum because he felt young boys in the saddle were dangerous, whereas John Porter would have preferred only four and a half stones so as to give apprentices more chances of getting a ride in a race (Day, 1880; Porter, 1896).

Why the weights are so low is not clear but probably had something to do with owners realising that carrying less poundage lessened the risk of the breakdown of valuable thoroughbred racing stock, especially as younger horses began to be raced. Whatever the reason it forced all riders, apart from those blessed with natural lightness, to eat little and combat even that with a regimen of long walks in heavy clothes, Turkish baths, and purgatives. George Barrett and some other jockeys took a different approach and ate well then forced themselves to vomit (Spencer, 1900). Yet even jockeys with no apparent weight problems often found themselves trying to sweat off that additional pound to gain a mount in what was a very competitive job market in which there were always more jockeys chasing rides than there were rides available. In the close season, which pertained to flat-racing till the development of the all-weather course in the late twentieth century, many jockeys would allow their weight to balloon but they then had to face the wasting process again. Archer, for example, had a winter weight of around eleven stones (Welcome, 1967).

There were two major health risks associated with this weight-watching masochism. One was that the rigours of losing weight often lessened jockeys' ability to control the half ton of horseflesh on which they were mounted. Striking a balance between sufficient strength and reduced weight was a constant problem. Worse still was that the earlier minimum weights encouraged owners and trainers to use child jockeys who could do little if their mount proved troublesome. In the Goodwood Stakes of 1856 *Chevy Chase* could not be controlled by his diminutive rider, a boy called Hearden and he brought down seven other horses and put two jockeys in hospital for several weeks (Astley, 1895).

The other health issue was that wasting so weakened their constitutions that, like poor Archer, they were susceptible to disease and illness. Indeed some commentators felt that tuberculosis was almost an occupational disease (Fairfax-Blakeborough, 1937; Weston, 1952). Dehydration and long periods of inadequate nutrition reduce the ability to concentrate (on horseback at 35–40 mph!), affect the body's thermostatic qualities, and deplete liver glycogen – all of which can lead to accidents or serious illness (Evans, 1998). Wasting certainly contributed to the premature deaths of Victorian riders Tom French, John Charlton, and Tom Chalenor, all of them Classic winners; John Wells, twice champion jockey; and, of course, Archer himself (Tanner & Cranham, 1992).

One rationale for racing was that horses that performed well in the racecourse test could be used to breed remounts for the army. Indeed the Sovereign's Plates were flat races subsidised for such military breeding purposes. Yet there is an inconsistency here between the weights carried and the objective to be attained. Put simply, few military officers weighed less than eight or even nine stones. Overall jockeys weights can be considered illogical, artificial, and, of course, a danger to their health.

Alcohol for Sport

Many jockeys resorted to alcohol as part of their weight watching. In the early nineteenth century Frank Butler, the first Triple Crown winner, followed a champagne-based diet to help restrict his weight to 8 stones 7 pounds (Tanner & Cranham, 1992). Later in that century, the tragic Fred Archer allegedly breakfasted on a diet of castor oil, a biscuit and a small glass of champagne for the bulk of his racing life (Welcome, 1990). For these riders alcohol was seen as perhaps a psychologically-satisfying way of taking a minimal level of calories.

For other nineteenth-century sportsmen, however, alcohol was viewed as a positive aid to athletic performance. Bottle holders at prize fights were instructed by Vincent Dowling (1868), editor of *Bell's Life in London*, that

> A bottle of brandy-and-water should be in readiness when a stimulant becomes necessary after long exertion, but this should be used with moderation; and at times, especially in wet, cold weather, about a table-spoon of neat brandy may be given – this ought to be of the best quality.

Doubtless on occasions alcohol was also used to give the fighters extra 'bottom' or courage. Pugilists themselves were told that that 'strong ale' is the athlete's drink and given advice that

> with respect to liquors, they must always be taken cold; and home-brewed beer, old, but not bottled, is the best. A little red wine, however, may be given to those who are not fond of malt liquor, but never more than half a pint after dinner. The quantity of beer, therefore, should not exceed three pints during the whole day (An Operator, 1828).

Cider was also recommended as a base for a sweating liquor, the latter part of the training regimen of Captain Robert Barclay Allardice who gained fame in 1809 for winning a £16,000 challenge to run a thousand miles in a thousand hours (Radford, 2001). Barclay was not alone in his consumption of alcohol as an aid to strength and stamina. Another record-breaking pedestrian, Foster Powell, renowned for his walks from London to York and back in less than six days, was reported to take wine or brandy with water during his perambulations (*Say's Weekly*

Journal, 6 Oct. 1787).

The use of alcohol by athletes should be seen in the context of a society in which many of the population utilised alcoholic drinks as thirst quenchers or for physical stamina. In an age when clean, piped water was a rarity, consuming alcohol in which the water supply had been purified to some extent was rational from a health point of view. Moreover it was generally believed that intoxicants imparted stamina: whenever extra energy was needed resort was had to alcohol (Harrison, 1994).

Such ideas took a long time to change. At the end of the nineteenth century cricketers still resorted to alcohol during a day's play and were being advised that when playing on a hot day 'beer and stout are too heady and heavy' and 'gin and ginger beer is too sickly sweet' and that 'shandy-gaff, sherry or claret and soda are the most thirst-quenching, the lightest and the cleanest to the palate' (Steel & Lyttelton, 1893). A writer in 1890 suggested to Scottish footballers that

> there can be no harm in a glass or two of sound ale or a little light wine such as hock or claret at dinner. The glass of port afterwards I confess I think unnecessary as long as the training process is well borne. If, however, a man shows any sign of falling with the state known as "overtrained", that is to say, when the reducing process is too rapid or too severe, a little port or dry champagne at meals may be found beneficial (Medicus, 1888/89).

The rowing expert, R.C. Lehman (1898), noted that the Oxford boat-race crew in the 1890s were allowed a glass of draught beer or claret and water with their lunch, two glasses with their dinner, and a glass of port with their dessert. Occasionally, champagne was substituted for the other drinks, but only when they had 'been doing very hard work, or when they show evident signs of being over-fatigued, and require a fillip'. In the same decade H.L. Curtis (1892) suggested moderate consumption of alcohol as part of a sportsman's regime but warned against smoking and drinking coffee.

Yet by 1888, in his advice to athletes, Montague Shearman (1888) leaned towards the increasing trans-Atlantic tendency to adopt 'the system of training upon water alone, and taking no alcohol in any shape during training'. He left it to doctors to decide if alcohol was 'nutritious to any degree' but noted that it was universally acknowledged 'that it is very hard to digest, and this alone should be a strong argument against its use'. Nevertheless he accepted that if a sportsman was 'accustomed to drink beer or wine, it is a hard thing to say that the athlete should give up either and take to water if he doesn't like it'. He had seen men well trained 'upon beer, upon claret, and upon weak whisky-and-water'. However, he warned that 'any other wines ... are bad in training, as they excite the nerves and interfere with sound and quiet sleep'. He allowed that 'if a man is getting stale, good strengthening wine may do him a world of good', though he stressed that 'as long as an athlete is not in this state, the glass or two of port, which he often recommended to take, is exceedingly likely to do harm, and can hardly do any good'. All in all the 'general principle' should be 'the less alcohol ... the better'.

Writing slightly earlier, the Reverend Beveridge was adamant that

> much liquid of any kind ought not to be imbibed by the training athlete; and there is one kind of liquid which must not be imbibed at all, namely that which is alcoholic in its nature. There is no use whatever of a man going into training if he intends, at the same time to use intoxicating liquors (*Scottish Athletic Journal*, 13 Oct. 1882).

Beveridge was a member of the teetotal lobby which claimed that 'medical science has proved beyond a doubt the injuriousness of spirituous liquors to the human frame' (Weir, 1992).' This was countered by the *Licensed Trade News* which argued that 'the whole field of physical culture is filled with the best of men doing the best of work on alcohol in moderation'. It added that 'where moderation marks the guarded way, the result of alcoholic liquor consumed, such liquors as are represented by a good sound, wholesome glass of beer, there is nothing to come near it as a thirst quencher, a dietetic, a support and a stimulant' (*Licensed Trade News*, 27 Aug. 1910). Alcohol producers lent support to the trade. The 1880s saw the start of advertisements professing the fitness-aiding qualities of alcohol. Grant's Morella Cherry Brandy claimed that it 'strengthened and invigorated the system,' as was proved by Captain Boyton who drank it whilst swimming the Straits of Dover. Indeed the gallant captain was quoted as finding it 'not only palatable and refreshing, but most effective in keeping up nerve and strength' (*Scottish Athletic Journal*, 1 Dec. 1885). Clearly the advice being provided for sportspersons was confusing and contradictory.

When considering the consumption of alcohol by sportspersons, other than in a recreational context, there is a need to distinguish between that which was actively promoted by trainers and coaches and that simply encouraged by the nature of the occupation. For example, fast bowling in cricket, even in an English 'summer', led to a thirst that was often quenched in the luncheon and tea intervals. A problem here was that at such times the professional cricketers mixed with the general public many of whom were pleased to buy a drink for their heroes. In the 1890s county cricket administrators complained about the public buying drinks for players (Minutes of Lancashire C.C.C., 31 Jan. 1890; Minutes of Leicester C.C.C., 11 June 1894). Indeed the Yorkshire chairman claimed that the 'demon drink' had cost his side the county championship and the Warwickshire secretary appealed to the public not to treat the county's professionals (Cricket, IX, 1890; Duckworth, 1974).

For most participants sport is a recreational stress reliever, but for elite athletes it can be a stress-creator, often producing severe pre-competition anxiety. Not all athletes could cope unaided with this and resorted to anti-anxiety drugs, including alcohol. Some seem to have handled this without overtly damaging their health. In the mid-nineteenth century 'Stonehenge', a writer on rural sports, cited instances of young men drinking one to two gallons of strong ale a day for many months 'without any great injury'. It was, he added, 'astonishing what quantities of intoxicating drinks may be imbibed without much injury, provided that a corresponding amount of exercise is taken' Stonehenge, 1857). At senior level in football the old pros had the attitude that you could always sweat out last night's drinking at training, and that 'the beginner is only too apt to be led by the old stagers' remains as true today as in 1906 when the secretary of the football players union wrote the comment (Cameron, 1906).

However, not all could cope. Pugilist Henry Pearce, the 'Game Chicken', made 'too free with his constitution' and 'in company with sporting men frequently he poured down copious libations at the shrine of Bacchus' so that 'his health was impaired' (Ford,

1976). In horseracing the low weights required caused problems as the effects of alcohol are often aggravated by the lack of food: indeed nutrition expert Professor Michael Lean suggests that 'alcoholism is a probable effect of being starved' (Targett, 1998). It is thus no surprise to learn that in Victorian horseracing Bill Scott, winner of nine St Legers, George Fordham, fourteen times champion jockey, and Tommy Loates, champion in three seasons towards the end of the century were alcoholics Mortimer, Onslow & Willett, 1978; Collingwood, 1967).

Whether professional sportsmen have a greater tendency towards alcoholism than other occupational groups is conjectural given the inadequate statistical information. However there are features of a career in sport that could encourage its emergence in those participants genetically or otherwise predisposed towards the addiction. In most sports there are anxieties associated with the pressures of performance, constant job insecurity and retirement at an early age. There is no place to hide on the sports field. Every time they play sportspersons are subject to public and professional appraisal; and often their performance depends not just on themselves but on their team-mates and on the opposition. Cricket, for example, is a team game within which the individual is often isolated, worrying about his own form even in the midst of team success: as is clear from David Frith's (1991) study of cricketing suicides, some of whom first turned to drink as they could not handle the pressure of perpetual uncertainty. Indeed insecurity is the hallmark of a career in professional sport. It stems from many sources including fear of injury, loss of form, threats to jobs from newcomers, and the inevitable short shelf-life of professional sportsmen. Every day the professional faces the possibility of no work tomorrow: losing in a tight finish, dropping an important catch, being injured in a tackle can all lead to non-selection.

For footballers in particular there was ample opportunity to indulge in drinking. Unlike golfers, who had to spend most of their time on course maintenance and playing with club members, and cricketers, who often had a full day's play several times a week with travel to follow, professional footballers had time on their hands. The training regimes operated by many clubs demanded attendance at the ground for only a few hours a day. Indeed a typical pre-1914 training programme would involve nothing at all on Monday; on other days a 10.00 morning arrival time with a brisk five mile walk to follow unless the weather was inclement when there might be skipping or Indian club and punchball work (Bassett, 1906).

Conclusion

The minimum weight allowed today in British flat racing in 7 stones 10 lbs with top weights carried by the horses rarely exceeding 9 stones, neither figure is really representative of the adult population at large, particular for males who dominate the jockey profession. Modern jockeys thus still have to watch their weight but no longer have to do what Archer and his contemporaries did. When Michael Turner became Chief Medical Advisor to the Jockey Club in the early 1990s, one of his first decisions was to treat jockeys as athletes and offer them scientific advice on nutrition and weight control. Jockeys now increasingly use the gym as well as the sauna (Evans, 1999). Yet, even after Turner began his rein, Willie Carson noted that 'bulimia is not a secret in the weighing room' and leading jockeys, Walter Swinburn and Steve Cauthan allegedly were both bulimic (McGowan, 1997; Reid, 1998). To remain employed jockeys have to flirt with potential eating disorders (Tolich & Bell, 2008). As in the past too, many jockeys turn to alcohol, whether in the belief that it will help them sweat in the sauna or as a satisfying and tension-easing alternative to food (Johnston, 1998).

The relationship between alcohol and sporting performance has changed over the past century. Traditionally, alcohol was seen as an aid to strength, stamina and courage. But today, apart from a few sports that require a steady hand for aiming, such as darts, shooting or archery, alcohol is no longer regarded as a performance-enhancing drug. It is now acknowledged that alcohol depresses the nervous system, impairs both motor ability and judgement, reduces endurance, and, as a diuretic, can disturb electrolyte balance and cause dehydration, all of which are detrimental to effective sports performance (Stainback, 1997; Reilly, 1996). Yet there is still a line of thought that argues that alcohol can act as a performance enhancer, especially in team sports, football in particular (Reilly, 1996).

Amateur sports teams have a long tradition of treating each other to refreshments, alcoholic or otherwise, after a match.

That so many early football clubs were attached to public houses by sponsorship, changing rooms, or ground provision both encouraged and facilitated this. Significantly the move into professionalism in football in the late nineteenth century undermined the alcoholic reciprocity between clubs, though at least one team, Dumbarton, elected to continue the after-match socials whenever the opposing team was agreeable, as they felt 'that it would be a pity should it ever be considered necessary – on account of the demands of professionalism, or for any other reason – to eliminate every source of relaxation and enjoyment from the life of the football player, and reduce the game to a mere sordid pursuit (*Scottish Sport*, 4 Sept. 1893). It is noteworthy that this club suffered a sharp decline in their onfield success.

In contrast professional football now often sanctions alcohol consumption. In the British game pre-season team bonding often takes the form of team-drinking sessions. Pat Nevin, ex-chairman of the Professional Footballers Association, maintains that at the start of the football season this is sometimes more desired by managers than absolute fitness (Stewart, 1997). Teams are collections of individuals who may not necessarily get along with each other. On top of personality differences, there is the friction brought about by competition for places. Older players may be wary of newcomers, unwilling to pass on the lessons of experience for fear that it might hasten their journey down the inclined plane to sporting oblivion. The young bloods, aware that few of them will become established in the team, may not assist each other as much the coach might desire. Alcohol is sometimes regarded as a panacea to these problems in that drinking sessions are seen as a way of bringing team-mates together (Atkinson, 1998; Molby, 1999). Yet there is a downside. Mark Bennett of the charity Alcohol Concern put it clearly: 'when you get young men earning enormous sums of money, with enormous amounts of free time and a heavy drinking culture, you have some key indications for an alcohol problem' (*Daily Telegraph*, 13 Oct. 1998).

With increased scientific knowledge on weight loss and alcohol consumption, it might have been expected that their deleterious effects would now a thing of the past. Unfortunately this view is only partially valid. Archer and Hicks may be long gone but others, be they bulimic jockeys or alcoholic sportsmen, have taken their place.

References

An Operator 1828 *Selections from the fancy*. London.
Astley, J.D. 1895 *Fifty years of my life*. London.
Atkinson, R. 1998 *Big Ron: a different ball game*. London.
Bassett, W. I. 1906 The day's work in *The book of football*. London, 110–113.
Cameron, J. 1906 in *Spaldings Football Guide*.
Collingwood, F. 1967 The tragedy of Thomas Loates, *The British Racehorse*, Oct. 1967, 427–8.
Curtis, H.L. 1892 *Principles of training for amateur athletics*. London.
Day, W. 1880 *The racehorse in training*. London.
Dowling, V. 1868 *Fistiana, or oracle of the ring*. London
Duckworth, L. 1974 *The story of Warwickshire cricket*. London.
Evans, G. 1998 Medical cabinet. *Guardian*, 15 May.
Evans, R. 1999 Dunwoody a non-runner in the retirement stakes. *Daily Telegraph*, 22 March.
Fairfax-Blakeborough, J. 1937 *The analysis of the turf*. London.
Ford, J. 1976 *Boxiana*, London.
Frith, D. 1991 *By his own hand: a study of cricket's suicides*. London.
Hansard, 3rd series, vol 156, 11 February 1860; vol 159 12 June 1860.
Harrison, B. 1994 *Drink and the Victorians*. Keele.
Johnston, M (racehorse trainer) 1998 Radio 5, 4 June.
Kent, J. 1892 *The racing life of Lord George Cavendish Bentinck*. London.
Lucas, C.P. 1905 *The Olympic Games 1904*. St Louis: Woodward & Tiernau.
McGowan, B. 1997 Top jockey's great race to beat eating disorder. *Daily Express*, 27 March.
Medicus 1889–90 Football from a medical point of view. *Scottish Football Annual*.
Middleton, I. 2000 The developing pattern of horse racing in Yorkshire 1700–1749: an analysis of the people and the places PhD De Montfort University.
Molby, J. 1999 Real lives. *Total Sport*, 17 November.
Jamie Reid, J. 1998 Cool Clear Walter. *Guardian*, 5 June.
Mortimer, R., Onslow, R. & Willett, P. 1978 *Biographical encyclopedia of British flat racing*. London.
Porter, J. 1896 *Kingsclere*. London.
Radford, P. 2001 *The celebrated Captain Barclay*. London.

Reilly, T 1996 Alcohol, anti-anxiety drugs and sport, in Mottram, D. R., *Drugs in sport.* London.
Shearman, M. 1888 *Athletics and football.* London.
Spencer, E. 1900 *The great game.* London.
Stainback, R.D. 1997 *Alcohol and sport.* Champaign, Ill.
Steel A.G. & Lyttelton, R.H. 1893 *Cricket.* London.
Stewart, D. 1997 *Alcohol: The Ethical Dilemma* MA University of Warwick.
Stonehenge, 1857 *Manual of British rural sports.* London.
Tanner M. & Cranham, G. 1992 *Great jockeys of the flat.* Enfield.
Targett, J. Slim chance, *Sunday Telegraph Magazine,* 29 November
Tolich, M. & Bell, M. 2008 The Commodification of Jockeys' Working Bodies: Anorexia or Work Discipline? In McConville, C. *A Global Racecourse: Work, Culture and Horse Sports.* Melbourne.
Weir, J. 1992 *Drink, religion and Scottish football.* Renfrew.
Welcome, J. 1967 *Fred Archer and his times.* London.
Welcome, J 1990 *Fred Archer: a complete study.* London.
Weston, T. 1953 *My Racing Life.* London.

'Remembering Us Year After Year': The Glasgow Charity Cup 1876–1966[1]

Abstract
Before the First World War Glasgow was the football capital of the world and also the most extensively municipalized city in Britain. Civic pride and enthusiasm for football came together in the promotion of the Glasgow Charity Cup. First played for in 1875, it was the major charity football competition in Britain for almost 90 years, raising the modern equivalent of nearly £11 million. This article will outline the history of the rise and eventual decline of the Glasgow Charity Cup and examine how the organisation of the competition and the disbursement of its revenues were influenced by developments within football and changes in social welfare.

Keywords: Charity, entertainment tax, fans, football, Glasgow, philanthropy, professional sport, Scotland, social welfare.

Introduction
When Glasgow, the second largest urban area in Britain, held its International Exhibition of Industry, Science and Art in 1901, the 11.5 million visitors witnessed the city's triumphs not the abject poverty and deprivation that affected many of its inhabitants.[2] Its industrial economy, heavily dependent on shipbuilding, engineering and the metal trades, created employment in times of boom but was also subject to significant cyclical slumps, as in 1885 when 70 per cent of the shipyards were idle with consequent adverse effects on related sectors.[3] The hardship was aggravated by the Scottish Poor Law which forbade any assistance to an able-bodied man out of work.[4] The slums of the

congested urban tenements meant that tuberculosis, bronchitis and pneumonia were significant causes of death, and sickness was an ever-present threat to life and livelihood.[5] Some of the visitors, however, might have watched a football match arranged as part of the Exhibition festivities, perhaps unaware that their gate-money would be used to aid the sick and needy of the city, something that Glasgow football clubs had been doing for nearly thirty years.

Football was a significant element of the city's popular culture. From the 1870s Glasgow was at the epicentre of football development in Scotland. One historian puts it more strongly: writing in a British, if not an international context, Goldblatt argues that '... the new sport of football acquired its leading edge, its most modern expression, in a single city. In the years before the First World War that city was Glasgow.'[6] Both the Scottish Football Association (SFA) and the Scottish Football League (SFL), the two organisations that controlled football in Scotland, had been housed in the city since their foundation in 1873 and 1890 respectively. Glasgow teams dominated the competitions organised by these bodies. On its establishment the SFA immediately inaugurated a national cup contest which was won by a Glasgow side twenty-five times before 1914. Moreover, until 1887 when the SFA prohibited its members from participation, some Glasgow clubs also performed creditably in the English FA Cup, Queen's Park reaching the final on two occasions in the 1880s and Rangers a semi-final. When the SFL was formed five of the ten constituent clubs hailed from Glasgow; a decade later the League had expanded to eleven clubs, seven of which were Glasgow-based. Between 1890/91 and 1913/14 the league trophy left Glasgow on only three occasions.

Success brought support. By 1914 the aggregate capacity of the grounds of the SFL clubs in Glasgow was over 300,000.[7] Hampden Park, owned by Queen's Park, was the largest stadium in the world and in 1906 hosted a crowd of 121,452 for a Scotland versus England match. Ibrox, home to Rangers, could hold some 75,000 and Celtic Park over 63,000. No other country could match these sports stadia as a trio or any city the number of major soccer clubs within its boundaries. Furthermore, in this, the most densely populated city in Britain, a well developed transport infrastructure, including the municipally-owned tramways, made Glasgow's football grounds accessible.

Most football matches in Glasgow in the 1870s were friendlies, though a few of these were played for local good causes or to raise funds in the aftermath of a specific tragedy or disaster such as a major fire at Bridgeton in 1876.[8] In the latter part of that decade, however, the funding of charity through football was put on a formal, regular basis by the inauguration of the Glasgow Charity Cup, the competition which later featured at the International Exhibition.[9] Three years after its foundation the SFA, confident that it had become 'a very prominent public institution' and that the matches held under its auspices had given considerable pleasure to thousands of spectators, felt that it would be 'a graceful as well as a rightful act ... to close the season with a match for the benefit of some Charitable Institution.' A game was accordingly played in April 1876 between Glasgow and Dumbartonshire which raised £100 for the Glasgow Western Infirmary.[10] Around the same time a group of Glasgow merchants also organised a charity football contest, but by 1878 the two competitions had merged into one which was run by the Glasgow Charity Cup Committee (GCCC), a joint board of merchants and SFA representatives. Often referred to as the Merchants' Cup, this Glasgow Charity Cup competition spanned nearly ninety years and raised nearly £350,000 (nearly £11 million in 2008 prices) for good causes.[11]

This article outlines the history of the rise and eventual decline of the Glasgow Charity Cup. Divided into three time periods, it examines how the organisation of the competition and the disbursement of its revenues were influenced by developments within football and changes in social welfare.

Emerging Patterns in Football and Charity 1876–1914

By 1914 a pattern had emerged of the competition being held post-season in May, with six competing city-based clubs, four of them playing in a first round with the other two joining at the semi-final stage.

In earlier years, however, the number of clubs and who they were could vary from season to season. In 1885 there were five teams, in 1887 eight, but only four in 1889. The choice of teams was at the discretion of the GCCC and no criteria were published.

When SFA cup-winners Vale of Leven queried its non-selection in 1890 it was simply told that those chosen were 'the most suitable'.[12] Throughout the 1880s some leading non-Glasgow teams were invited to participate; probably because they would attract Glasgow spectators keen to see how their own sides would fare against elite opposition. Hibernian from Edinburgh played both in 1887 and 1888. Nearer home there were often places for Renton, Dumbarton and Vale of Leven, successful sides from the west of Scotland. Until the 1891 competition, the first after the establishment of the SFL, clubs used SFA meetings to make recommendations about the composition of the charity tournament, but the GCCC, with merchant representation in the majority and in the chair, remained of independent mind. In 1885, for example, there was a movement by a group of clubs to expand the competition to eight clubs. The SFA went so far as to select the eight from ten nominations, but when one of the omitted clubs protested to the GCCC, the Committee refused to join the debate and opted to have only four clubs.

Although a few would occasionally refuse to play on grounds of principle or protest, generally clubs wanted to participate in the Glasgow competition. When the Glasgow Charity Cup was first played for there was only one major competition, the Scottish FA Cup, for the Glasgow clubs to enter. Early defeat in this could render the rest of the season meaningless in terms of trophy aspirations. The Charity Cup, scheduled towards the end of the season, offered an opportunity for a club to finish on a high note. This prospect of redemption from earlier failures still remained even after the inauguration of a Glasgow Cup in 1887 and the SFL three years later. However the league competition did offer regular competitive fixtures and this signalled a change in the balance of power within Scottish football with consequences for the Charity Cup.

In 1891, in protest at the GCCC's refusal to alter match dates, the newly-formed SFL insisted that Celtic, Rangers and Third Lanark drop out of the tournament. Without these leading teams, the Charity Cup, consisting of Airdrieonians, Partick Thistle, and Queen's Park who played Northern in the final, raised only £150. Moreover the League flexed its muscles and organised its own charity competition which brought in £820.[13] A lesson learned, the Committee gave way and next season switched its fixtures to dates after the League season ended, but the SFA Annual General Meeting also passed a rule saying that all matches including charities and friendlies had to have their permission.[14] In turn the League dropped its charity tournament and the official records encompass the revenue from both the 1891 charity cups, though labelling the League contribution as coming via a supplementary charity committee.[15] Aware of the drawing power of the leading clubs, the GCCC often capitulated to their demands, though usually after a show of resistance. Hence, at the instigation of the clubs, the Committee approved neutral venues (1894), allowed players SFA-cup tied for other clubs to play in the Charity Cup matches (1902) as well as accepting that clubs could switch match dates by mutual agreement.

The establishment of the SFL had other consequences for the charity competition. Those teams with support from virtual village populations could not compete on a regular basis with the city clubs and their resources; so, after only a few years, out of the SFL went twice cup-winners Renton, seven times cup finalists Vale of Leven, and winners of the first two league titles, Dumbarton. This was reflected in the constituent teams of the Glasgow Charity competition which from 1894, with the occasional exception, became Glasgow-based. Celtic, Queen's Park, Rangers and Third Lanark were a regularly chosen quartet. One variation was in 1902, following the disaster at Ibrox in which 26 fans were killed and over 500 injured when a wooden stand collapsed at a Scotland-England match. An attempt to secure more funds for the relief of victims and their families saw the competition broadened 'under the exceptional circumstances' to include St Mirren and Morton from the west and the Edinburgh duo of Heart of Midlothian and eventual winners Hibernian.[16] The experience of the expanded tournament tempted the organisers to add Hibernian and Hearts to the established foursome, but Hearts could not accept the invitation and they were replaced by St Mirren. The 1904 competition reverted to the traditional four Glasgow clubs, but expansion became permanent with the addition of Partick Thistle the next year and Clyde in 1907.

One other development in Scottish football that had an impact on the fund-raising activities of the charity cup competition was the authorisation of professionalism in 1893. All the competing clubs – except for Queen's Park who remained staunchly amateur – immediately began to claim for their players' wages. Initially the Charity Cup Committee insisted that it only pay 'an allowance towards expenses', so Rangers' claim for £49 was reduced to £34, Celtic's £38 to £25 though Third Lanark was granted its full £15. However by 1896 contributions towards wages were clearly acknowledged. At times they were a significant proportion of the gate-money as in 1903 when wages of £242 took 29% of the £840 gate.[17] Also possibly indicative of a change in attitude by the clubs was that the Committee yielded to them on the matter of refreshments; four years after a policy of 'no tea to be given after the game' was declared in 1896, each finalist was receiving a bottle of whisky, a dozen beer and a dozen minerals.[18] Actual donations from the clubs were rare till the twentieth century. In 1899 Celtic donated £15 from its match expenses though no other professional club followed suit till 1906 when most rebated part of their expenses. By 1910 giving back at least 10% was standard practice. Two years later the Secretary of the Charity Cup Committee wrote to all participating clubs requesting them 'to consider a reduction in your expenses for this season's competition'. Whether this embarrassed the clubs is a matter of conjecture but in 1914, when unfavourable weather affected the money raised, neither Rangers nor Celtic charged expenses and the other professional clubs reduced their charges. All clubs also began to provide their own refreshments.[19]

Before 1914 there were less changes on the charity side than on the football one, though there was a special call for help in 1908 when an industrial slump, the worst since 1870s, saw unemployment rise to over 20%. The GCCC gave £200 to the Glasgow Unemployed Distress Relief Fund and £25 for the same cause in Govan and Partick.[20]

As philanthropy historian Prochaska has noted 'the charitable are free to choose the objects of their concern and make decisions about them independent of external control.'[21] Most money was dispersed at the discretion of the GCCC though, initially, some was allocated to any non-Glasgow teams in the competition who then distributed it to charities of their own choosing. What charities were selected by the GCCC and how much each received was public knowledge, the details being published annually in the Glasgow press. Unfortunately, however, even the GCCC minutes do not reveal how or why the recipients were chosen. References were occasionally made to a Deed of Assignment (alas untraceable) when some requests were turned down. For example, St Mary's Catholic Institute in Edinburgh was informed that the Deed made 'no stipulation for other than charitable' organisations and these could not be outside 'Glasgow or the West of Scotland'.[22]

Who was eligible is to an extent discernable from the actual disbursements. The instigators of Glasgow's charity football matches appear to have had two major groups in mind when they drew up the earliest lists of beneficiaries – hospitals and homes. After the initial SFA donation to the Western Infirmary in 1876, the proceeds of the 1877 match (£130) were settled on the Home for Incurables. At the same time £250 was raised via the Merchants' Cup competition, to be divided between the Western and Royal Infirmaries. The same institutions shared the gate monies in 1878. The following year, the first in which a merged competition took place, saw the number of recipients rise to eight, with the addition of Mr Quarrier's Orphan Homes, Dunoon Seaside Homes ('a boon and a blessing for ... many a weary and suffering one'[23]) and charities representing the deaf and dumb, the blind, and the poor of Alexandria (Dumbartonshire). However, more than half the money raised, £300 from a total of £545, was donated to the Glasgow Unemployed Fund, the matches taking place in spring 1879 during the period of economic crisis following the City of Glasgow Bank collapse.

Thereafter the list of charities expanded rapidly with 19–24 beneficiaries in the period 1880–83, two-thirds of which were hospitals or homes. A further aspect of the early distribution list was its emphasis on women and children, always amongst the poorest and most needy in Victorian society. By 1883 the major city infirmaries had been joined by the Lenzie Convalescent Home (where half of the beds were reserved for the Infirmaries' patients), the Maternity Hospital, the Hospital for Sick Children, the Ophthalmic Institution and the separate Eye Infirmary, the Lock Hospital and the Ear Infirmary. The Home for Deserted Mothers, the House for Infirm and Imbecile Children, and the Night Asylum for the Houseless were among the 'houses of shelter' supported by the GCCC. Other charities to benefit at this time included the Dumbarton Benevolent Society, the Magdalen Institution and the Widows' Friend Society, which relieved 'destitute Christian widows in Glasgow.'[24]

While most of these were entirely appropriate, others had a hint of the risqué, or were at best unpopular. The Lock Hospitals, located in several British cities, were said to be 'unattractive to philanthropists' as their patients were generally prostitutes and a cure for venereal diseases was viewed as an incentive to immorality. Glasgow's first Magdalen Asylum was established in 1815 and later merged with a second society to form the Magdalen Institution, for the repression of vice and to provide a temporary home for 'females who have strayed from the paths of virtue.' Even maternity or lying-in hospitals were said to be a dubious choice for charitable funds as the morally righteous were concerned that some unmarried women were being admitted. But ignorance on the part of donors allowed the Glasgow Eye Infirmary to be 'warmly regarded by the subscribing public,' unaware that some of the eye conditions being treated were the result of venereal diseases.[25]

The amounts donated to those institutions lucky enough to be supported by the Glasgow Charity Cup matches were not large but they were regular. Although the annual donation could be as little as £5–10 (roughly £375–750 in current prices), the fact that it could be relied on was probably helpful. Of the 24 charities listed in 1883, three-quarters were funded until either they or the Cup itself ceased to exist. Eight hospitals received money up to the advent of the National Health Service in 1948; the Magdalen Institution was resourced until its closure in 1959; and the Widows' Friend Society, Dunoon Seaside Home and the Mission to the Outdoor Blind were still obtaining charitable funds in 1966, the final year of the Charity Cup.

Both the scale and the extent of giving continued to grow throughout the late Victorian era but while donations fluctuated widely from year to year, the number of charities receiving aid moved steadily upwards. The 24 charities of 1883 had become 54 by 1890 and 67 by 1900. They peaked at 80 in 1908 and remained at no lower than 72 for the next thirty years. The stability of the distribution list was such that a printed, rather than a handwritten, roll of recipients was pasted annually into the *Charity Cup Minute Books* from the turn of the century. Medical charities and residential homes continued to dominate. St Andrews Ambulance (from 1884), the Dental Hospital – funded wholly by philanthropic effort – the Samaritan Hospital for Women (from 1889), and the Cancer and Skin Institution (from 1896) were amongst the new beneficiaries, along with refuges and orphanages. The young remained a priority with children's day nurseries, the Society for the Prevention of Cruelty to Children and the 'poor children's dinner tables' – providing one hot meal per day — added to the list. The even quainter sounding Children's Fresh Air Fund and the Foundry Boys Fair Holiday Excursion Fund both had their origins in religious movements, the former set up by the Glasgow United Evangelical Association to take children into the country for a fortnight, the latter an initiative of the Foundry Boys' Religious Society – 'for the religious, educational and social elevation of boys and girls'.[26] The highlight of a year spent in drill classes, religious meetings and musical entertainments was the Fair Week trip to a camp at Inveraray Castle, at a cost per child of five shillings (25 pence). The annual contribution from the Glasgow Charity Cup would usually have paid for 20 children to participate.

No discussion of football, charity and Scotland can ignore the sectarian issue. Celtic was founded in 1888 specifically to support local Catholic charities and first played in the Glasgow Charity Cup the following year. Immediately the first overtly Catholic charities – the Society of St Vincent de Paul, the Little Sisters of the Poor and the Children's Refuge at Whitevale – were added to the list, amidst a general expansion of recipient charities most of which would have been available to the public generally, irrespective of religion. Another eight Catholic charities joined the list before 1914 including, in 1904, the Roman Catholic Discharged Prisoners Aid Society funded alongside a similar named organisation (less the religious descriptor) which had been in operation since 1856 and in receipt of Charity Cup money from 1900.

Charity matches did not just benefit the recipients of the money raised. Many of the fans who paid to watch the games may have belonged to that half of working-class and artisan families who gave regularly to charity in the 1890s but, as well as helping others, they were also consumers purchasing entertainment.[27] The members of the GCCC who disbursed the funds gained power, publicity and additional status by subscribing to voluntary hospitals and residential charities.[28] And what of the football clubs themselves? As well as gaining a favourable image and the chance to win a trophy, there is also the question of whether charity began at home. Alex Wylie, a trustee of the GCCC from 1889, maintained 'charity was the noblest object that any young man in the full flush of health could devote himself to, and the players had excelled themselves this year in relieving those whose physical condition was in such a marked contrast to their own'.[29] But was it totally disinterested behaviour? The money donated to hospitals and homes was often used as subscriptions for lines which entitled the GCCC and the participating clubs to nominate persons for beds and for convalescence: and this could and did include footballers.[30] In 1882 a letter had been sent to the Western Infirmary asking what they intended to do in the future as several persons sent by the SFA had not been admitted. Whether these were players is not stated, but, thirty years later, the GCCC lambasted the Victoria Infirmary after two players had to wait several weeks for admission despite their injuries.[31] The incident led to a letter being sent to all three major infirmaries asking 'if you are prepared to facilitate the entrance of an injured football player to your institution'.[32]

Although virtually ignored by the historians of philanthropy, the nineteenth-century charity football match was as innovatory a fund-raiser as the 'charity bazaar, flag day or deed of covenant'.[33] The success of the Glasgow Charity Cup spawned a host of imitators and by the end of the 1880s there were at least nineteen other Scottish charity competitions of note being played.[34] Even more significant was the influence south of the border where major charity cups were inaugurated in London, Sheffield and Birmingham modelled on that of Glasgow.[35] Such competitive charity fixtures provided a symbiotic relationship between football and charity: the teams gained meaningful fixtures and the charities obtained money.

However the Glasgow competition remained the most successful in terms of attendance and fundraising. This can be attributed to the concentration of elite clubs within the conurbation which made many games local derbies. All these clubs had their coterie of fans who identified not just with their club but also the area of the city that the team represented be it, among others, Rangers from Kinning Park and Ibrox (with sizeable support also in Govan and Hyndland), Third Lanark from Govanhall and the Gorbals, Clyde from Bridgeton and Rutherglen, Partick Thistle from Maryhill, Partick and other areas in the west end, and Celtic from Parkhead and Irish catholic communities in the east end and northern districts.[36] A set of communities looked to their team for entertainment, reinforcement of civic pride, and, of course, defeating local rivals. As shown in the appendix small contributions via the turnstile produced significant sums for distribution to charitable activities

Marking Time 1915–1946

The Scottish FA Cup was not held between 1915 and 1919 and, although the Scottish League continued to function during the First World War, the quality suffered as teams were often depleted by having lost men to the services or to war work at home. However, perhaps because of the non-existence of the national knockout competition, the Glasgow Charity Cup continued to attract good crowds. In the immediate post-war years football boomed. The Scottish FA Cup was resurrected; teams were at full-strength; and spectators, many of them back from the frontline, thronged to watch the games. In line with other tournaments attendance at Glasgow Charity Cup games soared. Inevitably this fell away but good crowds were maintained for most of the inter-war period. A prime reason for this was the dominance of Rangers who won the league title on all but five occasions. Often by late January their triumph was virtually assured and attendances throughout the league declined as matches became meaningless. Even Celtic and Rangers themselves might muster crowds of only 12,000 for such games. In contrast the Glasgow Charity Cup provided some excitement at the end of an often predictable season. There was always a chance in a knockout tournament that luck or a one-off performance could bring victory to any of the Glasgow teams.

There were no innovations in the structure or composition of the Charity Cup throughout this period. However, in 1937 the GCCC took up an invitation from the Corporation of Glasgow to organise an additional match against a team selected by the Rosebery Charity Cup Committee, its Edinburgh equivalent, as part of a sports carnival to celebrate the coronation of King Edward VIII. They were offered £100 towards their funds but negotiated £250 plus the surplus after expenses, eventually receiving £1487.[37]

Although Glasgow's heavy industries made a major contribution to the war effort, the inflexible structure of the city's economy with too large a proportion of resources in traditional, but declining, activities meant that its workers suffered heavily in the inter-war depression and failed to benefit significantly from the growth of new industries in the 1930s. In 1933 three in every ten of the insured population was unemployed.[38] The economic experience exacerbated social problems, particularly those associated with congested living conditions: in 1935 29% of the city's homes were officially designated as overcrowded.[39] Although the National Insurance Act of 1911 began to offer a basic income during sickness and, for some, during unemployment, even by 1939 less than half the population was covered.[40] As always, immorality, crime and alcoholism were both a result of and a contributory factor to poverty and illness. Hence throughout the inter-war years there was a continued demand for charitable relief towards which the revenues of the Glasgow Charity Cup contributed.

The introduction of an entertainment tax in 1916 gave the GCCC an opportunity to extend their charitable donations.[41] The tax, initially a penny on a sixpence entry fee, had to be collected but was later remitted and the GCCC used the lump sums obtained to endow beds first in the infirmaries and then, during the 1920s and early 1930s, in several residential homes and specialist hospitals. The demand for football appears to have been price inelastic and thus provided a windfall gain to the Committee.

The *Glasgow Evening News* in 1930 claimed 'the task of allocating money to 72 different institutions was by no means an easy one'.[42] The continued use of a printed list suggests that this was not the case and most of the charities which received donations before the First World War continued to do so throughout the inter-war years. The minutes of the GCCC show that fresh applications were rarely entertained and certainly not from various miners' organisations who applied for funds to run soup kitchens during their strike in 1921.[43] Of the 76 charities receiving aid in 1914, 63 continued to be funded in 1936 and 53 in 1946. Newcomers in the inter-war period receiving at least £25 regularly were the David Elder Infirmary, the Elder Cottage Hospital, the Glasgow

Nursing Association, and intermittently the St. Vincent de Paul Country Home. New recipients of regular smaller sums were the Anderston Health Association, the Catholic Nursing Society, Garnethill Girls Refuge, St Charles Institute and St Vincent School, Tollcross. Somewhat ironically when the GCCC opted to revise the list in 1941 and included two new organisations, the Scottish Convalescent Home for Children and the Scottish National Homeopathic Hospital, the cheques to both were returned their premises had been taken over for war purposes.[44]

A Brave New World 1947–1966

The establishment of the National Health Service in Scotland after the Second World War effectively nationalised the majority of voluntary hospitals and thus undermined the basic donation strategy of the Glasgow Charity Cup Committee.[45] In 1946 52.5% of their funds had gone to hospitals. They thus sought and obtained permission from the SFA to depart from their original charter 'and be allowed to include in their list of donations such organisations, either local or national, recognised as eligible for exemption from the entertainment tax, whose objects are solely to social welfare or the encouragement of youth.' The immediate decision was to double the level of donations to extant charities on their list with the balance going to organisations concerned with health and fitness (which they regarded as preventative medicine), institutions associated with the treatment of war wounded, and 'special cases'.[46] Glasgow Corporation itself took steps to reduce another problem. Almost 50,000 municipal homes were built in the immediate post-war period to ease the pressure of accommodation demand and a clearance programme began in the 1950s to redevelop inner-city Glasgow and relocate much of its population.[47] Nevertheless, despite a state-funded health service and improved housing, letters to the GCCC appealing for funds demonstrate that even in the world of the welfare state there were new demands for financial assistance. Not many were given it. The minutes from the early 1950s are replete with applications not being entertained and reductions in the amounts given to those on the list. The newcomers that replaced the hospitals of the donations list were the Association for Relief of the Incurables, Bellevue Children's Home, the British Empire Cancer Research (replacing the money going to the Cancer

Hospital), the Central Council for Physical Recreation, the Children's Holiday Home, the Children's Welfare Home, the City of Glasgow Society for Social Services, Earl Haig Fund, Erskine Hospital (for ex-servicemen), Glasgow Hospital Auxilaries Association, Hazlewood Nurses Home, the Playing Fields Association, St John Foundation Hospital, Scottish Convalescent Home for Children, Scottish Physiotherapy Hospital, Scottish Veterans Garden City Association and the YMCA Forces Fund. Many of these were eligible under the old criteria.

Like health and housing, football too changed after the war; but not as quickly. The immediate post-war years witnessed huge crowds at competitive soccer matches including the Glasgow Charity Cup with consequent record donations. Yet inexorably its status as a football tournament declined. The League and Scottish Cup titles had always been the more important with the Glasgow Cup and Charity Cup increasingly being seen as consolation competitions. Both the latter tournaments suffered from the late 1950s when the glamour (and financial rewards) of playing in European competitions beckoned and neither of these Glasgow-based cups offered an entry route.

By 1961 the Chairman of the Cup Committee was expressing his disappointment and concern at the almost uninterrupted decline in the annual amounts collected over a period of years. The Committee 'generally agreed that the competition no longer achieved its purpose' and it was agreed to play it one more time only with the winners to retain the trophy.[48] Rangers refused to enter so eventually a Glasgow Select game was played against Manchester United though in October rather than the traditional May. Although Glasgow lost, the city's charities gained as, in real terms, more money was distributed than in any year since 1951. No wonder one recipient thought 'the Committee are to be congratulated on the reorganisation of the competition'.[49] This from a single game rather than a cup competition! Moreover both Scottish Television and the BBC paid for broadcasting rights.[50] The Committee seized on this path to salvation and successive seasons witnessed matches against Manchester United again, followed by Chelsea and Tottenham. Each year however, receipts declined. One reason was the difficulty of getting Rangers and Celtic players to participate and they were the 'backbone of the Glasgow XI'.[51] Risking injury to key players in post-season matches had been a different proposition to asking them to play in October when all Scottish titles were still up for competition.

A nadir was reached in 1966 when, after Liverpool were unable to accept an invitation, the second choice of Leeds United failed to ignite any enthusiasm and only £1,072 was available for distribution, the lowest amount in real terms for ninety years. Donations were reduced to only £16 per organisation. William Martin of the British Sailors' Society was philosophical in his acknowledgement to William P. Allan, Secretary of Glasgow Charity Cup Committee:

> 'I appreciate your remarks regarding the diminishing of receipts but this is a thing over which we have no control and, as you say, possibly next year's match will help'[52]

But there were no further matches. Manchester United declined an invitation. Arsenal agreed to come but the match was cancelled because of atrocious weather and it proved impossible to secure a fresh date.

In vain the Committee invited Real Madrid, Manchester United and its City rival. Spare dates were hard to find especially when the Committee could not offer any financial guarantees. Until the proposed Arsenal match the visiting team had been paid travel and hotel expenses; its players rewarded with £20 each in money orders or premium bonds (so as not to break the maximum wage rules operating in England); and the club itself offered £1,000 to distribute to its chosen charities. However, in view of the 'disappointing return' from the Leeds match 'it was decided not to undertake any commitment to Arsenal FC and to await the outcome before reaching a conclusion.'[53] Although the London side had been willing to take a chance, others were not.[54]

Even had significant opposition been available, fans were not willing to see them play against a Glasgow side weakened by the withdrawal of Old Firm stars. Suggestions to attract fans ranged from the fanciful of having the Portuguese superstar Eusebio as a guest player, through providing extra entertainment via the US Air Force Band playing before the game and a five-a-side match between Celtic and Rangers at half-time, to the desperate resort of securing publicity by inviting the local press to cocktails! In July 1968 the Committee discussed 'the question of the future of the Glasgow Charity Cup and were unanimous in their concern and apprehension'.[55] This was the last entry in the Minute Book.

Conclusion

The International Exhibition of 1901 culminated several decades of civic pride, exemplified in Glasgow's architecture, creative cultural life, unrivalled open space and parkland, and municipalisation, the most extensive in Britain which by 1900 included the city's water, gas and electricity supplies, the tramways and the telephone system.[56] Set in this context, the development of the Charity Cup competition can be seen as a further example of Glasgow's pioneering efforts to provide for its citizens: relief for the less fortunate and entertainment for the football fans.

It was a cooperative form of benevolence. It gave merchants and other leading citizens the opportunity to overtly demonstrate their philanthropic role whilst most of the money came from working-class football followers who simultaneously bought entertainment and helped others.[57] Once it had become a permanent feature of the fixture list, withdrawing from the Glasgow Charity Cup does not appear to have been contemplated by the football clubs. There would have been too much loss of image and anyway it was a cheap, convenient and overt way for a club to support charity.

Table One:

Glasgow Charity Cup and FA Charity Shield: Comparison of Money Distributed to Charity (£)

Period	Glasgow Charity Cup	FA Charity Shield
1909–1914	7885	2564
1915–1919	11750	Not played
1920–1929	46630	7587
1930–1939	37500	8981
1940–1948	41165	Not played
1949–1959	102455	37629
1960–1966	50437	56279

Source: Calculated from data in *Minutes of Glasgow Charity Cup Committee* and *Minutes of Football Association.*

The Glasgow tournament was the first major charity cup competition and was 'for long the most successful, in financial terms, local competition in Britain'.[58] Over its existence the Glasgow Charity Cup raised the modern equivalent of nearly £11 million and when compared specifically with the Football Association Charity Shield in England, as shown in Table One, was a substantially greater fundraiser. One reason for this was that, for most of its life, it was a tournament rather than a one-off game which meant that several matches were played, each contributing to the revenue stream. Yet for almost ninety years the generous football fans of Glasgow were prepared to pay to attend these, perhaps because as well as supporting their teams they were aware that the proceeds went to local charities.[59] Philanthropy implies a redistribution of income but in the case of the Glasgow Charity Cup it did not mean from the rich to the poor but from football supporters to those receiving aid from institutions selected by the Charity Cup Committee. Many recipients, like the Glasgow Home for Deserted Mothers, which had received aid from 1880, were grateful to the GCCC for 'remembering us year after year.'[60]

Appendix: Glasgow Charity Cup Statistics 1875–1966

Season beginning	Matches	Gate Receipts* (£)	Tax Rebate (£)	Donations to Charity (£)	Donations (2007 £)	Charities Aided
1875		?		200	14400	
1876		?		380	27360	
1877		?		420	30240	
1878		?		545	40875	9
1879		?		510	39780	23
1880		?		520	39000	23
1881		?		450	34200	19
1882		?		750	56250	23
1883		?		345	26220	24
1884	4?	?		600	46800	34

68] *How the Game was Played*

Season beginning	Matches	Gate Receipts* (£)	Tax Rebate (£)	Donations to Charity (£)	Donations (2007 £)	Charities Aided
1885	3?	?		520	42120	40
1886	3?	?		380	31160	?
1887	7?	?		1200	98400	?
1888	7?	?		1050	86100	?
1889	3?	?		1700	137700	?
1890	3?	?		900	72900	?
1891	3?	?		970	77600	?
1892	5	1168		1000	80000	58
1893	4	670		540	43200	58
1894	3	1528		1380	113160	61
1895	3	1169		1000	83000	63
1896	3	1380		1100	91300	65
1897	3	1599		1400	114800	66
1898	3	993		750	61500	66
1899	3	1152		950	76950	68
1900	4	1032		825	63525	69
1901	4	1055		810	61560	68
1902	8	950		550	41800	68
1903	6	838		500	38000	67
1904	3	1382		1100	83600	69
1905	5	873		600	45600	70
1906	4	997		830	63080	69
1907	5	1657		1400	105000	70
1908	6	2746		2250	168750	80
1909	5	1850		1500	112500	79
1910	5	1245		1000	74000	77
1911	5	1420		1130	83620	77
1912	5	1600		1305	93960	77

Remembering Us Year After Year [69

Season beginning	Matches	Gate Receipts* (£)	Tax Rebate (£)	Donations to Charity (£)	Donations (2007 £)	Charities Aided
1913	5	1833		1500	108000	77
1914	5	1589		1450	104400	77
1915	5	1519		1450	92800	79
1916	5	2092		2000	108000	79
1917	5	2270	401	2150	92450	79
1918	5	2317	700	2150	75250	76
1919	5	4214	1299	4000	128000	76
1920	5	5742	1628	8000	224000	78
1921	5	5405	1589	6400	198400	77
1922	5	4331	1240	6200	223200	79
1923	5	4022	1138	5100	193800	77
1924	5	2787	781	3950	150100	75
1925	5	3027	541	2830	107540	73
1926	5	3327	599	4400	167200	74
1927	5	2653	493	2500	97500	72
1928	5	3661	698	4500	175500	73
1929	5	2881	528	2750	110000	72
1930	5	3832	715	4950	202950	73
1931	5	4335	811	5200	223600	74
1932	5	2925	581	3800	167200	74
1933	5	2444	485	3135	141075	77
1934	5	2821	560	3250	146250	74
1935	5	2325	460	2650	116600	77
1936	5	3233	594	3655	160820	79
1937	5	2540	469	3150	135450	79
1938	5	3625	667	4110	172620	78
1939	5	3167	576	3600	147600	78
1940	5	1986	356	2250	78750	77

Season beginning	Matches	Gate Receipts* (£)	Tax Rebate (£)	Donations to Charity (£)	Donations (2007£)	Charities Aided
1941	5	2058	593	2520	78120	70
1942	5	2590	745	3200	92800	70
1943	5	3492	1788	5130	143640	77
1944	5	3612	2206	5650	152550	79
1945	6	6428	4081	10210	265460	82
1946	5	8173	1847	9800	245000	83
1947	5	7814	1699	9250	222000	81
1948	5	10754	2251	12700	279400	67
1949	5	10189	808	10600	233200	68
1950	5	12841	1071	13576	285096	66
1951	5	11550	887	11904	226176	65
1952	5	8600	686	8720	156960	65
1953	5	7805	1962	9340	168120	65
1954	5	7124	1833	8560	154080	64
1955	5	?	tax ended	7610	129370	64
1956	5	?		6900	110400	64
1957	5	?		10230	163680	66
1958	5	?		5940	89100	66
1959	5	?		9175	137625	66
1960	5	?		4745	71175	65
1961	1	?		3805	57075	64
1962	1	?		14160	198240	67
1963	1	?		7985	111790	66
1964	1	?		12035	156455	68
1965	1	?		6535	84955	67
1966	1	?		1072	12864	67

Source: **Calculated from data in** *SFA Annuals, Minutes of Scottish Football Association, Minutes of Glasgow Charity Cup Committee,* **and** *Glasgow Charity Cup Committee Cash Book.*
Notes: *excludes entertainment tax.

Bibliographical references

AIRD, A., *Glimpses of old Glasgow*. Glasgow: Aird & Coghill, 1894.
BERRIDGE, V. Health and medicine. In: THOMPSON, F.M.L. (Ed.) *The Cambridge social history of Britain 1750–1950* Volume 3. Cambridge: Cambridge University Press, 1993, p.171–242.
CARLS, K. Glasgow 1901. In: FINDLING, J.E.; KIMBERLEY D.P. (Eds.). *Historical dictionary of world's fairs and expositions 1851–1988*. Westport Connecticut: Greenwood, 1990, p. 172–173.
CHECKLAND, O. *Philanthropy in Victorian Scotland*. Edinburgh: John Donald, 1980.
CHECKLAND, S. *The upas tree: Glasgow 1875–1975*. Glasgow: University of Glasgow Press, 1977.
GIBB, A. *Glasgow: the making of a city*. London: Croom Helm, 1983.
GOLDBLATT, D. *The ball is round: a global history of football*. London: Viking, 2006.
JACKSON, N.L. *Association football*. London: George Newnes, 1900.
MAVER, I. *Glasgow*. Edinburgh: Edinburgh University Press, 2000.
MAVER, I. *No mean city: 1914–1950s: neighbourhoods*. Available at http://www.theglasgowstory. Accessed 16 May 2008.
MUIR, J.H. *Glasgow in 1901*. Glasgow: William Hodge, 1901.
PROCHASKA, F.K. Philanthropy. In: THOMPSON, F.M.L. (Ed.) *The Cambridge social history of Britain 1750–1950* Volume 3. Cambridge: Cambridge University Press, 1993, p.357–394.
ROBERTSON, F.H.C. *The Glasgow merchants' charity cup*. Association of Football Statisticians Report No. 25, 1982.
ROBINSON, R. *History of Queen's Park F.C. 1867–1917*. Glasgow: Hay Nisbet, 1920.
SMOUT, T.C. Scotland 1850–1950. In: THOMPSON, F.M.L. (Ed.). *The Cambridge social history of Britain 1750–1950* Volume 1. Cambridge: Cambridge University Press, 1993, p. 209–280.
SPARLING, R.A. *The romance of the Wednesday 1867–1926*. Sheffield: Leng, 1926.
TREBLE, J.H. Skilled sectionalism, unemployment and class in Glasgow. In: FRASER D. (Ed.). *Cities, class and communication*. Hemel Hempstead: Harvester Wheatsheaf, 1990, p. 127–151.

ARCHIVES HELD AT SCOTTISH FOOTBALL MUSEUM, GLASGOW.
Minutes of Scottish Football Association.
Minutes of Glasgow Charity Cup Committee.
Letter Books of Glasgow Charity Cup Committee.
Cashbook of Glasgow Charity Cup Committee.
Letter Book of J.K. McDowell.

NEWSPAPERS
Glasgow Evening Times.
Scottish Sport.

ANNUALS
Athletic News Football Annual.
SFA Annual.

References

1. The author is grateful to the Nuffield Foundation for financial assistance, to Dr Joyce Kay for research assistance, and to the staff of the Scottish Football Museum for access to their archives, library and knowledge.

2. CARLS, K. Glasgow 1901. In: FINDLING, J.E.; KIMBERLEY D.P. (Eds.). *Historical dictionary of world's fairs and expositions, 1851–1988*. Westport Connecticut: Greenwood, 1990, p. 172–173.

3. For an overview of the Glasgow economy with specific reference to unemployment see TREBLE, J.H. Skilled sectionalism, unemployment and class in Glasgow. In: FRASER D. (Ed.), *Cities, class and communication*. Hemel Hempstead: Harvester Wheatsheaf, 1990, 127–151.

4. SMOUT, T.C. Scotland 1850–1950. In: THOMPSON, F.M.L. (Ed.). *The Cambridge social history of Britain 1750–1950*. Volume 1. Cambridge: Cambridge University Press, 1993, p. 255.

5. For general information on Glasgow's history see MAVER, I. *Glasgow*. Edinburgh: Edinburgh University Press, 2000. On the Scottish economy see SMOUT. Scotland, p. 209–227.

6. GOLDBLATT, D. *The ball is round: a global history of football*. London: Viking, 2006. p. 68.

7. GOLDBLATT, *The ball is round*. p. 68.

8. *Glasgow Evening Times*, 17 March 1877.

9. So successful had the competition become that the Exhibition

organisers paid £1050 to the Glasgow Charity Cup Committee for the right to host the tournament. *Minutes of GCCC*, 5 April 1901. Scottish Football Museum, Glasgow.

10. *Scottish Football Association Annual 1876–77*. Glasgow: SFA, 1877, p. 27, 45. The SFA stated that £200 was handed over to charity and this appears in the [retrospective] official records of the Charity Cup. Where the other £100 came from is unknown.

11. For statistics see the Appendix. The actual date of the first acknowledged game for the Glasgow Charity Cup is unclear and is currently being researched by Dr Joyce Kay of the Department of Sports Studies at the University of Stirling.

12. *Minutes of SFA*, 28 March 1890. Scottish Football Museum, Glasgow.

13. *Minutes of SFA*, 24 March 1891, 2 April 1891; ROBINSON, R. *History of Queen's Park F.C. 1867–1917*. Glasgow: Hay Nisbet, 1920, p.181–2; Scottish Sport, 5 April 1892, p. 4.

14. *Minutes of SFA*, 12 May 1891. Ironically, after the Charity Cup Committee faced reality and switched to more suitable dates for the League teams, Queen's Park, a stalwart of the Charity Cup but a club that refused to join the League for a decade, did not play in the 1893 tournament as it ended its season before League fixtures were complete and hence before the Charity Cup competition began. *Minutes of GCCC*, 18 April 1893.

15. *Athletic News Football Annual 1894*, p.109.

16. *Minutes of GCCC*, 17 April 1902.

17. *Cashbook of GCCC*. Scottish Football Museum, Glasgow.

18. *Minutes of GCCC*, 4 June 1895, 5 June 1896, 9 April 1896, 18 April 1900.

19. *Minutes of GCCC*, 7 June 1899, 9 June 1905, 8 June 1910; letter 23 March 1912; *Glasgow Evening Times*, 10 June 1914.

20. *Minutes of GCCC*, 13 May 1908.

21. PROCHASKA, F.K. Philanthropy. In: THOMPSON, F.M.L. (Ed.), *The Cambridge social history of Britain 1750–1950* Volume 3. Cambridge: Cambridge University Press, 1993, p. 392.

22. *Minutes of SFA*, 13 June 1887.

23. AIRD, A., *Glimpses of old Glasgow*. Glasgow: Aird & Coghill,1894, p.203.

24. AIRD, *Glimpses of old Glasgow*, p. 202–207.

25. CHECKLAND, O., *Philanthropy in Victorian Scotland*. Edinburgh: John Donald, 1980, p. 185, 192–194, 233–237.

26. AIRD, *Glimpses of old Glasgow*, p.199.
27. PROCHASKA, F.K. Philanthropy, p. 358.
28. BERRIDGE, V. Health and medicine. In: THOMPSON, F.M.L. (Ed.) *The Cambridge social history of Britain 1750–1950* Volume 3. Cambridge: Cambridge University Press, 1993, p.204; PROCHASKA, Philanthropy, p. 374.
29. Press cutting in *Minutes of GCCC*, 13 May 1908.
30. Letters to Sir John Primrose 12 June 1913 and to Mr Anderson 12 June 1913. *Letter Book of J.K. McDowall*, Scottish Football Museum, Glasgow.
31. *Minutes of SFA*, 5 May 1882; *Minutes of GCCC*, 29 May 1913.
32. *Letter Book of J.M. McDowell*, 12 March 1913.
33. PROCHASKA. Philanthropy, p. 384.
34. Calculated from *SFA Annuals*.
35. This was certainly the case for the Sheffield and London tournaments and most likely for the Birmingham one given the long relationship between the Football Associations in the two cities. JACKSON, N.L. *Association football*. London: George Newnes, 1900, p. 153; SPARLING, R.A. *The romance of the Wednesday 1867–1926*. Sheffield: Leng, 1926, p.49.
36. Queen's Park was a special case because of its unique position in Scottish football and its support spread across the south side beyond the Mount Florida district. Moreover by 1914 both Celtic and Rangers, for a variety of reasons, were drawing fans from across Glasgow. For a view of football in the life of the Glasgow working man see MUIR, J.H. *Glasgow in 1901*. Glasgow: William Hodge, 1901, p. 192–3.
37. *Minutes of GCCC*, 30 March 1937, 12 April 1937, 31 August 1937.
38. MAVER. Glasgow, p. 207.
39. MAVER, I. *No mean city: 1914–1950s: neighbourhoods*. Available at http://www.theglasgowstory. Accessed 16 May 2008. See also CHECKLAND, S. *The upas tree: Glasgow 1875–1975*. Glasgow: University of Glasgow Press, 1977, p. 35–40.
40. BERRIDGE. Health and medicine, p. 229.
41. *Minutes of GCCC*, 16 April 1916.
42. *Glasgow Evening News*, 14 May 1930.
43. *Minutes of GCCC*, 18 May 1921.
44. *Minutes of GCCC*, 19 June 1941, 14 April 1942, 5 April 1943.
45. BERRIDGE. Health and medicine, p.238.
46. *Minutes of GCCC*, 25 June 1948, 25 March 1949.
47. GIBB, A. *Glasgow: the making of a city*. London: Croom Helm, 1983,

p.160–168.
48. *Minutes of GCCC*, 3 August 1961.
49. W. Martin to W.P.Allen, 24 October 1962. *Letter Books of GCCC*.
50. D. Paterson to W.P.Allen 13 July 1962; D. Livingston to W.P. Allen 10 August 1962. *Letter Books of GCCC*.
51. *Minutes of GCCC*, 18 July 1968.
52. W. Martin to W.P.Allen, 24 December 1966. *Letter Books of GCCC*.
53. *Minutes of GCCC*, 8 December 1967.
54. *Minutes of GCCC*, 14 February 1967.
55. *Minutes of GCCC*, 18 July 1968.
56. SMOUT. Scotland, p. 252.
57. Prochaska, unaware of the nineteenth-century football matches, sees the charity sports event as a modern continuation of the idea of combining charitable activity with recreation as with the jumble sale, dinners and balls, concerts and Sunday School marches [PROCHASKA. Philanthropy, p. 383–384].
58. ROBERTSON, F.H.C. *The Glasgow merchants' charity cup.* Association of Football Statisticians Report No. 25, 1982, p. 19.
59. Glasgow also had the perpetual rivalry between Celtic and Rangers. In 64% of the years when they were drawn together their tie provided over 40% of the total gate revenue for the tournament. Moreover average aggregate gate receipts were 5–9% higher when the two played each other and from 1934 they were 16–19% higher when they met in the final..
60. M. Jenkins to W.P. Allen, 18 October 1962. *Letter Books of GCCC*.

Sports Without Rules: Hunting, Shooting and Fishing in Edwardian Britain[1]

Writing of football in 1905, sporting commentator G.B. Pollock-Hodsoll declared that as 'a sport strictly controlled by regulation' it differed from those 'such as hunting and fishing where practically everything is left to the individual to honour in the breach or the observance.'[2] This study will explore the Edwardian field sports of hunting, shooting and fishing which operated around a set of conventions and rituals rather than formalised rules.[3]

The basic premise is that most country sports did not require formal, written rules because either they were not competitive (in the sense of having acknowledged winners and losers) or they were not associated with gambling. Where these factors were involved then written rules did emerge as in coursing and cockfighting.[4] The few written rules in hunting, shooting and fishing were essentially local ones often concerned with financial matters such as when hunting subscriptions or capping fees should be paid.[5]

Field Sports in Edwardian Britain

Hunting, shooting and fishing were major sports which one critic estimated had £14 million expended on them annually.[6] *Baily's Hunting Directory* for 1906/07 identified 203 packs of foxhounds in Britain (including Ireland) 136 of harriers, 71 of footharriers and beagles, 22 of otterhounds and 21 of staghounds. In 1902 62,501 sporting gun licences were issued in Britain; and in one branch of shooting by 1911 over a third of the total land area in the Scottish crofting counties was devoted to deer stalking.[7]

In 1910 7,308 rod licences were issued for salmon fishing and a further 59,655 for other forms of angling.[8]

Although there was some continuity from the mid-nineteenth century, by the Edwardian period major changes had occurred in the techniques and organisation of field sports. In shooting, the traditional walking up, where dogs were used to flush out birds to be shot by the approaching guns, was giving way to the *battue* where vast numbers of birds, bred specifically for game purposes, were driven by lines of beaters towards stationary shooters.[9] Although grouse, unlike pheasants and partridges, were not reared artificially for shooting, like the *battue* birds they were increasingly driven towards the guns.[10] In some areas too deer stalking was being replaced by the driving of the beasts towards the shooter.[11] In game fishing the dry-fly technique had developed, creating a geographical division between the south and the rest of the kingdom.[12]

Associated with some of these changes was the entry of newcomers into country sports, particularly as some fishing rights and shooting beats became tradable commodities, available not just to individuals but also to syndicates.[13] Field sports witnessed a broadening of participation from the socially-ambitious middle-class and plutocrats from trade and industry seeking formal social acceptance from the landed gentry. As one commentator put it 'the newly rich ... discovered the covert-side as a social club of some distinction'.[14] In hunting, the impact of the agricultural depression led to subscription packs replacing many of those owned and operated by an individual master and the introduction of 'capping' fees for visitors with the result that the sport had been 'invaded ... by an army of strangers who have little or no connection with the neighbourhood', but who considered that hunting was 'a fashionable occupation of the winter ... which a wealthy man ought to do.'[15]

Whether the wives and daughters of these wealthy men also became involved is unresearched, but there appears to have been increased participation by women in rural sports. The *Edinburgh Review* of 1909 reported that more females were now involved in the hunting field and in 1913 one authority reckoned that 'at any fashionable meeting' about a third of riders would be women.[16] Although not quantifying the number of participants, one female shooter reckoned that, as the Edwardian era approached, it had been acknowledged by sporting men that women were able to shoot.[17] Fishing, a more gentle art of killing, appealed to some women more that the physicality of hunting or shooting as, in the opinion of one female practitioner, 'of all sports there is none more entirely suited to the powers of women than fly-fishing'.[18] By the end of the Victorian era there were 'already not a few angling champions of the gentler sex ... especially as fly-fishers'.[19] The editor of a book specially aimed at sportswomen argued that in the last decade of the nineteenth century 'women have come to be reckoned as a power in the land in the matter of sport'.[20]

The Unwritten Rules

These changes in organisation and participation raised concern among traditionalists that convention, custom and etiquette were being forgotten or ignored.[21] Such unwritten rules were seen as necessary to the 'harmony and well being' of the sport.[22] Many of these

> 'unwritten laws of sport ... relate chiefly to one's duty to one's neighbour and to those rules of social intercourse and etiquette in the due observance of which the chief pleasure and profit of sport undertaken in the company of others must necessarily and mainly depend.'[23]

In hunting and shooting

> 'the sportsman forms part of a more or less numerous society where a blunder or a selfish action on the part of any one of its members may go far to spoil other people's amusement.'[24]

Thus in hunting it was stressed that all participants 'depend on each other and thoughtless or selfish action from the Master down to the humblest follower on foot, may spoil the pleasure of the whole field' and 'unwritten laws demand that all who go hunting should remember their duties to the Master, to each other and to those over whose land they ride.'[25]

Obeying the conventions was, of course, a way of making social differentiations. As with all sports, field sports too had their own language, terminologies known primarily by the cognoscenti. Only true hunters would know to count hounds in couples, including half couples when a pack had an odd number; only true anglers would be aware that the sink-and-draw method of fishing used dead bait to imitate the movements of a sick minnow; and only true shooters would recognise the jouking circle made by roosting partridges. Yet, although such knowledge could be used to separate the informed from the parvenu, it was conventions of behaviour that really differentiated between true sportsmen and others.

    Field sports were not a peculiarly British recreation, but they were perhaps ritualised to a far greater extent in Great Britain than elsewhere. They had to be undertaken in an appropriate manner. This gave opportunities to ridicule the 'funny foreigner' who wore the wrong clothes and failed to understand the conventions.[26] Dressing in the proper hunt uniform was seen as a matter of etiquette.[27] If full dress was not affordable a top hat, black coat, boots and tweed or cord breeches was acknowledged as a suitable alternative, though this immediately labelled the wearer.[28] In shooting many proprietors or tenants devised their own pattern of tweed to blend into local colours of the hill and the wearing of this estate tweed or tartan became a cultural practice.[29] In angling social distinctions were often reflected in fishing methods and catch. Game fishing, like game shooting, was for wealthier participants and used artificial flies as lures for salmon and trout whereas coarse fishermen – the name says a lot – used natural baits for varieties of other indigenous fish.[30]

    Although many conventions were a check on social acceptance, others were less socially constructed. Some customs were merely acknowledgement of commonsense and common courtesy. Hunters were expected to make way at all times for hunt servants and not to get in the way of the hounds;[31] shooters were encouraged to keep to time and, if early, not to embarrass their host by shooting at small birds while waiting;[32] and anglers were reminded that noise should be kept down.[33] Other conventions, however, were designed to ensure that participants were safe, that good sport was had, and that animals were humanely treated.

    Some 'rules' were there as a matter of safety. Field sports could be hazardous pursuits: anglers risked deep and fast water; hunting required riding at speed and the jumping of fences; and shooting involved dangerous weapons. It was often argued that 'no one ought to shoot until he can shoot well.'[34] The correct handling of firearms and the desirability of controlled shooting, the two major ways to avoid gunshot accidents, featured extensively in instruction books.[35] Indeed, according to one authority advising beginners in the sport, 'the rules of etiquette to be observed in the field when out shooting all tend to ensure safety.'[36] In hunting it was emphasised that 'crowded gateways are dangerous and are to be avoided' and 'casualties ... may be avoided if a rider restrains himself from taking his own line.'[37] Hence hunters were advised not to cut in front; to await their turn at gates; and that it was wrong to ride too close behind another hunter, particularly when jumping, as this could cause serious accidents.[38] Loose horses too could lead to trouble and riders were advised to catch these 'even if it spoils your run.'[39] Horses that were 'kickers' were generally identified in some way such as having red ribbons attached to their tails, but this did not exempt the rider from further care and he should not allow the animal into a crowded gateway.[40] Hunters were cautioned to have regard for 'the safety of the pack' and 'exercise a certain discretion in riding on the hounds' backs.'[41]

Other conventions were there to create good sport by ensuring that there would be sufficient quarry available either on the day or in the future. An awareness was cultivated among anglers as to the size and number of fish that should be taken.[42] In shooting the traditionalists advocated restraint in the volume of killing, hence their criticism of the *battue*, a disapproval not eased by the fact that most of the birds shot by the stationary guns had been bred in large numbers specifically for that purpose.[43] Although cub hunting was a rehearsal for the full chase and pre-season education for young hounds, care had to be taken not to kill too many of the young foxes or resort might have to be had to the 'bagged' fox, the sin that no huntsman would openly talk about.[44]

Good sport could also be interpreted as fair play both to one's companions and to the prey. Riding too near to the hounds, disturbing the scent of the fox, and taking one's own line could all be deemed inappropriate behaviour as could fishing almost on top of a fellow angler. Shooting birds across a neighbouring gun was similarly disapproved of.[45] Even killing birds 'which would make a more sporting shot for another gun may be within the letter but it is outside the spirit of the sportsman's convention'.[46] There was criticism of the introduction of the telescopic sight as being 'grossly unsporting' as it made shooting much too easy.[47] Some even felt that it was unsportsmanlike to stalk capercailzie during the spring mating season when the prolonged and loud love-call of the male made him easily detectable.[48]

What all true sportsmen insisted on was that cruelty had no part in their sport and that all quarry should be killed as humanely as possible. A typical statement would be that of fishing enthusiast, Percy Seton, who proclaimed that

> 'the one great unwritten law which should govern all field sports – out duty towards the creatures that we destroy for our amusement and which should therefore be killed as mercifully as possible.'[49]

Thus, in his sport, salmon, for example, should be despatched by a blow to the head not left to struggle for life out of the water.[50] In shooting no real sportsman would risk wounding birds by firing very long shots or continuing to shoot at deer as long as they were in sight.[51]

Setting and Enforcing the 'Rules'

Conventions were not imposed from above. Indeed there were few national organisations for field sports. In 1884 country sports enthusiasts responded to a complaint from W.S. Seton-Karr that 'there [was] no such thing as a central agency' by establishing the National Sports Defence Association to protect their pursuits from political and moral opposition. Next year it was renamed the Field Sports Protection and Encouragement Association, becoming the Field Sports and Game Guild in 1908 when it merged with the Game Guild, an organisation that sought to prevent the illegal trade in game and game eggs. However membership was voluntary and the organisation looked to defend the interests of hunters, shooters and anglers rather than control their actions.[52]

Fishing had the Fly-fishers Club, founded in 1884 to encourage discussion on technical details of angling, fishing laws and river pollution.[53] Additionally the Freshwater Fisheries Act 1878 gave power to any district to form a local body for protection of fisheries within its bounds.[54] Again the focus was outward rather than inward. Fox-hunting had its Masters of Foxhounds Association which emerged as a formal body in 1881 and which 'may be regarded as forming the legislative body in all matters appertaining to the hunting field.'[55] Their main concern seems to have lain with settling disputes over boundaries and gaining access to coverts. No national organisation within fields sports seems to have had any authority to impose rules on any particular sport.

Most 'rules' within field sports were developed and applied at the level of the hunt, shoot or fishing club. Hence real power in hunting lay with the individual Master of Hounds. As a writer in *Baily's Magazine* put it 'a master of hounds must be recognised as one from whose judgements there is no appeal.'[56] It was his (and very rarely her) responsibility to provide good sport for all hunt followers, partly by exerting discipline over their behaviour during the chase. Mr W.M.Wroughton, often referred to as 'the ruler of the Pytchley', was considered an excellent example – firm but courteous, 'capable at all times of holding a position from which he can see the hounds and control their following' while still securing fair play to his huntsman and full freedom to his pack.[57]

How the conventions were learned is conjectural. For those whose families had been long associated with rural sports the customs would have been handed down through the generations, the youngsters literally being blooded in the hunting field and absorbing the conventions of shooting and angling via social osmosis. For others there were instruction books and articles in sporting journals, some of them specifically for females and the young, all of which emphasised the etiquette of field sports.[58]

If conventions were imposed at the local level then so presumably was discipline. The great unfathomable is what sanctions were taken against those who transgressed the unwritten rules. Research at the level of the individual hunt and fishing or shooting estate might reveal instances but such work is beyond the scope of this paper. There may be a clue in one reason for the formation of the Association of Hunt Secretaries, founded with the support of the Masters of Fox Hounds Association in 1904. It was to exchange information on capping, poultry claims, subscriptions 'and the establishment of a private black list for the use of secretaries.'[59] Otherwise we are left with wondering to what extent transgressors faced social censure and paid 'the penalty of that social ostracism which is usually meted out to dishonourable men'.[60]

One writer claimed that in hunting 'a kindly latitude is generally shown to the modest sinner against its unwritten laws.'[61] This presumably did not cover the 'master or keeper' who shot a fox in hunting counties who had 'to suffer the pains and penalties of social ostracism'.[62] Not observing the etiquette of hunting and shooting created 'an extraordinary amount of ill-feeling and resentment and those 'jealous shots' who took birds rightly those of fellow shooters were 'generally disliked'.[63] It was claimed that in shooting those 'delinquents' who took pot shots at long distances 'may feel pretty sure that their sins are duly noted by their entertainer [i.e. host].'[64]

Another unresolved query is how much the reality matched the rhetoric. It has been noted that the 'gentrified code of honour' often failed to match the practice particularly when shooting overseas and collecting specimens for trophy and natural history purposes.[65] Even in Britain female rider, Lady Mabel Howard, claimed that

> 'hunting is practically a selfish pastime, *chacun pour soi*. You may, perhaps, pull back at a fence or hold a gate for a fellow hunter, but when that supreme moment has come, and "gone away" echoes ... it is generally a case of *sauve qui peut*, and no one thinks of any one but himself or herself in the general scramble which ensues in order to get a good start.'[66]

However the very fact that there were complaints suggests that the concept of acceptable behaviour was not an invented tradition and that in some quarters at least there was a norm of behaviour within the various field sports from which others were deviating. That the 'unwritten' rules appeared so often in print may have been part of a conservative resistance movement to change in which old-school adherents sought to educate newcomers not steeped in the traditions of the sport.

The Law

Whereas most sports had game rules, hunting shooting and fishing had game laws which set the parameters for field sports by determining who could participate, where they might occur, and even when they could take place.[67]

There is general agreement that the game laws were 'blatant class legislation', set within the law of property, which awarded the aristocracy and landed gentry an exclusive privilege to kill certain birds and animals.[68] Tenant farmers who wanted to kill to protect their crops and labourers who wanted kill in order to eat were legally prevented from doing so in the interests of the landed elite who wanted to kill in the name of sport.[69] The basic qualification to kill game – to be a [country] landowner – survived intact until 1831 when certified persons who had purchased a licence *and* who also had permission of the landowner to shoot were allowed to participate. Not till the Ground Game Act of 1880 were tenants finally given the right to shoot game on their holdings, though their landlord still retained his own rights and could restrict those of the rent-payer in the tenancy agreement.[70]

Angling had its own legal regulations. Public fisheries can exist only in tidal waters so all fisheries in inland waters are by definition private.[71] Here the riparian owners had exclusive rights to fish and allow others also to do so, though with the proviso that no-one could not bar the passage of migratory fish (salmon and sea trout) heading upriver for spawning.[72] Thirty years after game licences were instituted fishing licences made their debut. These were brought in partly to fund the administrative costs of fishing regulation, but also as a means of controlling the numbers who could fish and what methods they could use.[73] Yet, even with a licence, permission had to be obtained from the property owners from whose river banks the angler wished to cast their lines and, from the 1870s, more owners were asserting their own rights to fish and reducing the degree of free access, especially where salmon and trout were concerned.[74]

Fox hunting faced fewer legal barriers. Foxes were classed as vermin and had no protection under any game laws; not did they belong to any property owner. Moreover, participation in the hunt traditionally had been open to all, including local farmers over whose land the hunt would traverse.[75] However, hunters had no legal freedom to ride over a farmer's land unless he or his landlord had authorised such action. In essence, with the connivance of those over whose land they rode, hunters ignored the law of trespass for the duration of the chase.[76] Yet a heavy toll in terms of loss of poultry and damage to hedges and crops was exerted from farmers every year by those who exercised their sporting rights.[77] Farmers tolerated this, partly because compensation was often paid; sometimes because they had to accommodate the desires of their landlords who generally supported hunting; but also because they offered deference to those whose activities were commonly regarded as beneficial to rural communities. The hunts maintained that they bought local products, kept foxes down, provided hospitality and entertainment to the rural populace, sponsored farmers' races, and patronised district agricultural societies.[78] Additionally it could be argued that, although hunting had no legal close season, conventionally it was operated as a winter sport when there were less crops at risk; and generally cub-hunting did not start till after the local harvest had been gathered.[79]

Although they enjoyed exclusive rights to fish and shoot, property owners could not totally choose when they wished to partake in these pursuits. By the Edwardian period all forms of game had a close period in which their killing was legally prohibited, usually the breeding and weaning seasons.[80] Legal close seasons and size limits for certain species of fish date back to the thirteenth century. Impositions since then were generally made for fish stock conservation and breeding purposes. From 1818 magistrates could fix close seasons for their particular locality which led by 1860 to the opening of fishing beginning anywhere between 31 December and 30 April and closing starting between 31 August and 15 January![81] A close season for game fish was brought in with the Salmon Act of 1861 and others for coarse fish in the 1870s.[82]

Growing Tensions

As field sports changed, some new conventions emerged and some old ones were undermined. The increasing involvement of women in rural pursuits led to queries as to how *manly* sports could be enjoyed by female participants. Yet generally the resistance movement accepted those women who were prepared to perform like men; it was others, those who attempted to bring more feminine attributes into the countryside, that were derided by male and female participants alike. Publications advised women on correct procedures. Specifically they were counselled on appropriate dress in fishing ['quiet colours, heather mixture and the like'], in shooting ['some dark or neutral tinted material that will not be conspicuous on the moor'], and in hunting [skirts 'off the saddle (not) too scanty to be unbecoming].[83] Additionally huntswomen were warned – by one of their own – to trot, not gallop, between coverts and 'never trade on the chivalry of the opposite sex, for this is what makes them unpopular in the hunting field'.[84] This was reinforced by a male writer who proclaimed that 'if a woman hunts she should in some little things forget that she is a woman ... [and] not expect those same courtesies in the field which are lavished on her in the drawing-room.[85] Indeed one experienced male hunter reckoned that those who sought it had 'attained in the hunting field the much talked-of equality of man.'[86] Women anglers who were prepared to wear the appropriate attire for wet and muddy river banks do not appear to have faced resentment; in fact the author of a major instruction text welcomed 'lady fishers'.[87] In shooting, however, they were advised that they were 'out of place' in the *battue* and big shoots and even at smaller shoots 'luncheon should be the signal for the prudent sportswoman to retire'.[88]

There was greater controversy about the change in attitude by some shooters to large bags of game. Walk-up shooters could not be certain what birds or how many their dogs would flush out. In contrast the *battue* guaranteed large numbers to shoot at and the rapid shooting vital to 'success' was assisted by the development of the breech-loading shotgun and the employment of men to load them.[89] In turn this led to social cachet being gained from the numbers killed, particularly when printed and verbal announcements were made of 'scores'.[90] Bags such as the 1,300 partridges shot in a day by the king's party at Sandringham in 1904 would have been considered 'reprehensible and unreasonable' in earlier years.[91] And still were in some shooting circles. To the rough shooter, brought up to flush the birds with dogs, the mass slaughter of the driven partridge or pheasant by 'gunners rather than hunters' was a basic breach of shooting etiquette in the first place, being 'a style of sport which finds little favour in the eyes of genuine sportsmen'.[92] It may have tested marksmanship but it was not physically demanding and required no field craft; like the equally detested trap pigeon shooting it necessitated no knowledge of the natural environment.[93] Even one supporter of the *battue* 'with sorrow and shame ... confessed that gunners of the exterminating class are just now too abundant. The number is increasing of men who go shooting without idea or conception of the *sport* of pursuing game, but with the sole desire of firing off as many cartridges as possible in the shortest space of time, and with the least exertion.'[94]

The slaughter of the *battue* was considered bad enough by the traditionalists but the practice of driving deer to where they could be ambushed was only for 'featherbed sportsmen'.[95]

There was also tension between the followers of the hunt and game preservers. In 'many hunting counties there has been an influx of non-resident shooting tenants, whose only object is to obtain a big head of game without regard to the hunting proclivities of their neighbours'.[96] Historian John Lowerson has argued that the pheasant-shooting syndicates of 'new men' were a problem as they hadn't the nerve to acquire the art of riding and viewed hunting with distaste or at best a lack of empathy.[97] Keeping foxes alive so that the hunting season could progress was a threat to the birds being raised in the coverts. A bidding war could occur in which the hunt might pay a keeper if a fox was found in the coverts of a shooting tenant but the tenant might offer him more to keep them fox-free.[98] Actual hunting could be even more disruptive to game if the riders ventured at speed through the domicile of the game.[99] Lord Willoughby de Broke, a keen follower of the hounds, had no doubt 'foxes and pheasants can be simultaneously preserved but it requires a surgical operation of the most radical nature to get the fact into the heads of most keepers.' He advised compliance with the wishes of game preservers but, significantly added, 'by no means, and for no man, stop your hounds when running.'[100]

What annoyed many of the traditionalists was that many of the newcomers to the sport were ignorant of the conventions of field sports. This was particular the case in hunting where the urban hunting men were not

'as a rule [like] the genuine sportsman ... who has been brought up to the sport from boyhood and understands country life, knows something of farming and crops, and what hounds are doing, when to ride, and when to avoid following the huntsman in every cast he makes, which must occasionally be over crops that he and his whips *only* do little damage to.'

One critic of the new entrants felt that 'a practical and theoretical exam ... which should include etiquette' should be taken by all those wishing to hunt.[101] This reflected the complaint of the Duke of Beaufort who felt that hunting was being spoiled by the 'sheer want of knowledge of the unwritten laws of the hunting field' by the large numbers of 'ignorant' participants.[102] One estimate was that 'about a quarter of the mounted crowd were ignorant of all the laws, written and unwritten, which govern ... the noble game of hunting'.[103]

It was the actions of these parvenus that undermined the rural relationships built up over the years between sportsmen and farmers. At the turn of the century several Masters of Hounds felt they had to apologise for some followers 'riding over crops, particularly roots and seeds'[Hambledon],[104] 'a lot of ramshackle huntsmen who had not the slightest idea of the crops over which they were riding'[Badsworth];[105] and 'the serious damage and annoyance to farmers which is caused by riding over wheat, turnips and clover seeds'[Zetland].[106] It was becoming increasingly important '... in all ways try to keep friendly with the farmers, for on them depends the continuation of hunting.'[107] The sheer numbers now hunting brought problems: 400 to 500 riders careering through cultivated fields wrought unprecedented damage to crops and fences. In the midst, and aftermath, of agricultural depression, farmers were protecting their fields with wire – including the barbed variety – and were even destroying foxes. Landlords were less able to insist that their tenants bowed to the desires of the hunt as the supply of potential renters fell away.[108] The situation was aggravated by the growing number of outsiders who were hunting but not spending anything in the district on horses or forage thus disrupting traditional rural relations.[109] As one observer put it 'the character of the hunting field ... lost the social significance of local surroundings'.[110] Compensation became critical. Hunts were advised that a serious loss to a farmer such as death of livestock caused by hounds or hunters should be paid for liberally and at once, preferably by a collection from those out hunting that day.[111] Although paying for poultry killed by foxes was a moral not a legal obligation, one hunt secretary noted that 'a generous spirit in dealing with claims generally saves the life of many a fox'.[112]

Conclusion

In most Edwardian sports, published constitutive rules set the formal rules of play; auxiliary rules specified and controlled eligibility; and regulatory rules placed restraints on behaviour independent of the sport itself. In cricket, for example, the MCC set the playing rules for the game; likewise the Rugby Football Union, the Football Association and the Jockey Club in their respective sports.[113] There is nothing in such constitutive rules or in the nature of sport itself which determines who can and who cannot play: exclusion is a cultural creation specific to sports in a certain domain at a particular time. It was the organisers of events and competitions who set such auxiliary regulations as with the residential qualifications for country cricketers or the anti-professional rules in most amateur sports. Both constitutive rule-makers (governing bodies) and auxiliary rule-makers (promoters), as well as participating clubs, also imposed regulatory rules. These were independent of both the game and competition but serve to reinforce expected behaviour, such as the dress codes that were common in Edwardian golf clubs.

In field sports all such rules remained largely unwritten. Constitutive rules in most sports serve to make the particular sport more difficult: golf would be easier if the ball could be thrown out of the bunker and the lbw and offside rules in cricket and football have added complexity to those games. In field sports there were no such published rules but the easy routes were still frowned upon and participants voluntarily imposed difficulties on their activities. Recreational anglers thus used rod and lines not the nets of professional fishermen and shooters fired their guns at birds on the wing not on the ground. Additionally field sports adherents adopted other conventions designed to ensure good sport in a safe environment, exhibit humanity to their prey, and operate as a mechanism of social differentiation.

Yet all this took place within an overarching set of regulations imposed nation-wide by statute law. Here was a major difference with those sports that had formal rules. The law had been resorted to in Georgian England to settle disputes, normally over betting, at a time when there was a virtual absence of final authority within the sports themselves.[114] However, as central rule-making authorities consolidated their positions, there was less recourse to the courts. By Edwardian times cricket and football might be involved in legal actions if a player was killed, particularly if the written rules of those games had been transgressed; otherwise the sports were left to keep their own house in order.[115] In contrast the very existence of much hunting, shooting and fishing was based on what the law did or did not allow.

References

1. The author thanks the British Academy and the Carnegie Trust for funding the project and Dr Joyce Kay for research assistance.
2. Pollock-Hodsoll, G.B.: "The Unwritten Laws of Sport: Football", in: 21 *Badminton Magazine* (1905), 489–494, p.493.
3. For the purposes of this article field sports, also here called rural or country sports, involve the pursuit and killing of animals, birds and fish. Hunting, shooting and fishing are collective titles for field sports which have several subsets. In the period studied animals hunted included deer, foxes, otters and hares; shooting encompassed deer stalking, wild fowling, covert shooting using beaters and rough shooting using dogs; fishing was generally divided between game fishing for a select group of freshwater fish, especially salmon and trout, and coarse fishing for other river fish. In Britain, hunting with dogs is generally distinguished from hunting with guns, the latter being classified as shooting. For an overview see Billett, Michael: *A History of English Country Sports*. London 1994 and Collins, Tony, Martin, John & Vamplew, Wray: *Encyclopedia of Traditional British Rural Sports*. Abingdon 2005. Contemporary description can be found in Suffolk and Berkshire, Earl of, Peek, Hedley & Aflalo, F.G.: *The Encyclopaedia of Sport*. London 1900.
4. On coursing, see, H.H.D.: "English Coursing Fields" in: 2 *Gentlemen's Magazine* (1869), 571–585 and Sirius: "The Waterloo Cup" in: 10 *Gentlemen's Magazine* (1874), 292–298. Cockfighting developed a complex set of rules under which the determination of victory and the role of the bird handlers was carefully defined. Although not specifically attributed to any particular source, a set of 19 rules for cockfighting was published in both Cheny's *Racing Calendar* for 1743 and Heber's *Racing Calendar* in 1751. Middleton, Iris: "Cockfighting in Yorkshire During the Early Eighteenth Century", in: 40 *Northern History* (2003), 129–146.
5. See, for example, "Sporting Intelligence [Glamorgan Hunt]" in: 75 *Baily's Magazine* (1901), p. 392 and "Sporting Intelligence [Warwickshire Hunt]" in: 79 *Baily's Magazine* (1903), p. 233.
6. Salt, Henry S.: "The Sportsman at Bay", in: 16 *International Journal*

of *Ethics* 4 (1906), 487–497, p. 491.

7. Lowerson, John: *Sport and the English Middle Classes 1870–1914*. Manchester 1995, p.38; Orr, Willie: "The Economic Impact of Deer Forests in the Scottish Highlands 1850–1914", in: 2 *Scottish Economic and Social History* (1980), 44–58, p. 47.

8. Annual Report of Proceedings Under The Salmon and Freshwater Fisheries Acts for 1911. *Parliamentary Papers* 1912/13 XXVI, Appendix 3.

9. "Old-Fashioned Sportsmen" in: 63 *Saturday Review* (1887), pp. 404–5.

10. Durie, Alastair: "'Unconscious Benefactors': Grouse Shooting in Scotland, 1780–1914", in: 15 *IJHS* 3 (1998), 57–73, p. 62.

11. "Deer-Stalking", in: 58 *Saturday Review*, (1884), p.9.

12. Watson, A.E.T.: *The Young Sportsman*. London 1900, p.11.

13. Durie: "Grouse Shooting", p. 64.

14. Henry, Hugh: "Etiquette in the Hunting Field", in: 83 *Baily's Magazine* (1905), 106–10, p.107.

15. Collins, Martin & Vamplew: *Encyclopedia*, p. 113; Henry: "Etiquette", p. 107; "Hunting", in: 166 *Edinburgh Review* (1887), p. 396.

16. "Nimrod", in: 209 *Edinburgh Review* (1909), 146–167, p. 153; Hughes-Onslow, Major Arthur: "Then and Now: Hunting", in: 36 *Badminton Magazine* (1913), 126–140, p. 136.

17. Lowther, Gwendoline: "Shooting", in: Slaughter, Frances E. (ed.): *The Sportswomen's Library*. London 1898 volume 1, 109–124, p. 109. On the more prominent see Ruffer, Jonathan Garnier: *The Big Shots*. London 1977, pp. 88–90.

18. Slaughter, Frances E.: "Trout and Other Fly Fishing" in: Slaughter: *Sportswomen's Library* volume 2, 220–234, p. 221.

19. Cholmondeley-Pennell, H.: *Fishing*. London 1889, p. 114.

20. Slaughter, Frances E.: "Englishwomen and Sport" in: Slaughter: *Sportswomen's Library* volume 1, 1–9, p. 6.

21. For the purposes of this study no significant distinction will be drawn between custom, convention and etiquette, terms which generally seem to have been used interchangeably to embrace acceptable behaviour and practices within field sports.

22. Henry: "Etiquette", p. 106.

23. Seton-Karr, Sir Henry: "Unwritten Laws of Sport: Big-game Shooting", in: 20 *Badminton Magazine* (1905), 487–496, p. 487.

24. Seton, Percy: "Unwritten Laws of Sport: Fishing", in: 20 *Badminton Magazine* (1905), 615–621, p. 615.

25. Hughes-Onslow: "Unwritten Laws", p. 16.
26. MacKenzie, John M.: "Review of Ruffer: *Big Shots*" in: 8 *IJHS* 1 (1991), 155–156, p. 156.
27. Henry: "Etiquette", p. 109.
28. Hughes-Onslow: "Unwritten Laws", p. 22..
29. Hart-Davis, Duff: *Monarchs of the Glen: A History of Deer-Stalking in the Scottish Highlands.* London 1978, p. 177.
Wightman, Andy, Higgins, Peter, Jarvie, Grant & Nichol, Robbie: "The Cultural Politics of Hunting: Sporting Estates and Recreational Land Use in the Highlands and Islands of Scotland", in: 5 *Culture, Sport, Society* 1 (2002), 53–70, p. 55.
30. Phillips, Ernest: "In Defence of Coarse Fishing", in: 83 *Baily's Magazine* (1905), 460–467.
31. Hughes-Onslow: "Unwritten Laws", p. 16.
32. Granby, Marquis of: "The Unwritten Laws of Sport: Shooting", in: 20 *Badminton Magazine* (1905), 254–262, pp. 258–9.
33. Watson, *Young Sportsman*, p. 389.
34. Buxton: "Shooting", in: 70 *Fortnightly Review* (1901), 832–845, p. 834.
35. "A Gun-Room Causerie" in: 75 *Baily's Magazine* (1901), 46–48, p. 46; Watson: *Young Sportsman*, pp. 528–530.
36. Walsingham, Lord & Payne-Gallwey, Sir Ralph: *Shooting.* London 1906, p. 33.
37. Caldecott, R.: "Fox-Hunting", in: *English Illustrated Magazine* (1886), 414–423, p. 421.
38. Hughes-Onslow: 'Unwritten Laws", p. 19.
39. Henry: "Etiquette", p. 109.
40. Hughes-Onslow: "Unwritten Laws", p. 19.
41. Suffolk and Berkshire, Earl of: "Fox-Hunting", in: 2 *Pall Mall Gazette* (1894), 204–207, p. 206.
42. Watson: *Young Sportsman*, p. 28.
43. "Covert-Shooting, Past and Present" in: 57 *Saturday Review* (1884), 274–5.
44. Hughes-Onslow, Major Arthur: "Cub-Hunting", in: 35 *Badminton Magazine* (1912), 195–201.
45. Walsingham: *Shooting*, p. 37; G.T.T.B.: "The Etiquette of the Shooting Field", in: 83 *Baily's Magazine* (1905), 390–394, p. 392.
46. Buxton: "Shooting", p. 842.
47. Hart-Davis: *Monarchs*, p. 177.
48. H.B. MacPherson: "In the Haunts of the Capercailzie", in: 29

Badminton Magazine (1909), 495–504, p.498.
49. Seton: "Fishing", p. 621. See also MacKenzie, John: *The Empire of Nature: Hunting, Conservation, and British Imperialism.* Manchester 1988.
50. Malmesbury, Susan, Countess of: "Salmon Fishing", in: Slaughter: *Sportswomen's Library* volume 2, 186–217, p.189.
51. Walsingham: *Shooting*, pp. 35, 86.
52. McKenzie, Callum C: "The Origins of the British Field Sports Society", in: 13 *IJHS* 2 (1996), 177–191, pp. 177–179.
53. Field, Basil: "Fly-Fishing", in: 55 *Fortnightly Review*, 494–509, p. 496.
54. "The Progress of Angling", in: 179 *Edinburgh Review* (1894), p. 227.
55. George F Underhill: "Fox-Hunting and Agriculture", 43 *Nineteenth Century* (1898), 745–754, p. 751.
56. Henry: "Etiquette", p. 107.
57. "Mr. W.M. Wroughton MFH", in: 76 *Baily's Magazine* (1901), pp. 407–8, p. 408.
58. See, for example, Menzies, Mrs Stuart: "Skirts and Guns", in: 37 *Badminton Magazine* (1913), 753–761; Watson: *Young Sportsman*, passim; Lowther: "Shooting", p. 112.
59. "Association of Hunt Secretaries", in: 82 *Baily's Magazine* (1904), 48–50.
60. Underhill: "Fox-Hunting", p. 750.
61. Henry: "Etiquette", p.107.
62. Underhill: "Fox-Hunting", p. 752.
63. Menzies: "Skirts and Guns", p. 759.
64. Watson: *Young Sportsman*, p. 533.
65. Gillespie, Greg & Wamsley, Clive: "Clandestine Means: The Aristocratic British Hunting Code and Early Game Legislation in Nineteenth-Century Canada", in: 22 *Sporting Traditions* 1 (2005), 99–119, p. 109.
66. Howard, Lady Mabel: "A Riding Party", in: 11 *Badminton Magazine* (1900), 319–329, p.319.
67. The following discussion is simplified for purposes of clarity. In practice the game laws were complex and nuanced. Fuller detail on angling regulations can be found in Howarth, William: *Freshwater Fishery Law.* London 1987; on deer shooting in Orr, Willie: *Deer Forests, Landlords and Crofters.* Edinburgh 1982, pp. 51–65; and on winged-game shooting in Munsche, P.B.: *Gentlemen and Poachers: The English Game Laws 1671–1832.* Cambridge 1981 and Hopkins, Harry: *The Long*

Affray: The Poaching Wars 1760–1914. London 1985.
68. Munsche: *Gentlemen,* p. 163.
69. Howkins, Alun: "Economic Crime and Class Law: Poaching and the Game Laws, 1840–1880" in: Burman, Sandra B. & Harrell-Bond, Barbara E.: *The Imposition of Law.* London 1979, 273–287.
70. Howkins: "Economic Crime", p. 277.
71. Howarth: *Fishery Law,* p. 8.
72. Bartrip, Peter: "Food for the Body and Food for the Mind: The Regulation of Freshwater Fisheries in the 1870s", in: 28 *Victorian Studies* 2 (1985), 285–304, p. 286.
73. Howarth: *Fishery Law,* p. 99.
74. Bartrip: "Food", p. 286.
75. Itakowitz: *Peculiar Privilege,* p. 23.
76. Davenport, W. Bromley: "Fox-Hunting", in: 13 *Nineteenth Century* (1883), 978–991, p. 978; Underhill: "Fox Hunting", p. 746.
77. Henry, Hugh: "Riding to Hunt and Hunting to Ride", 78 *Baily's Magazine* (1902), 413–417, p. 414.
78. Itakowitz: *Peculiar Privilege,* pp. 132–134; A Hunt Secretary: "A Few Suggestions as to Wire and Poultry Funds", in: 78 *Baily's Magazine* (1902), 375–379, pp. 378–379.
79. Itakowitz: *Peculiar Privilege,* p. 122; Watson: *Young Sportsman,* p. 345.
80. De Montgomery, J.E.G.: "State Protection of Animals at Home and Abroad", in: 18 *Law Quarterly Review* (1902), 31–48, pp.32–33, 37–38.
81. Howarth: *Fishery Law,* pp. 16–17.
82. De Montgomery: "State Protection", p. 39; Bartrip: "Food", p. 286; MacLeod, Roy M.: "Government and Resource Conservation: The Salmon Acts Administration 1860–1886", in: 7 *Journal of British Studies* 2 (1968), 114–150, p. 124; "The Progress of Angling", in: 179 *Edinburgh Review* (1894), 226–245, p. 227.
83. Malmesbury: "Salmon Fishing", p 197; Lowther: "Shooting", p. 123; Burn: "Fox-Hunting", p. 39.
84. Burn: "Fox-Hunting", pp. 23, 30.
85. Haig-Brown, Alan R: "Women and Sport", in: 83 *Baily's Magazine* (1905), 250–27, p. 251.
86. Dale, T.F.: *Fox-Hunting in the Shires.* London 1903, p. 274.
87. Cholmondeley-Pennell: *Fishing,* pp. 113–116.
88. Lowther: "Shooting", pp. 139, 134.
89. Hopkins: *Affray,* p. 213.

96] *How the Game was Played*

90. Hopkins: *Affray*, pp. 247–9.
91. Watson, A.E.T.: *King Edward VII as a Sportsman*. London 1911, p. 24; Buxton: "Shooting", p. 834.
92. Sharp, H.: *The Gun: Afield and Afloat*. London 1904, p. xiv; "Our National Sports and Pastimes", in: *British Almanac and Companion* (1878), 46–65, p. 53.
93. McKenzie, Callum: "The British Big-Game Hunting Tradition, Masculinity and Fraternalism with Particular Reference to the Shikar Club", in: 20 *Sport Historian* 1 (2000), 70–96, pp. 73–75.
94. Watson: *Young Sportsman*, p. 533.
95. Ellangowan (Bertram, J.G.): *Outdoor Sports in Scotland*. London 1889 cited in Hart-Davis: *Monarchs*, p.189.
96. Underhill: "Fox-Hunting", p. 752.
97. Lowerson: *Middle Classes*, p. 36.
98. Borderer: "The Fox and His Enemies", in: 75 *Baily's Magazine* (1901), 6–10, p. 7.
99. "Hunting", in: 166 *Edinburgh Review* (1887), p. 393.
100. De Broke, Lord Willoughby: "Advice on Fox Hunting", in: 11 *Badminton Magazine* (1900), 591–601, pp. 591–2.
101. Robinson, Mrs Stennard: "Some Ladies Who Ride to Hounds", in: 21 *Badminton Magazine* (1905), 661–676, p. 662.
102. Cited in Coaten, Arthur W: "Hunting Prospects and Changes", in: 21 *Badminton Magazine* (1905), 272–286, p. 273.
103. Wynter, Maud V.: "With the Devon and Somerset", in: 35 *Badminton Magazine* (1912), 145–153, p. 148.
104. "Sporting Intelligence" in: 75 *Baily's Magazine* (1901), p. 77.
105. "Sporting Intelligence" in: 73 *Baily's Magazine* (1900), p. 228.
106. "Sporting Intelligence" in: 80 *Baily's Magazine* (1903), p. 486.
107. Burn: "Foxhunting", p. 34.
108. Itakowitz: *Peculiar Privilege*, pp. 152–175.
109. "Hunting", in: 63 *Saturday Review* (1887), 441–442, p. 442; "The Decline of Fox-Hunting", in: 79 *Saturday Review* (1895), 343–344.
110. Underhill: "Fox-Hunting", p. 746.
111. Willoughby: "Advice", p. 598.
112. A Hunt Secretary: "Suggestions" p. 377.
113. For a more detailed discussion see Vamplew, Wray: "Playing with the Rules: Influences on The Development of Regulation in Sport", in: 24 *IJHS* 7 (2007), 843–871.
114. Brailsford, Dennis: *A Taste for Diversions*. Cambridge 1999, p.173.
115. Grayson, Edward: *Sport and the Law*. London 1978, pp. 31–33.

Captains Courageous: Gentlemen Riders in British Horse Racing, 1866–1914

Gentlemen riders played a significant role in British horse racing before 1914, particularly in National Hunt, where higher weights and less stringent legislation encouraged greater participation than on the flat. Men from the hunting field and the military took their skills and courage to the racecourse and often competed successfully against professional riders. However, racing's intimate association prevented an amateur ethos from emerging and too many gentlemen riders were guilty of dubious practices. National Hunt racing was a sport in which shamateurism developed on a considerable scale, with supposedly amateur jockeys making money from the sport.

The first day of June 1904, a wet Wednesday at Epsom Downs, saw leading professional jockey Kempton Cannon pilot St Amant home to win the Derby, the blue-riband classic of the British turf. Three lengths behind was second favourite John o'Gaunt in the Cambridge blue and white colours of Sir John Thursby but under an amateur, his half-brother George. Behind George were six other professionals. 'Mr' Thursby had already ridden his sibling's horse into second place in the Two Thousand Guineas that year, again beaten by St Amant. This was not the end of his riding achievements in the classics. Two years later he repeated his Derby feat on Picton and in 1908 was yet again second in the Two Thousand Guineas, this time on Sir Archibald. Four places in elite races says much about Thursby's riding skills, but that was the sum of success by amateur riders at the highest level of British flat racing.

Over fences the situation was very different.[1] Between 1871 and 1885 gentlemen riders won 12 Grand Nationals, the premier event of the National Hunt calendar, five more between 1885 and 1897, and a further three by 1915. In their riding 'careers' Roddy Owen won 254 races and Arthur Yates 460, including 67 in season 1872-3, a record for an amateur.[2] Several amateurs actually won the National Hunt riders' championship including John Randolph ('Jack') Anthony, one of three Carmarthenshire brothers who all became racehorse trainers. This study will consider why the majority of amateurs rode under National Hunt rules, attempt to define the term 'gentleman rider' and suggest that there was no place for the amateur ethos in horse racing.

The amateur in British racing

Victorian and Edwardian racing possessed two distinct strands: races on the flat and those over jumps, be they fences or hurdles.[3] Flat racing had the longer history, dating back in organized form to the seventeenth century, a time when many owners rode their own horses. During the nineteenth century it became increasingly commercialized, professionalized and subject to the authority of the Jockey Club[4], and as a result the owner-rider was gradually sidelined. Nevertheless, in 1870 at least 60 amateurs, riding for themselves and other owners, still took part in open races against professionals, gaining 23 wins and a further 43 places. While most of these riders participated at only one meeting, almost a third competed at two or more, though usually within a particular area. By 1911, however, there were no gentlemen competing against the professionals.

This was partly attributable to Jockey Club legislation. The intervening years had seen the licensing of jockeys (from 1880) and the introduction in 1889 of Rule 96 which stated that 'Any gentleman wishing to ride in races on even terms with jockeys shall obtain a permission, current till revoked, from the Stewards of the Jockey Club, and make a donation of £5 to the Bentinck Benevolent Fund.' When lists of licensed jockeys and gentlemen riders were published in the Racing Calendar from 1897, it became easier to establish the numbers involved. In that year there were 35 amateurs, around 12 per cent of the total of approved jockeys and riders. In 1901 the number of gentlemen had risen to 39, but this had collapsed to only nine by the next season. The reason for this was an amended Rule 96: 'Any gentleman wishing to ride in races other than those open to gentlemen riders must obtain an annual permission from the Stewards of the Jockey Club and pay a yearly subscription of 5 sovereigns to the Bentinck Benevolent Fund.'[5]

Clearly only nine gentlemen in 1902 were serious enough about their sport to be willing to pay each season for the pleasure.[6] Yet even these seldom rode against professionals. In contrast to George Thursby, who competed in 18 open races, securing nine wins and four places, the others totalled 12 such races between them and gained only one third place. Four of these were part of a group of 36 amateurs who rode in flat races specifically for gentlemen riders under the Rules of Racing. Gentlemen thus had not abandoned the flat, merely shifted the focus of their competition; but even those races purely for gentlemen riders or welter races in which professional jockeys could compete against the amateur with a seven-pound penalty were lessening in number. In 1870, 39 courses offered 64 such races; in 1913, 18 courses staged 39.

Even in 1870 gentlemen riders rarely rode in open competition in major races or at elite racecourses. Thursby aside, few amateurs could give the professionals a run for their money. George Baird, who initially raced as Mr Abington to hide his activities from his trustees, inherited a fortune from his ironmaster father and another from his uncle. He virtually bought his way to the gentlemen riders' title between 1885 and 1891 by spending money on quality horses, but in his title-winning year of 1889 he gained 48 of his victories against professional opposition.[7] Arthur Coventry, later to become Jockey Club starter, could also hold his own: a fellow amateur, George Lambton, brother of Lord Durham, remembered champion professional Fred Archer saying that there was no jockey living who could give Mr Coventry five pounds.[8]

Weight was a major reason why so few amateurs became successful flat jockeys; too much of the good life had to be sacrificed to achieve the low levels necessary. George Baird, however, wasted as hard as he rode. His last ride was on his 31st birthday, when he got down to only nine stones and five pounds to ride Alice to victory in the Edinburgh Gold Cup at Musselburgh. Like all the jockeys in the Derby, George Thursby weighed out at just nine stones, but this was towards the upper level in conventional flat racing. In 1850 the minimum weight set by the Jockey Club was a mere four stones and although this rose to five stones and seven pounds in 1875 it remained at this level until after the First World War.[9] Few riders, even professionals, raced at these weights, but they are an indicator that weights carried by runners on the flat could be artificially low. It was not always so. In the mid-eighteenth century nine stones seems to have been the minimum for normal thoroughbred racing, and hence at that time owners could often ride their own horses without serious disadvantage. The emergence of lighter weights probably owes something to gambling owners and most of them were realizing that not only did this lessen the risk of a valuable horse breaking down under the weight of a heavy jockey but it could also improve the chances of beating other animals with heavier riders. Nevertheless although the lighter weights carried on the flat might have deterred some potential amateur jockeys, its effect should not be exaggerated. On one-fifth of the occasions in which amateurs rode on the flat against professionals in 1870 they weighed out at nine stones or under, and of the nine gentlemen licensed to compete against professionals in 1902 four were able to ride at such a weight.

In contrast, in National Hunt racing perhaps because of its origins in the hunting field the weights carried were on average two to three stones higher than on the flat and even greater in many of the events restricted to amateurs. Gentlemen riding over jumps thus could maintain a more normal physique. Steeplechasing had emerged from matches between individuals over hunting country, eventually becoming races for several participants over constructed courses. Commercialization began in the 1830s, first at St Albans and then at Aintree, where the Grand National was inaugurated.[10] Most National Hunt racing was over fences, but there were also hurdle races run at a faster pace, often involving flat-race horses seeking to extend their careers. The sport became formally organized in 1866 with the formation of the National Hunt Committee, which also began to issue licences to riders. There was a substantial expansion after the 1870s following the Jockey Club imposition of a minimum prize-money regulation for flat racing, which pushed many race committees to convert to National Hunt racing where there was no such rule.[11] In 1911 there were 235 professional jockeys who had received licences to ride but, in contrast to the situation on the flat, the list also contained 55 qualified (i.e. amateur) riders. Yet these were listed only if they qualified by 'election' rather than by status as a gentleman or farmer (see Appendix) so the actual number of amateur riders was significantly higher. Most National Hunt races were open to all comers, but many more than on the flat, especially at meetings hosted by hunts and racing clubs, were restricted to amateur riders, usually socially defined but often with the addition of residential, occupational or hunting qualifications. Hence there were substantial openings for the amateur rider to compete either against professionals or just among fellow gentlemen riders.[12]

If 1902 is examined in detail it is apparent that, although some amateurs rode at only one or two local meetings, there was a hard core of about 25 who raced at multiple meetings, both against professional riders and other amateurs. The races they took part in were a mixture of National Hunt flat races, open welter races, steeplechases and hurdles; unlike flat racing no race specifically stated that it was for 'gentlemen riders'. Of the 1,626 races in the National Hunt calendar, 225 (14 per cent) were competed for by professionals only. Amateur riders took part in the remainder. In 201 races (12 per cent) only amateurs competed, but in 1,200 (74 per cent) jockeys were a mixture of amateurs and professionals. Over 12 months amateurs won about a third of these open races, which suggests that many gentlemen riders were competent in the saddle and able to compete effectively with professionals.

For those who felt that even National Hunt racing had become too professionalized, there remained point-to-point events run over natural terrain with no prize money at stake. Popular from the 1880s, these were for horses that had been hunted and amateur jockeys who had ridden to hounds. Here no licence was required, merely a certificate from the local master. Indeed most were hosted and organized by local hunts, even when the races were for members of the Stock Exchange or the legal fraternity of the Pegasus Club. Initially each meeting set its own rules, but in 1913 the Master of Hounds Point-to-Point Association established a national set of regulations, an unanticipated outcome of which was that between 1913 and 1929 women were allowed to compete against men.[13] However, there is no place here for further consideration of this purely amateur version of the sport.

Origins of the gentlemen riders

So who or what was a 'gentleman rider'? In flat racing, unlike most other sports, there was a long history of professionalism. Gentlemen riders were by implication those licensed to ride who were not professionals, men who did not receive payment for their services and who had not served an apprenticeship in a training stable. In practice this led to social standing being a key distinguishing factor. In jump racing there was far greater elasticity of definition. One Yorkshire rider in the 1830s had no doubts as to his eligibility: 'I subscribes to a pack o' dogs. I hunts three days a week. I drinks wine to my dinner. And I keeps a mistress!'[14] Three decades later, however, there were complaints that 'grooms, broken-down riding masters and stable-keepers' were riding as 'gentlemen' and an appeal was made for 'a rule to be framed of sufficient strength' to prevent such misrepresentation.[15] When the National Hunt Committee established its regulatory code in 1867, the term 'gentleman rider' emerged as a complex and exhaustive definition designed to exclude persons of inferior social status. To be eligible a man had to belong to one of a select list of clubs, be a magistrate, a peer or an officer of either service on full pay or bear a courtesy title. Persons of lower social standing could be balloted in, but they had to be nominated by men holding the club or commission qualification. There had been modifications to these rules by the end of the century, particularly after the reorganization of the National Hunt Committee in 1883. The list of approved clubs was extended and farmers (and their sons) with a minimum occupation of one hundred acres became eligible, but those seeking entry by ballot had to he proposed and seconded by members of the National Hunt Committee itself.[16]

It may have been elitist, but the 'career' of a gentleman rider was not for the dilettante. Horse racing was a sport that demanded courage: more than in football and rugby, both of which had become more civilized with the prohibition of hacking; more than in cricket, which had a hard missile but protective pads and a bat with which to defend oneself. Racing was the supreme test of sporting courage. Trying to control 500 kilos of horseflesh travelling at 2540 kilometres an hour while sometimes also attempting to jump obstacles en route is not an activity for the faint-hearted. National Hunt riders are always just one fall away from paralysis. Modern statistics show that a fall can be expected every 14 rides over jumps and hurdles and an injury every eighty.[17] Admittedly, riding styles and tactics have changed since the late nineteenth century, but so too has protective equipment and medical knowledge; hence it is likely that racing then was at least as dangerous as it is today. As Fox Russell, a cross-country rider in the third quarter of the nineteenth century, recorded:

> I have had my fair share of accidents, and have broken ribs, collar bones, and arm, some two or three times each, and once sustained a slight concussion of the brain, but have never been seriously, that is, dangerously, injured in my life except once, when a horse rolled on me.[18]

Some were less fortunate. The inaugural St Albans Steeplechase in 1830 saw the first recorded National Hunt fatality when Mr Stretfield's mount Teddy the Tyke fell over a gate and crushed his rider.[19] The first two decades at Sandown, a course opened in the 1870s, witnessed the deaths in falls of Greville Nugent, Mr Goodwin and Captain Boyce. Lord Rossmore was also killed in a racing fall, this one at Windsor.[20] Jump racing also proved fatal to several leading amateur riders such as George Ede and Charles Cunningham. Old Etonian George Ede, who rode as 'Mr Edwards', had 306 winners between 1856 and 1870 including a victorious Grand National on The Lamb.[21] When riding in a hurdle race at Aintree in 1870, the day after participating in another National, his mount Chippenham fell and rolled on him. Ede died without regaining consciousness.[22] A serious fall in 1890 from which he never fully recovered contributed to the early death of 'Charlie' Cunningham who, in one three-year period, won 144 out of 276 races, a remarkably high percentage.[23] Hugh Nugent, second in the Grand National of 1902, died later that year after a fall in a hurdle race in Ostend.[24] To get into the saddle knowing that injury was not just possible but highly probable required bravery of a special kind. This aspect of manliness, unlike that of the middle-class (amateur by implication) footballer, rugby player or cricketer, was not the direct product of a public-school education as no public school in the period studied offered hunting or riding, let alone racing, as an extracurricular pursuit.[25] So where did it originate?

One avenue would be via the military, an institution still obsessed with the horse and in which the ability to travel on horseback at high speed was an admired trait. Allegedly the first St Albans Steeplechase, organized by hotelier Thomas Coleman, was at the behest of officers from the 1st Life Guards following a dinner at Coleman's Turf Hotel.[26] Military meetings themselves started as races casually organized by cavalry officers, though some, like the Grand Military Gold Cup, became permanent features of the National Hunt social and racing calendar. Some jump meetings organized for military men often had a course deliberately more severe than at conventional steeplechases. At Aldershot, for example, 'the water jump is of a width to test the stride of a horse; there is an open brook, unguarded in any way; a drop over one of the obstacles' so that 'altogether the course more nearly resembles the typical fair hunting country'.[27] To one supporter, writing in the late 1880s, it was unfortunate that other, less testing courses were now being chosen to host military events 'principally for social reasons'.[28]

Turning to individual military riders, it was Captain 'Josey' Little who won the Grand National on Chandler in 1848.[29] The late 1860s and early 1870s saw two colonels, Knox and Harford, win Grand Military Steeplechases but also participate widely and successfully in non-military events.[30] Captain E.R. ('Roddy') Owen, the 'acknowledged head of the active soldier brigade', was an army officer who had 254 winners from 812 mounts in the decade from 1882 and then, immediately after winning the Grand National on Father O'Flynn, gave up the sport to focus on his army career.[31] Captain Lee Barber won many races and was described by George Lambton as 'the Fred Archer of the soldiers'.[32] Captain Arthur Smith too had a name as a fine horseman and rider to hounds.[33] Two officers in the Northumberland Fusiliers, Charles Lambton and Captain Whitaker, also had reputations as horsemen.[34] A correspondent in Bell's Life argued that senior officers encouraged their juniors to ride in steeplechases 'because it excites that courage, presence of mind and skill in horsemanship without which their glorious achievements of Balaclava and Inkerman would never have been recorded'.[35] There were other equally practical reasons: the writer added that it also checked 'riotous living and its worst accessory, the use of the gaming table'.

Another source of courageous horsemen, and to some extent associated with the military, was the hunting field where chasing Reynard involved jumping real fences. The Vale of Aylesbury Steeplechase, first run in 1835, was the brainchild of a party of hunting men dining at Crockfords.[36] Hugh Owen, brother of Roddy, was rated as 'one of the best men to hounds in England'.[37] George Ede lived with Lord Poulett at Waterloo and assisted him with the mastership of the Hambledon Hunt.[38] Maunsell Richardson, who won the Grand National twice, was a brilliant rider to hounds and eventually retired from the turf to concentrate on hunting.[39] Many others, less successful over jumps than these, also combined the two sports.

The courage was there but what about the skills? For professionals, these were developed through an apprenticeship in a training stables which involved not just riding horses but grooming them, feeding them and mucking out. No amateur would risk social contamination by sinking so low, though several would go as guests to training establishments and learn by helping to school the horses and ride them in trials and gallops. George Ede was taught by Ben Land, a noted cross-country rider and later trainer.[40] Others to follow this path included Captain Little, Thomas Towneley, 'Mr Thomas' (i.e. Mr T.F. Pickernell, who won three Grand Nationals), captains Scobell, Tempest and Henry ('Bee') Coventry, and Fothergill Rowlands, who gave up his medical practice to become a gentleman rider.[41] Arthur Coventry learned the tactics of race riding under the tuition of Tom Cannon, a professional jockey who became a trainer with a reputation for producing skilled apprentices.[42] In the 1880s there were hunters' flat races at almost every meeting, winter and summer, in which horses would carry heavy amateur riders. George Lambton maintained that these were an ideal nursery for amateurs to experience race-riding.[43]

Shamateurs and corruption

In many sports a distinctive amateur ethos emerged under the influence of the public schools, their old boys and other Corinthians. Its ideal(istic)-type central features focused on a 'contained competitiveness' in which the process of how the game was played was regarded as more important than the actual outcome, which itself should be acknowledged by 'gracious winners' and 'good losers'.[44] Part of this process was that both opponents and the rules should be respected. To the amateur, participation was all and no cognizance was taken of any need to entertain the spectator.

Although aspects of these features can be found among some gentlemen riders, no specific amateur ethos has been identified with horse racing. Even when racing featured in a series on the unwritten rules of sport in the Badminton Magazine, a periodical devoted primarily to field sports and an elite readership, there was no mention of gentlemen riders. Instead the emphasis was on honest and trustworthy relationships between owners and trainers, particularly in regard to insider information and betting.[45] Possibly it is this intimate relationship with gambling that prevented any real amateur ethos developing in the sport. As one historian of the Jockey Club aptly put it, 'betting is the manure to which the enormous crop of horse racing and racehorse breeding ... is to a large extent due'.[46] Such an involvement may have precluded style and process from undermining the necessity to win. In contrast, most other amateur-led sports had thrown off their Georgian inheritance and now viewed gambling with abhorrence: unlike racing they had cleansed their stables.

Gambling may also have encouraged corruption within racing even among its amateur participants. A common thread of the late nineteenthcentury debate over the introduction of professionalism into many sports was a concern that professionals, whose livelihoods were at stake, either would commit fouls to avoid defeat or be susceptible to corruption to ensure it. The experience of racing with its long history of paid jockeys and associated misconduct would not have calmed their fears. Yet research has suggested that amateur cricketers and rugby players, among others, were not averse to gamesmanship. So the question to be asked is whether the sporting conduct of gentlemen riders was better than that of their counterparts in other sports, particularly considering that horse racing was a sport driven by gambling. Clearly many gentlemen riders bet on racing. George Lambton, for instance, recalls that he had Lord Lurgan act as his commissioner to place most of his bets when he was riding.[47] Whether this was because they needed the money, wanted to add extra excitement to their ride, or just wanted to challenge the bookmakers with their (inside) knowledge is not known. Whether this led to deviant activity is also conjectural. One amateur rider often accused of unsporting practices was 'Mr Abington', one of the first gentleman riders to gain Jockey Club permission to ride on the flat against professionals. If many gentlemen riders can be seen as one of Emsley's courageous 'plucky chaps', George Baird, in contrast, was the middle-class version of the 'hard man', oozing toughness, exuding an air of menace and being not quite respectable.[48] In 1882 he was warned off by the National Hunt Committee for threatening to put a fellow rider over the rails. The Jockey Club extended the suspension to meetings under their jurisdiction, but the continental authorities did not follow suit and he continued to race in France. On his reinstatement in 1884 he appears to have ridden hard but more fairly, though he continually flouted Jockey Club regulations on running horses in other people's names, partly to create an impression that he was securing outside rides.[49] Yet many of the social establishment would argue that he was not even a gentleman, let alone a gentleman rider. His background was that of new money, made out of Scotland's industrialization, and his behaviour had little regard for social niceties. Baird may not have been the worst offender. The Earl of Suffolk and Berkshire argued that too many gentlemen riders possessed 'dubious integrity' and 'that the regular "wrong one" should continue to flourish in our midst as he does is the worst blot on the reputation of the Turf'. He felt that they got away with sharp practice because of the incompetence of some gentlemen riders, so that 'the gradual development of clumsiness into skilful knavery often passes unnoticed' by the stewards.[50]

Much illicit activity by amateur riders centred on trying to beat the definitional regulations which often restricted entry to those of particular social standing or locality. The defence of the gentleman rider was straightforward: those who committed these transgressions were not true gentlemen riders. Hence the term became a self-fulfilling descriptor which argued that gentlemen did not cheat and that anyone who did break the rules was thus not a gentleman. So it was that Arthur Coventry and his fellow author noted that it was a 'so-called gentleman rider' who took a small farm in a district hunted by several packs so that he might label himself a farmer and qualify for the local races.[51] Such races were eventually abolished as the local clerks of courses had become too lax regarding qualification and 'many people rode as gentlemen riders who were very far from meriting that distinction'.[52] It is noteworthy that in one of the few late-nineteenth-century stories to have a corrupt amateur rider as its focus, 'To Win a Race' by turf authority Alfred Watson, the villain is actually a professional masquerading as the appropriately named 'Mr Sharpe', a gentleman rider.[53]

National Hunt racing, like cricket, was a sport in which middle-class shamateurism developed on a significant scale. Admittedly, some clerks of the course took a lenient attitude to gentlemen riders of obscure pedigree, but mainly it was the economic qualification that was abused, with supposedly amateur jockeys obtaining retainers and liberal fees when they were not legitimately entitled even to out-of-pocket expenses. It was open to owners, however, to object to the suspect gentlemen riders. One such objection to Mr Frank Lotan, after he won the National Hunt Chase at Melton, led to his disqualification on the grounds of having received payment to ride on previous occasions and this brought the whole issue into the open.[54] Following the reorganization of the National Hunt Committee in 1883, the regulations were tightened, but some owners were still willing to condone shamateurism. They purchased the services of men qualified to ride on social grounds and found their way round the 'not having ridden for hire' regulations by laying a bet with the proceeds going as a present to the rider.[55] Some owners found that hotel and other expenses could make it dearer to put up a gentleman than pay a fee to a professional but presumably they thought it was worth it.[56]

A study of the 1902 season suggests a number of cases of shamateurism. Messrs Garnett and Gordon, both elected as qualified riders, raced at between 20 and 30 meetings that year; the two Nugents rode at between 35 and 45 meetings; and R.H. Harper and H.S. Sydney both attended over 40 meetings. And what about Frank Hartigan, a member of a prominent Irish racing family? As an amateur he travelled to 43 meetings at 23 different courses, mostly in the south but as far north as Nottingham and Liverpool. He won on 30 of his 125 mounts and was placed a further 34 times, a workload and success rate worthy of a paid rider. That he later turned professional and, in 1913, when a trainer, showed little respect for the rules by riding as Mr Hartigan with no evidence that he had ever been reinstated as a gentleman rider, gives credence to the claim that he was a shamateur. In contrast to these amateurs who sought to make money out of their sport, the often-maligned Mr Abington, as already noted, spent a fortune becoming a successful rider.

Conclusion

Many gentlemen riders were skilful enough to compete effectively against professionals, but why did amateurs risk serious injury or death in the name of sport? It can be hazarded that they were men of courage who sought the action and excitement that jump racing in particular provided. For the professional there was the carrot of income at least for the successful. For the amateur, as distinct from the shamateur, peer recognition and social kudos probably played a part. As huntsmen and cavalry officers, many were good horsemen and could compete effectively against their paid counterparts. But the times were changing. The deaths of many officers in the Boer War and the abandonment of hunters' flat races in the early twentieth century further contributed to the decline in the numbers of gentlemen riders. As National Hunt racing became more commercialized, owners sought the best riders and increasingly these were professionals who devoted themselves full time to their trade. In 1919 Harry Brown, the younger of two gentlemen rider brothers, won the National Hunt jockeys' title. He was the last amateur to do so.

Appendix
Riders, Gentlemen Riders, Qualified Riders, Jockeys etc: Rules 91 and 92 of National Hunt Racing

Rule 91

1) Persons who have never ridden for hire, and who are not otherwise disqualified under these Rules, need no qualification to ride in steeple chases or hurdle races unless the conditions of any such steeple chase or hurdle race requires a particular condition, but for welter flat races riders must be 'Qualified Riders' or Jockeys holding licences under these Rules.

110] *How the Game was Played*

2) Qualified Riders under these Rules are persons who have never ridden for hire, and who are qualified either [a] as Gentlemen, [b] as farmers, [c] by election, [d] Yeomen when riding at their own Regimental Meeting.

   a) Riders qualified as Gentlemen must be Members of the National Hunt Committee, the Irish National Hunt Steeple Chase Committee, or one of the following Clubs: Jockey Club, Turf Club of Ireland, Jockey Club of Paris, Jockey Club of Berlin, Jockey Club of Vienna, New Rooms at Newmarket, Bibury, Croxton Park, Ludlow, Southdown, Army and Navy, Junior Army and Navy, Guards', Cavalry, Navy and Military, United Service, Junior United Service, East India United Service, Arthur's, Badminton, Boodle's, Brooks', Carlton, Junior Carlton, Conservative, Devonshire, Oxford and Cambridge, New University, United University, Oriental, Pratt's, St James', Travellers', Turf, Union, Wellington, White's, Windham, Western Meeting (Ayr), Kildare Street (Dublin), Sackville Street (Dublin), Hibernian United Service (Dublin), Stephen's Green (Dublin). Or that they be persons holding commissions under the Crown, or bearing titles in their own right, or by courtesy.

   b) Riders qualified as farmers, must now be farming at least 100 acres of land, and their Sons if following the same occupation. A 'Farmer' shall be understood to mean one who resides permanently on his farm, working it himself, and deriving therefrom his principal and ostensible means of subsistence.

   c) Persons not qualified as 'Gentlemen Riders' or 'Farmers' who are desirous of becoming 'Qualified Riders' must send their names in for election, with the names of their proposer and seconder, who must be members of the National Hunt Committee, to the Registry Office for publication in at least one Calendar month before the day of the election. The names of the persons elected must be submitted annually to the Committee at the General Meeting on the second Monday in December, for re-election. The fee to be paid for election, or re-election, is 1 sov.

Rule 92

Should any Qualified Rider at any time ride for hire, he shall thereupon cease to be a 'Qualified Rider', or should his name appear upon the Forfeit List, or he be reported by the Committee at Tattersall's as being a defaulter for bets lost on horse racing, he will, at the discretion of the Stewards of the National Hunt Committee, lose his qualification, and if he be a qualified rider by election, his name may be erased from the list of Qualified Riders.[57]

References

1. All calculations are based on information drawn from the *Racing Calendar*. The research was supported by a British Academy grant.
2. David H. Munroe, *The Grand National 1839 1931* (London, 1931), pp. 99–101.
3. For more on the history of the structure of racing see Wray Vamplew and Joyce Kay, The encyclopedia of *British horseracing* (London, 2005).
4. This is really a misnomer in that it was for the rulers of racing not riders. For more detail on the Jockey Club and its regulatory powers see Wray Vamplew, 'Reduced horsepower: The Jockey Club and the regulation of British horseracing', *Journal of Entertainment Law*, 2 and 3 (2003), pp. 94 111.
5. Minutes of Jockey Club, Racing Calendar 1901, p.lxix (our italics). It has not been possible to determine why the terminology changed from 'on equal terms' to 'other than those open to gentlemen riders'.
6. A search of the results for 1902 suggests that a further four rode either without permission or obtained it during the year and then did not renew it for the following season.
7. Roger Onslow, *The squire: A life of George Alexander Baird gentleman rider 1861 1893* (London, 1980).
8. George Lambton, *Men and horses I have known* (London, 1986, facsimile of 1923 first edn), p. 156.
9. Such weights contradict the oft-used nineteenth-century rationale for horse racing, that it was the racecourse test which produced horses from which to breed army remounts. Army officers rarely weighed less than eight stones!
10. John Pinfold, 'Where the champion horses run: The origins of Aintree racecourse and the Grand National', *International Journal of*

the *History of Sport*, 15 (2) (1998), pp. 13751.
11. John Tolson and Wray Vamplew, 'Facilitation not revolution: Railways and British flat racing 18301914', *Sport in History*, 23(1) (2003), pp. 1034.
12. Although jump and flat racing were separately organized, there was no strict demarcation between riding under either code. In 1902 roughly a fifth of professionals were licensed under both codes and 34 of the 45 amateurs who
raced on the flat also raced under National Hunt rules.
13. A few women did ride against men in the 1920s, sometimes successfully. Michael Williams, *Point-to-pointing in our time* (London, 1998), pp. 45, 25.
14. Quoted in John Fairfax-Blakeborough, *The analysis of the turf* (London, 1927), p. 143.
15. The Gentleman in Black, 'Gentlemen-jockeys', *Baily's Magazine*, XI (1866), p. 5.
16. Earl of Suffolk, 'Gentlemen riders', *Badminton Magazine*, II (1896), p. 495.
17. Based on information supplied by Dr Michael Turner, senior medical advisor to the Jockey Club. A further breakdown suggests a fall every eight mounts over fences and every 27 over hurdles.
18. Fox Russell, *In scarlet and silk* (London, 1896), p. 221.
19. Michael Williams, *The continuing story of point-to-point racing* (London, 1970), p. 19.
20. Roger Munting, *Hedges and hurdles* (London, 1987), p. 132.
21. 'Our twelve best of today: Gentlemen riders', *Baily's Magazine*, LXXXI (1904), p. 39.
22. Edward Spencer, 'Some turf casualties', *Baily's Magazine*, LXVI (1896), p. 273.
23. Munroe, *The Grand National*, p. 109.
24. 'Our twelve best of today', p. 42.
25. Information supplied by Professor Timothy Chandler, Kent State University. Of course the fact that the boys did not have these activities at school does not mean that they did not participate fully as 'young gentlemen' during the holidays.
26. Williams, *Point-to-pointing in our time*, p. 19.
27. Arthur Coventry and Alfred E. Watson, 'Steeplechasing', in Earl of Suffolk and Berkshire, ed., *Racing and steeplechasing* (London, 1889), p. 327.
28. Ibid., p. 347.

29. It should be noted that the military rank of the famous Captain Becher, commemorated in Becher's Brook at Aintree, was in fact an honorary one in the Buckinghamshire Yeomanry, but this allowed him to compete as a gentleman even though it was common knowledge that he was receiving payment for riding. Vamplew and Kay, *Encyclopedia*, pp. 4344.
30. 'Our twelve best of today', p. 41.
31. 'Captain E.R. Owen', *Baily's Magazine*, LIII (1890), p. 218; Lambton, *Men and horses*, p. 30.
32. Lambton, *Men and horses*, p.73.
33. Munroe, *The Grand National*, pp. 11011.
34. Lambton, *Men and horses*, p. 197.
35. Quoted in Michael Seth-Smith et al., *The history of steeplechasing* (London, 1966), p. 42. See also C. Stein, 'Soldiering and sport', *Baily's Magazine*, LXXIV (1900), pp. 23540.
36. Williams, *Point-to-pointing in our time*, p. 20.
37. Lambton, *Men and horses*, p. 29.
38. Seth-Smith et al., *The history of steeplechasing*, p. 47.
39. Munroe, *The Grand National*, p. 96.
40. Seth-Smith et al., *The history of steeplechasing*, p. 47.
41. Earl of Suffolk, 'Gentlemen riders', p. 497; Seth-Smith et al., *The history of steeplechasing*, p. 45.
42. 'Mr Arthur Coventry', *Baily's Magazine*, LXXIX (1903), p. 238.
43. Lambton, *Men and horses*, p. 24.
44. Norman Baker, 'Whose hegemony? The origins of the amateur ethos in nineteenth-century English society', *Sport in History*, 24 (1) (2004), p. 1.
45. Alfred E. Watson, 'The unwritten laws of sport: racing', *Badminton Magazine*, XX (1905), pp. 36573.
46. Robert Black, 'The Jockey Club and its founders', quoted in Wray Vamplew, *The Turf* (London, 1975), p. 197.
47. Lambton, *Men and horses*, p. 70.
48. Clive Emsley, Hard men: *Violence in England since 1750* (London, 2005), p. ix.
49. Vamplew and Kay, *Encyclopedia*, pp. 4243.
50. Earl of Suffolk, 'Gentlemen riders', p. 500.
51. Coventry and Watson, 'Steeplechasing', p. 314.
52. Lambton, *Men and horses*, p. 25.
53. Watson, the turf correspondent for the *Illustrated London News*, wrote the entry on horse racing for the *Encyclopaedia Britannica*, was

an editor of the Badminton Library and penned several authoritative studies of the racing world, using the more libellous material in fictional form, most of which appeared in *Longman's Magazine*.

54. Earl of Suffolk, 'Gentlemen riders', p. 496.
55. Ibid., pp. 4956.
56. 'The amateur', *Baily's Magazine*, LXXX (1903), p. 252.
57. Source: *Racing Calendar: Steeple Chases Past* (London, 1906), pp. livlv.

Reduced Horse Power: The Jockey Club and the Regulation of British Horseracing

The Jockey Club, founded in 1752 has influenced racing for two centuries and controlled it by consent of the racing industry since the 1870s. Despite legal challenges and public criticism of a self-perpetuating, private club governing a major British sport, it maintained its pre-eminent position until the 1990s. In 1993 it began to share power with the British Horseracing Board though retaining the regulatory and disciplinary role. Failure to take full cognisance of human rights legislation, media publicity over corruption in the sport, and a conflict of interest via its ownership of racecourses led to proposals for a new, independent governing body.

Introduction

In February 2003 the Jockey Club announced that it was relinquishing its position as regulator and disciplinary authority of the British turf. It had ruled the sport by consent for well over a century,[1] but had come to the conclusion 'that in today's changing environment, the perception of a private club regulating a major British sport could be damaging to racing's interests.'[2] In its place it has proposed an independent body with an independent chairman, six executive directors, only two of which would be nominated by the Club, plus an unspecified number of non-executive directors. If the details of funding, financial accountability and cost control can be resolved, it is envisaged that the new body could be operating in 2004.

In the Beginning

In 1752 the *Sporting Kalendar* gave notice of 'A Contribution

Free Plate to be run for at Newmarket in April ... by horses the property of the noblemen and gentlemen of the Jockey Club at the Star and Garter in Pall Mall'.[3] This was the earliest mention of the Jockey Club that has been found in print and although some authorities date the foundation as 1750 the Jockey Club itself now accepts 1752 as its date of origin.[4] There is no documentation on the reasons why the Club was established but, by implication from its actions in the early years, it was to organise horse races at Newmarket for its members. It should be emphasised that, although several owners rode their own animals, the term 'jockey' did not infer a rider.[5] The Jockey Club rooms were exclusive premises with no place for the hired professional. In the late nineteenth century the Club probably had around 100 members.[6] Elections for new members were held twice a year. Candidates had to be nominated by existing members; at least nine members had to vote; and two black balls were sufficient to exclude.[7]

There is no evidence that at the outset the Club had any interest in governing British racing though it was a role that this private body was to occupy for many years. When it first began to exert any control outside its own domain is unclear. One historian of the Club has argued that 'as many of the early members of the Club were among the richest and most influential men in the country, it is not surprising that the Club *rapidly* acquired authority and prestige.'[8] However, three caveats need to be made on this statement. First, there was no list of members of the Club published until 1835. It has been argued that many can be identified as owners running horses in races restricted to Club members or from names attached to Jockey Club resolutions, but in fact there were very few of the former (and these were poorly subscribed) and the only names attached to resolutions were those of the stewards and committee members, so the bulk of the membership remained anonymous. Second, the same historian also suggested that 'the character and habits of many of the Club's early members' was such as to render any suggestion that the Club sought to govern or reform the turf 'ridiculous'.[9] Third, apart from an isolated instance in 1757 when it was asked to adjudicate on a dispute arising from a meeting at the Curragh in Ireland, there is no other mention in either Jockey Club records or the *Racing Calendar* of the Club having – or seeking – any influence in the eighteenth century beyond its immediate jurisdiction.[10]

At Newmarket, however, it was a different story with the Club attempting to control racing matters on the Heath, the vast stretch of land around the town that had been used from the sixteenth century as gallops, training grounds and racetrack. Initially parts of the Heath may have been common land but it was certainly in private ownership by the late eighteenth century and possibly before. In 1758 it enforced compulsory 'weighing in' after a race with any jockey failing to do so being banned from riding again at Newmarket.[11] The members also took a collective decision that 'any servant belonging to a member of the society [i.e. the Jockey Club]' found engaged in illegal acts relating to betting 'shall be dismissed his service, and no further employed by any member of the society.'[12] Thirteen years later it was agreed that 'all disputes relative to racing at Newmarket should for the future be decided by the three Stewards, and by two referees to be chosen by the parties concerned.'[13] Until 1770 the Club had only one steward but from then on there were three, one being replaced annually in rotation with the official in his final year being senior steward with the power to nominate the replacement steward. The same order of 1771 gave the stewards full powers 'to conduct racing affairs generally at Newmarket, and also all matters connected with the payment of stakes and forfeits.'[14]

Perhaps an indication of the power that it had consolidated came in 1790 when, after the inconsistent running of his horse *Escape*, the Prince of Wales was informed that if he continued to employ Sam Chifney as his jockey no gentleman would start against him at Newmarket. Although possibly aimed more at the servant than the master, it showed that the Club would not be deferential if the integrity of the sport came under question.[15]

Bidding For Power?

By this time the Club may have been seeking to formalise its influence in the wider racing world. In 1807 the *Racing Calendar* began to publish the results of certain 'Adjudged Cases', already decided by the Jockey Club, presumably as a guide to local stewards throughout the country, though they also served to draw attention to this function of the Club and perhaps encouraged the sending of disputes to it for judgement.[16] Nine years later the Club published a note in the *Racing Calendar* that 'persons who may be inclined to submit any matters in dispute to the decision of the Stewards of the Jockey Club were at liberty to do so'. For the first time the Club was volunteering to intervene when requested to do so. However, conditions were laid down:

> The matter in dispute must relate to horse racing. The parties must agree on a statement of the case in writing; request the opinion of the Stewards of the Jockey Club thereon, and agree to abide by their decision; and such agreement must be signed by both the parties. If the dispute should not occur at Newmarket, the reference must come through, or with the sanction of, the Stewards of the races where it happened. Except the case arise [sic] at Newmarket, they decline giving any opinion where facts alone are in dispute, such as complaints of foul riding, etc. All such cases are most effectually investigated on the spot, whilst the matter is fresh in the memories of the witnesses, where their attendance is most easily procured, and their credibility best understood.[17]

Yet the number of cases published in the *Racing Calendar* remained low – a total of eleven in 1826 had only risen to nineteen by 1833 – and most of these came from courses in the south of England. This suggests a limited take-up of the offer to adjudicate.

In 1832 the *Racing Calendar* contained a notice to the effect that the Jockey Club Rules and Orders applied only to racing at Newmarket and that it had no authority to extend them to any other racecourse. However, it was noted that 'for the sake of greater uniformity and certainty', the Club recommended the adoption of the same rules to the stewards of other races. Then came the crunch statement that 'the Stewards of the Jockey Club will not receive any references of disputes from any places except those at which the Rules and Regulations of Newmarket shall have been declared to be in force in the printed articles of those races.' This could be interpreted as either a retreat to isolation or possibly an attempt to force other meetings to accept the Newmarket Rules. Before 1750 most race meetings were organised via articles of agreement that allowed for local conditions and were signed by participating owners.[18] Possibly these were re-enacted year by year at those meetings held regularly. Not until 1751 were any general 'Laws of Racing' made available to assist those running meetings. These appeared in Pond's *Sporting Kalendar* and had nothing to do with the fledgling Jockey Club. Not till the early nineteenth century did Weatherbys, the publishers of the *Racing Calendar*, start including 'Rules Concerning Horse Racing in General' on a regular basis. Nevertheless at this time the Rules and Orders of the Jockey Club said nothing about racing elsewhere. Moreover the general rules remained virtually unaltered till 1858 which suggests an unwillingness to impose a Club view more widely.

The bid for power – if there was one – was backed up both by social position and the force of law, though both had limited impact at the time. Beginning in 1835, the annual publication of the names of Jockey Club members in the *Racing Calendar*, an organ that commenced its list of racing abbreviations with D for Duke, E for Earl, M for Marquis and Ld for Lord, served to remind the racing world of the status of club membership. In a country that had limited democracy, social position was important both in its own right but also for political patronage and influence. Yet there is no evidence that provincial executives were in awe of the Club and most valued their independence, even when they were Jockey Club members themselves![19]

The law was used to establish the Club's right to 'warn off' undesirable characters from the Newmarket courses and training gallops. Not until the 1820s did the Club move to develop the penalty of 'warning off' from Newmarket Heath. The first instance, in 1821, was straightforward. A tout, William Taylor (alias Snipe), accepted the punishment for watching a trial with a telescope and refusing to say who employed him to do so.[20] Six years later George Hawkins was less amenable when 'warned off' for taking umbrage over a decision regarding a bet and swearing at Lord Wharncliffe on the Heath. The Duke of Portland took action against Hawkins for trespass and the magistrates at Cambridge Assizes backed the Club on the grounds that it had been invested in the proprietorship of the Heath as a tenant of the Duke since 1753.[21] From then on the Jockey Club consolidated this position by buying more land around Newmarket when opportunity and financial resources permitted, most significantly in the purchase of the Exning estate in 1882 and the Cheveley in 1919.[22] However, the 'warnings off' initially applied only to Newmarket and not to other racing venues till the later nineteenth century.

Whether the Jockey Club could have enforced any regulations in a country without effective transport and communication systems is debatable. How willing would local stewards and race committees have been to cede power to a distant central authority? Well into the nineteenth century regional racing was organised in pockets with local race committees setting their own card of events without regard to Jockey Club wishes. Even when Jockey Club approved starters, judges and handicappers were available in the mid-nineteenth century, meetings often continued to appoint their own officials to handle these functions. Not until the late nineteenth century, with the introduction of licences for courses, could any meaningful sanctions be used by the Club to back up its demands. Owners too do not appear to have voluntarily accepted Club suggestions. In 1762 the Jockey Club recommended that owners register their colours. Yet by 1794 only 38 appear to have done so out of about 300 known owners: even in 1833 the figure was just 150 from around 700.[23] This was not because they did not have colours to register. Race lists for several meetings in the late eighteenth and early nineteenth centuries, held in the archives of the National Horseracing Museum at Newmarket, note the colours worn by jockeys to identify the horses they were riding, but reference to the *Racing Calendar* shows that very few were 'officially' registered.

One critic in the 1830s felt that 'a tighter hand of control is needed if the English turf is not to decline'.[24] It was not forthcoming and the lack of firm direction in racing affairs was seen in several racing scandals in the following decade, in particular the winning of the 1844 Derby, the Classic race for three-year-olds, by Running Rein (in reality Maccabeus, a four-year-old).[25] Two weeks later a similar case of an over-age horse winning a major race occurred at Ascot when Bloodstone, winner of the New Stakes for two-year-olds, was revealed to be a year older than the animals it had beaten. Although no such deception appears to have been tried at Newmarket itself, that it was being attempted at elite meetings suggests that the racing stables were in need of cleansing. In both instances the Jockey

Club stood back and allowed objectors to the race results to go to law to obtain satisfaction, though it should be noted that Baron de Tessier, one of the Epsom stewards, had refused to release statements made to him to the Club.[26] A special meeting was called at which a series of resolutions were passed intimating that in future the Club itself would prosecute in all cases where fraud was intended as such offences were 'calculated to inflict an injury on the Turf by bringing racing into disrepute, and … deterring honourable men from entering into competition in which they run the risk of being encountered by such dishonest rivals.'[27]

Integrity also featured in the warning off of James Adkins in 1857. Adkins, a racehorse owner and keeper of a gambling house, lost an action in which he was sued for using loaded dice to fleece a customer. Although initially the Jockey Club ignored the matter, a letter from Lord Derby (copied to *The Times*) stimulated the stewards to action. It is, he ventured

> your duty as stewards of the Jockey Club to exercise a wholesome influence upon the character and respectability of the Turf.
>
> You cannot debar any man, whatever his position in society from keeping racehorses, nor do I recommend a wholesale and inquisitorial scrutiny into the character and conduct of those who do so; but when among their number are found those against whom flagrant cases of disgraceful fraud, and dishonesty, have been legally established, it appears to me clearly within your preserve to stamp them with your reprobation; and to exclude them from association on an equal footing with the more honourable supporters of the Turf.

He proposed – and the stewards concurred – that Adkins 'be warned off the Heath at Newmarket; and that no horse of which he may be, in whole or in any part, owner, be allowed to run over any ground over which the Jockey Club exercises jurisdiction.'[28] Yet such punishments still formally applied only to Newmarket and it was also in 1857 that the Doncaster stewards – all of them Jockey Club members – dismissed an argument that Newmarket rules about defaulters should apply to that northern meeting.[29] Huggins sums up the situation by arguing that up to the 1860s, outside Newmarket and a minority of elite courses, the Jockey Club was ineffective. It had some influence but little actual power except in Parliament.[30]

Here it did achieve something. In 1860 Lord Redesdale had proposed to set a minimum weight of seven stone for any flat race as he felt that some of the very low weights assigned in some handicaps were detrimental to improving the breed of horses and led to the exploitation of child riders.[31] The Club petitioned the House of Lords not to pass the Bill and submitted 'that all regulations respecting racing are better entrusted to the authority which has hitherto made rules for the encouragement of this great national amusement'.[32] After debate the Bill was withdrawn. That many members of the Club were also members of the Lords doubtless helped its case. When Parliament next intervened in horseracing in 1879 to put down speculative, ill-regulated metropolitan racing – meetings organised by publicans for sinners! – the Club did not object strenuously as it was in favour of their suppression.[33]

Yet its influence in racing remained incomplete. In 1869 Sir Joseph Hawley, a successful but unpopular owner, proposed motions to limit the amount of two-year-old racing. He was opposed by Admiral Rous, at the time the driving force within the Jockey Club, who raised the surprising argument that the Club had no authority beyond Newmarket. *The Times* voiced incredulity that 'if the day comes when the authority of the Jockey Club extends no further than "The Ditch" [a feature of the Newmarket landscape], it will be because its members were not equal to their position, and had not the courage to exercise for the public good the powers which rest in their hands.'[34]

Holding The Reins

A defining moment came in 1870 when the Club again revised the rules of racing and drew a distinction between 'recognised' and 'unrecognised' meetings. It was resolved that neither the programme nor the results of any British flat-race meeting would be published in the *Racing Calendar* unless it was advertised as being subject to 'the established Rules of Racing' as settled by the Jockey Club.[35] It soon followed that any owner, trainer, jockey or official who took part in such unauthorised meetings would be disqualified from recognised or authorised racing. From the beginning of 1877 it was specifically noted that warnings off applied to all places where the 'Rules of Racing, made by the Jockey Club at Newmarket' were in force.[36] In the 1870s the Club used its power virtually to restructure racing by ridding the sport of a mass of small-scale meetings. Some of these were disreputable affairs but others were simply local holiday meetings that the Club felt did not contribute to the improvement of the thoroughbred, still an official rationale for horseracing. From 1877 all meetings wishing to be recognised by the Club had to provide a minimum of 300 sovereigns in prize money for each day of racing. The net result was a dramatic decline in the number of authorised meetings, some of which gave up racing while others opted to turn to the cheaper, less-regulated National Hunt Racing.[37] The *Racing Calendar* shows a decline from 136 courses holding 193 meetings in 1869 to 66 courses hosting 114 ten years later. By the end of the century the number of courses had fallen to 49, though they held 127 meetings. The Club had abandoned any attempt to regulate lesser racing, concentrating instead on controlling the more significant meetings.

Jockey Club regulations applied only to one type of racing, that on the flat. In the 1860s the Club deliberately opted to bypass an opportunity to regulate the jumping branch of the sport. Steeplechasing had only begun in an organised form in the 1830s and the Club did not consider it to be proper horseracing. Although Admiral Rous, a virtual perpetual Jockey Club steward for several decades, advised the embryonic National Hunt Committee on the structure of their rules, the Jockey Club itself decided that it wanted no part in regulating this side of the sport. However, when formally established in 1866 most of the original members of the 16-man committee were also members of the Jockey Club; indeed Mr. W.G. Craven was actually senior steward at the time. Next year the Jockey Club deemed that hurdle races more properly belonged in the sphere of the National Hunt Committee and such races were no longer encompassed within the established *Rules of Racing*.[38]

The Club's grip on flat racing was further tightened during the last quarter of the century when it introduced annual licences for jockeys, trainers, officials and racecourses and reserved the right to revoke them or refuse a re-application. At the turn of the century the Club had no qualms about getting tough with jockeys, even leading ones, who broke its rules. Champion rider Otto Madden and major jockey Fred Rickaby were deprived of their licences for 'associating with bad characters'; another champion, American Lester Reiff, was warned off for not trying in a race at Manchester; and Tod Sloan, the Yankee who revolutionised English jockeyship with his monkey-on-a-stick style of riding, was told not to bother re-applying for his licence because of his gambling.[39] Warnings off were now reported to turf authorities in other countries who, under reciprocal agreements, generally extended them to all racing under their control.[40] Whereas Sam Chifney in the late eighteenth century had been excluded solely from riding at Newmarket, these malfeasant jockeys were shut out of not just British racing but also many foreign meetings.

Twentieth Century Challenges

Several legal challenges were mounted against the Club in the twentieth century. Two major ones concerned decisions to ban trainers from pursuing their careers after their horses had tested positive in dope tests. Accepting that it was virtually impossible to prove who had administered drugs to a horse, the Club had taken a pragmatic stance and opted to disqualify the trainer who had had responsibility for the care and security of the doped animal. In 1930 the stewards revoked the licence of a young trainer Charles Chapman whose horse *Don Pat* had tested positive for caffeine at Kempton Park. The findings and decision were fully within the powers conferred on them by the *Rules of Racing* and Chapman was bound by these regulations as a condition of his licence. Unfortunately the way that the decision was expressed branded Chapman as a crook rather than as a trainer who had been careless in his security and, in an attempt to clear his name, he sued the stewards for libel. Although the jury found for Chapman, the Jockey Club won its appeal on the grounds that in a strict sense the wording of the decision in the *Racing Calendar* was actually true (it was the press that had interpreted it differently), the stewards had acted in good faith, and anyway they were protected by privilege.[41] Another doping case that led to a lawsuit in 1948 was when trainer J. Russell had his licence withdrawn following inquiries into the running of one of his horses at Lincoln the previous year. He sued the

Jockey Club stewards for wrongfully taking away his livelihood but the action was dismissed on similar grounds to the Chapman case.[42]

The Club, however, was defeated in the 1960s when Florence Nagle challenged its right to refuse training licences to women. The Jockey Club had a poor comprehension of social change and stubbornly clung to its nineteenth-century view of what was a fit and proper role for women in racing so female trainers such as Nagle had to allow their head lad to hold the licence in his name. After two decades of fruitless campaigning, Nagle decided to take the Jockey Club to court to gain the right to train under her own name. At 72 she had no career to look forward to but pursued the issue as a matter of principle. Lord Justice Denning did not agree with the views of the Jockey Club and at the Court of Appeal in July 1966 pointed out that 'if she is to carry on her trade without stooping to subterfuge she has to have a training licence.'[43] The Club went on to allow women to race on the flat as amateurs from 1972 and compete against male amateurs from 1974, but resisted calls for female professional jockeys until 1976 when forced to concede this right by the Sex Discrimination Act.

A criticism constantly made against the Jockey Club was that it was (and is) an undemocratic organisation unrepresentative of racing in general. In 1870 Sir Joseph Hawley had proposed that 'the basis of the Club be extended and that not only gentlemen who are large owners of racehorses, but those who take an interest in racing as a means of preserving the breed of horses, be invited to become members.'[44] Needless to say the motion was not passed. Writing in the mid 1950s, one historian of the Jockey Club maintained that little had changed since Hawley's attempted reform, apart from the inclusion of Jewish members.[45] Businessmen and industrialists were for the most part still missing and the Club remained 'fundamentally aristocratic and conservative'.[46] He queried 'just how much longer the Jockey Club can continue to exist in its present form – basically a social club drawn from a very small circle'.[47] The answer was 'for some years to come'.

Amalgamation with the National Hunt Committee in 1968, a precursor to incorporation by Royal Charter in 1970 which required racing to have a unified controlling body, brought some new faces.[48] The next decade saw female members elected. But the Club continued to be dominated by a titled elite. Those on the left politically would always criticise undemocratic institutions. George Wigg, socialist Chairman of the Horserace Betting Levy Board, always proclaimed that 'the Jockey Club believe that my function is the plebeian task of collecting the money. Theirs is the aristocratic task of spending it'.[49] But even those more attuned to the concept of noblesse oblige began to feel that social position alone was insufficient to provide authority in a society where meritocracy was becoming more important to the decision-making process.

In his history of the Club published in 1958, Roger Mortimer argued that 'most fair-minded people will agree that with all its faults the Jockey Club has served racing well and has the best interests of racing at heart'.[50] However the list of faults that he enumerated was somewhat damning: 'a closed shop … hopelessly out of touch with the feelings of average supporters of racing … ingrained backwards-looking conservatism … set their faces against reasonable and progressive reform …' and occasionally applied 'disciplinary measures in a manner arbitrary and unjust'.[51] With a friend like this …

Writing on the Wall

Although the Jockey Club ran racing, it did not speak on behalf of all the industry's stakeholders.[52] Indeed there were too many diverse interests in the sport, each pushing their own agenda. Racing needed a united voice. Speaking in December 1989, Lord Hartington, the Jockey Club Senior Steward, commented that:

> It is of immense concern to me when the public, and particularly their elected representatives, complain that racing does not seem to be able to make up its own mind on how it sees the future. How can an industry which is apparently divided in its own vision of the way ahead ever hope to gather sympathetic support in Westminster and Whitehall?[53]

The Club no longer had the influence in Parliament that its aristocratic membership had brought in the nineteenth century. Nevertheless Hartington and Christopher Haines, the Chief Executive (the first and last) of the Jockey Club, lobbied hard and were able to gain a reduction in betting duty, VAT concessions for owners, and the acceptance of Sunday racing.[54] Despite these successes the end was in sight for the Club having sole control of British racing.

Indeed in June 1993 monopoly became duopoly with the formation of the British Horseracing Board to organise and direct the sport. A Select Committee inquiry into the financial structure of racing had reported in May 1991 that

> 'it is vital in their own financial interests for the fragmented racing industry, through co-operation between the Horseracing Advisory Council and the Jockey Club, to find and follow strong and unified commercial leadership. Racing's power structure must be modernised ... We believe that the racing industry will do itself a grave disservice if it does not unite behind a leadership with business acumen'.[55]

The Jockey Club took the hint, agreed to cede some power to a new body, and, with Lord Hartington at the helm, took a lead role in its creation. Hartington believed that unless the Jockey Club surrendered some of its power voluntarily the government, even a Tory one, might intervene, something to which he was vehemently opposed.[56] The remit of the new body included the important functions of strategic planning, finance, fixtures, training and education, public relations, negotiating racing's share of the betting levy and marketing the sport. Of its eleven members four came from the Jockey Club, two each from the Racecourse Association and the Racehorse Owners Association and three from the Horserace Advisory Council (subsequently known as the Industry Committee) in recognition of the numerous interests it supposedly represented, including trainers, breeders, jockeys, stable staff and racegoers. At the national level, the Jockey Club was left with the role of regulator, in charge of race-day stewarding, discipline and security as well having the general responsibility for the Rules of Racing.

Commenting in 1997, Lord Hartington, the architect of the British Horseracing Board, noted that:

> Now that the Club has returned to the role to which it is most suited, that of regulation, I am confident that it will continue to secure the admiration for British racing that it has achieved over the past 235 years ... I hope that the

combination of the Jockey Club and the British Horseracing Board, separate but inter-dependent organisations, will make a formidable and successful partnership in the service of British racing.'⁵⁷

He was wrong, both in his historical assertion and his predictive ability.

Previous groups that brought together various interests within racing – such as the Racing and Breeding Liaison Committee (1958), the Joint Associations' Liaison Committee (1964), the Bloodstock and Racecourse Industries Confederation (1974), the Racehorse Industries Liaison Committee (1976) and the Horserace Advisory Council (1980) – had not possessed any power and remained talking shops, technically consulted but rarely listened to by the Jockey Club. Some commentators had hoped that the Horseracing Advisory Council might have ushered in a new era but their hopes were dashed almost from the start. John Macdonald-Buchanan, the Senior Steward of the Jockey Club, immediately pointed out that 'it should be remembered that the Jockey Club has executive power and all the responsibilities that go with it. The Horseracing Advisory Council, on the other hand, is an advisory body, not obliged to make decisions and not therefore carrying the responsibilities of decision-making'.⁵⁸ Although Phil Bull, the Chairman of the Council, believed that it could use the power of the written and spoken word, he resigned after only a few months in office, complaining that the body was a charade that was not taken seriously by the Jockey Club.⁵⁹ Writing in 1985, the publisher of *Pacemaker*, a well-respected journal in the racing industry, declared that 'consultation has been increased, yet there has been no erosion of the Club's power base' and George (now Lord) Wigg was clear that the Council was 'wholly cosmetic, an instrument of the Jockey Club'.⁶⁰

Unlike its predecessors, however, the Board was more than advisory and had responsibility for the direction of racing. Nevertheless, that the Board was an idea of the Jockey Club led to suspicion that nothing might change. For a few years it appeared that this could be the case as few initiatives were taken in either the finances or the structure of racing, but when Peter Savill, an outspoken representative of the Racehorse Owners

Association, became Chairman in 1998 change was inevitable.[61] His view was that:

> If the sport is to prosper we need to improve its funding substantially and to compete both with racing internationally and with other sports and leisure activities here at home. We can only achieve these goals if the leadership of racing is more professional, democratic, efficient and united.[62]

A first step was to transfer one of the Jockey Club's four seats to representatives of the breeding industry.[63]

Into the New Millenium

In 2001 the Jockey Club underwent a corporate restructure to recognise its four major roles of regulating racing, supporting the work of the BHB, owning and running racecourses, and operating training facilities. The vital regulatory role was ring-fenced from the Club's other activities and became the specific responsibility of Regulatory Stewards who also appointed the members of the Disciplinary and Licensing Committees. But criticism of the Club was growing.

The Jockey Club has consistently argued that it has to act to preserve the integrity of the sport and consequently reserved the right to effectively end the racing career of anyone whom it felt brought racing into disrepute. A series of legal judgements in the early 1990s supported the Jockey Club's contention that it was a private and domestic body that derived its authority from the contractual relationship between itself and those who agreed to be bound by the Rules of Racing.[64] However this failed to take cognisance of changing legal interpretations, in particular the effect of human rights legislation.[65] In matters of disciplinary procedures within racing the Club acted as prosecutor, jury and judge, with proceedings generally held in camera. The six members of the Jockey Club regulatory committee were the six stewards of the Club and the Senior Steward was head of both groups. Although a new appeal board was established under an independent chairman, the mechanisms of disciplinary enquiries, in particular the intention to continue to hold meetings in private, left the Club open to legal challenge.[66]

There was also criticism that the Jockey Club, dominated by rich owners and breeders, could not be truly unbiased in making judgements about the sport and on those who work in the industry. Others noted that the Club, via its wholly owned subsidiary, the Racecourse Holdings Trust, was running 13 of Britain's 59 racecourses, including several major tracks, and that the fortunes and futures of these also influenced its perspective on events, particularly on fixtures and media rights. Savill, while having 'absolutely no doubt that the Jockey Club intends to act in racing's best interests' also believed that 'it had been heavily influenced by its ownership of Racecourse Holdings Trust'.[67]

Perhaps the real catalyst for change was media intrusion into the affairs of the Club. In October 2002 two television programmes, Panorama's 'The Corruption of Racing' and Kenyon Confronts, exposed not just examples of corruption within racing but the ineffectual efforts of the Club to combat it. It did the Club little good that a sacked Head of Security provided the media with much of their ammunition and that his replacement, while able to mastermind the breaking of the siege of the Libyan embassy in the late 1980s, could not spot a hidden microphone and camera and had made unguarded comments about the ineptitude of his employers.[68] British Horseracing Board Director and chair of its Industry Committee, Rhydian Morgan-Jones did not hold back. He accused the Club of 'institutional incompetence' and added that:

> Democracy depends on an independent judiciary, but a judiciary consisting of part-time amateurs appointed by and responsible to a self-electing club with clear conflicts of interest is hardly independent, let alone acceptable in 2002. You cannot have 200 self-elected rich toffs appointing amateurs to run integrity.[69]

Savill seized the opportunity. At first apparently coming to the defence of the Jockey Club, he noted that:

> ...the public have the perception that racing is governed by a group of people living in a time warp when the truth is that the Jockey Club is highly respected throughout the world of international racing; that their regulatory work in the area of setting rules, licensing and registration, standards of veterinary and medical care, discipline and stewarding is exemplary; and that their hands have frequently been tied

by the under-regulation of betting and the fact that corrupt behaviour in racing is, in some instances, not a criminal offence.

But he then went on to point out that 'effective regulation is the bedrock of a successful racing industry' and that British racing had 'effectively two governing bodies – BHB and the Jockey Club – whereas all other sports and racing jurisdictions have just one. In order to modernise our structure, I believe that we need to merge the governance and regulatory responsibilities of the two governing bodies into one'.[70]

Whilst refusing to admit that such criticism of the Club was the stimulus for change, it was acknowledged by John Maxse, Director of Public Relations for the Jockey Club, that 'it speeded up a process already under way'.[71]

The proposals for a new body were welcomed in several quarters, including by Richard Caborn, the Minister for Sport who, though his portfolio at the time did not encompass horseracing, had called for a more transparent regulator after the television exposés.[72] He acknowledged that 'strong independent regulation is essential to ensure that the worldwide reputation of British horseracing for integrity is maintained and enhanced.'[73] Even Savill, who at one time had hinted that his organisation might have wanted to be the regulatory authority, accepted that racing needed an independent regularity body.[74] British Horseracing Board Chief Executive, Greg Nichols, was 'generally supportive of a greater degree of independence, transparency and accountability in the proposals'.[75]

However there were critics and sceptics, including the Racehorse Owners Association and the Jockeys Association, who suspected that the plan was an attempt to overtly cede power but covertly to retain it.[76] They drew parallels with the 1980s when the Jockey Club had set up consultancy mechanisms by which other bodies in racing were listened to but not heard. They questioned the independence of the four non-Jockey Club executive directors and queried how the other non-executive directors would be chosen.[77] Michael Caulfield, Chief Executive of the Jockeys Association, argued that there must not be 'an exchange of one tweed suit for another', though, to be fair, he had earlier accepted that 'the Jockey Club has a huge degree of expertise and understanding which should not be lost on the back of dealing with perception or image'.[78] Indeed the Club insisted that it should retain a minority representation on the new regulatory board so as to provide continuity of experience.[79] The critics also pointed out that the Club would remain one of the four stakeholder directors in the British Horseracing Board. They also ventured that no one of influence had suggested that either the bookmakers or the punters should have a voice on the new body, yet they are two groups whose money is essential to the viability of the industry. Those who had little time for the Club also noted that it is not relinquishing its assets, including 13 racecourses and 2,800 acres of gallops in Newmarket and wonder if it will be satisfied with the role of estate management.[80]

Conclusion

Despite opposition from those who felt that it was morally wrong for racing to be run by a private club, one so exclusive that most of the talent in the sport was denied any opportunity to influence or implement policy, the Jockey Club survived unscathed for many years as the governing body of the turf. Those who complained were unwilling to do more than criticise. Perhaps they feared interference from government even more than they disliked being dictated to by an organisation in which bloodlines seemed to be as important as in horse breeding. Eventually, however, changing social, economic and political circumstances persuaded the Club itself to cede power; first to a power-sharing arrangement with the British Horseracing Board and later to a proposed independent racing authority.

In 1969 George Wigg, then Chairman of the Levy Board and adamant opponent of the Jockey Club, compared the latter organisation to 'a well kept veteran motor car, interesting for use on an occasional drive if you have the infinite time and patience and willingness to judge the article by its original quality and value'.[81] Three and a half decades on, the self-perpetuating oligarchy had come to the end of the road.

References

1. Although the broadsheet press and even the *Racing Post* (12 February 2003) seem to believe that the Jockey Club has ruled racing since the mid eighteenth century, this is patently untrue. Yet even

racing historians have tended to accept that the Club was in charge much earlier than it actually was (see M. Huggins, *Flat Racing and British Society1790–1914* (London: Cass 2000,175). As shown later in this article, the 1870s is perhaps the decade that marks the coming to power of the Club.

2. Christopher Spence, Senior Steward of the Jockey Club, quoted in Racecourse Association, *Update* February 2003, 9.
3. Quoted in R. Mortimer, *The Jockey Club*, (London: Cassell 1958), 10.
4. www.jockeyclub.co.uk
5. See W. Vamplew, *The Turf* (London: Allen Lane 1978), 77.
6. Mortimer, 12.
7. By the mid twentieth century three black balls were required, still hardly a democratic process.
8. Mortimer, 11.
9. Mortimer, 10.
10. Mortimer, 30.
11. Mortimer, 30.
12. *Racing Calendar* 1773 xxiii.
13. Quoted in Mortimer, 32.
14. 'Rules and Orders of the Jockey Club' in *Racing Calendar* (1771). This remained the situation till after 1945 but today there are seven stewards, five serving for three year periods and the Senior Steward and Deputy Senior Steward officiating for four.
15. The Prince stuck by Chifney and never raced again at Newmarket. In 1805 the Club entreated him to bury the affair and return, but though he promised to patronise the Heath again he never did. However, towards the end of his reign as George IV he hosted a dinner for members of the Club.
16. In 1771 the Club consolidated the positions of Keeper of the Match Book, Stakeholder and Club Secretary under James Weatherby. Two years later Weatherby began to publish his *Racing Calendar* which, although primarily concerned with providing information on meetings throughout Britain, also offered a vehicle for Jockey Club pronouncements. It was finally purchased by the JC in 1902.
17. 'Laws of Racing' in *Racing Calendar* (1816).
18. See I. Middleton, *The developing pattern of horse racing in Yorkshire 1700–1749: an analysis of the people and places*, Ph.D. thesis De Montfort University 2000, 60–68.
19. Huggins 178.

20. R. Black, *The Jockey Club and Its Founders* (1893), 82; 'Rules and Orders of the Jockey Club', *Racing Calendar* (1827).
21. G. Hawkins, *The Jockey Club* (1827), 8, 38–9; J. Whyte, *History of the British Turf* (London: 1840) vol. 2, 242.
22. R. Onslow, *The Heath and the Turf* (London: Baker 1971), 25.
23. J. Kay, 'The Actress, the Politician and the Brigadier: British Horseracing Through the Pages of Weatherby's Racing Calendar' in T. Gonzalez Aja (ed.), *Proceedings of the 5th International CESH congress*, (Madrid: CESH 2002), 371.
24. C.P. Apperley, 'The Turf', *Quarterly Review* XLIX (1833), 383.
25. M. Huggins, 'Lord Bentinck, the Jockey Club and Racing Morality in Mid Nineteenth-Century England: The "Running Rein" Derby Revisited', *International Journal of the History of Sport* 10.3 (1993), 295–312.
26. Baron de Tessier to Charles Weatherby, 18 June 1844, Weatherbys Archives.
27. Mortimer, 76.
28. Letter quoted in Mortimer, 96.
29. J. Fairfax-Blakeborough, *Northern Turf History* vol 3 (1950), 363.
30. Huggins, 174.
31. *Hansard*, (156) 16 February 1860; (159) 12 June 1860.
32. Mortimer, 110; Vamplew, 98.
33. *Hansard*, (240) 13 June 1878; (243) 14 February 1879, 17 February 1879.
34. Quoted in Mortimer, 87.
35. *Racing Calendar* 1870 xlv, rule 74.
36. *Racing Calendar* 1876 xxxii rule 5 (iii).
37. See J. Tolson & W. Vamplew, 'Facilitation not Revolution: Railways and British Flat Racing 1830–1914', *Sport in History* Summer 2003, 89–106.
38. M. Seth-Smith, etal., *The History of Steeplechasing* (London: Michael Joseph 1966), 52–59.
39. Mortimer, 138; W. Vamplew, 'The American Invasion of the English Turf: A Study in Sporting Technological Transfer' in J. Toleneer & R. Renson (eds), *Old Borders, New Borders, No Borders* (Leuven: Meyer & Meyer 2000), 219–226.
40. Select Committee on Betting 1902 V qq. 2453–54.
41. Mortimer 133–6; *Daily Telegraph*, 1 December 1931.
42. R. Mortimer, *The Flat* (London: Allen & Unwin 1979), 60–1.
43. Quoted in J. Tyrrel, *Running Racing* (London: Quiller 1997), 149.

For more on the Jockey Club and women in racing see W. Vamplew & J. Kay, 'Horse Racing' in K. Christensen, A. Guttmann & G. Pfister, *International Encyclopedia of Women and Sports* (New York: Macmillan 2001), 537–44.
44. Black, 361.
45. Mortimer, 89.
46. Mortimer, 173.
47. Mortimer, 176.
48. Although this had the disadvantage that any change to its constitution, however trivial, required Privy Council permission, it was seen as offering significant protection from political interference. Tyrrel, 141.
49. Quoted in C. Hill, *Horse Power* (Manchester: Manchester University Press 1988), 109.
50. Mortimer, 175.
51. Mortimer, 174.
52. See entry on 'Associations' in W. Vamplew & J. Kay, *Encyclopedia of British Horseracing* (London: Cass forthcoming).
53. *The Times*, 13 December 1989.
54. Tyrrel, 167.
55. *The Times*, 21 May 1991.
56. Tyrrel, 173.
57. Tyrrel, vii.
58. Quoted in Tyrrel, 160.
59. H. Wright, *Bull: The Biography* (Halifax: Timeform 1995), 223.
60. Tyrrel, 161–2.
61. Savill immediately declared himself as an independent chairman and no longer a representative of the owners and indeed subsequently severely criticised the ROA for some of its attitudes. *Racing Post*, 16 December 1998.
62. *Racing Post*, 16 December 1998.
63. *Racing Post*, 16 December 1998.
64. Neil Parpworth, 'Guarding the Game: Governing Bodies and Legal Intervention' in S. Greenfield & G. Osborn, *Law and Sport in Contemporary Society* (London: Cass 2001), 71–90.
65. *Daily Telegraph*, 4 January 2002. See also T. de la Mere & J. Mulcahy, 'A Sporting Chance', *Legal Weekly* 12 December 2002. It can be conjectured that human rights legislation, particularly at the European level, may have significant effects on the whole issue of disciplinary sanctions by sports administrative bodies.

66. *Jockey Club Press Release* 19 February 2001; *Daily Telegraph*, 4 January 2001.
67. *Racing Post*, 14 August 2001.
68. *Guardian*, 9 October 2002.
69. *Racing Post*, 11 October 2002. Elections are held each December and usually about five new members are selected. They are elected (for life) for their knowledge and experience of racing and the contribution that it is felt they could make to the regulation of the sport. Of the 84 'active' members in 2002 – defined by the Club as those of the 123 members under 70 years of age – 96 per cent are past or current registered owners, 54 per cent are breeders, 51 per cent act as racecourse stewards, 42 per cent are racecourse directors, 30 per cent have sat on the licensing committee, 29 per cent on the disciplinary committee, 26 per cent are ex-jockeys (mainly amateur) and 17 per cent are past or present holders of a licence or permit to train. Members are expected to sit on Jockey Club and other racing committees.
70. *BHB Press Release*, 11 October 2002.
71. Quoted in *Coventry Evening Telegraph*, 12 February 2003.
72. *Daily Telegraph*, 12 February 2003.
73. *Racing Post*, 12 February 2003.
74. *Racing Post*, 21 October 2002; *Guardian*, 12 February 2003.
75. *Express*, 12 February 2002.
76. *Racing Post*, 12 February 2002.
77. *Scotland on Sunday*, 2 March 2003.
78. *Racing Post*, 17 January 2003.
79. *Racing Post*, 12 February 2003.
80. *Sunday Mail*, 16 February 2003.
81. Quoted in Hill, 108.

A Modern Sport? 'From Ritual to Record' in British Horseracing

Abstract

The classic text on the modernisation of sport is Allen Guttmann's *From Ritual to Record*, published in 1978, in which he devised a series of seven key interrelated features deemed to illustrate how modern sporting contests differ from traditional games. Horseracing has never been measured against these criteria although it was one of the first organised sports in Britain and America. Using Guttmann's hypothesis, this paper assesses the extent to which British racing had modernised by the 1830s and considers whether this sport can in fact be judged by this or similar notions of modernity.

Still the seminal work for all students of modernisation in sport, Allen Guttman's *From Ritual to Record: The Nature of Modern Sports* was first published in 1978. It was the subject of two retrospective sessions at the North American Society for Sport History (NASSH) conference in 2000 and was recently the focus of a special issue of the journal *Sport History Review*. Basically Guttmann devised a paradigm designed to clarify the characteristics of modern sports. This identified seven systematically related, structural features of modern sport: secularism, equality, specialisation, rationalisation, bureaucratisation, quantification and the quest for records.[1] Some of these can be found in pre-modern sport but Guttman argues that they need to exist as an interrelated whole before a sport can be classed as having modernised.

Although horseracing was one of the first regularly arranged sports in Britain, no one to date has tested it against his conceptual framework. Indeed Guttmann himself scarcely mentions the sport except to note the dilemma in deciding whether a horse race is primarily a contest between horses or between jockeys.[2] Organised at local level the length and breadth of the country – in 1827 the *Racing Calendar*, the bible of the British thoroughbred sport, reported 137 meetings in 125 different venues – horseracing could claim to be the first truly national British sport. Major races such as the five Classics and the Ascot Gold Cup had been established before 1815 and by this time large crowds were often attracted to meetings, reputedly over 100,000 at Doncaster, Epsom, Manchester and York.[3] If any sport could be said to have 'modernised' by the early nineteenth century then horseracing would surely be in the vanguard.

Using Guttmann's characteristics, this study will assess whether horseracing had become a modern sport by the 1830s, a decade that predates a period of major change in British turf affairs. Thereafter, steeplechasing became a popular variety of the sport, the railway network began to exert an influence on the structure of racing, and the Jockey Club, under the stewardship of first Lord George Bentinck and then Sir Henry Rous, moved to regulate and discipline its participants. These developments pushed racing further along the modernisation track. The issue to be discussed here, through an analysis of Guttmann's seven categories in turn, is how far the sport had travelled down that road by the 1830s.

Secularism is taken for granted in modern sport, but Guttmann noted that, in both primitive and ancient society, sporting activities were linked with religious ceremonies. Native Americans and Aztecs raced or played ball games as part of rituals aimed at appeasing, invoking or honouring their deities while the Olympic games and other Greek athletic festivals took place amidst prayers, sacrifices and gifts to Zeus and a host of lesser gods. According to Guttmann, only when the dependence of sport on religion is broken and those physical activities begin to form part of ordinary life, 'partly pursued for their own sake, partly for other ends which are equally secular', can sport pass the first test of modernity.[4]

In assessing whether any given sport has successfully abandoned its religious roots, a distinction has to be drawn between sports *as* ritual and sports *with* ritual.[5] The former – the Cherokee stickball game, the Mayan-Aztec ball game – are religious in origin, requiring 'some sense of a supernatural being as well as a set of established rituals.'[6] When deities and spirits fade from the picture, rituals often remain, public or private, traditional or invented. The Olympic games were revived in their modern form in 1896, shorn of their sacred rites but still ripe with ceremony and symbolism. A raft of fresh initiatives has followed, from the ritualistic lighting of the Olympic flame on the opening day to the 'spontaneous' melding of separate national teams into one global family at the increasingly elaborate closing event. National anthems and flags vie with Olympic oath, hymn and medals in a two-week international orgy of ritual while daily in some small corner of field or locker-room, individual athletes prepare for contests with bizarre private acts to keep the demons at bay – the tying of left before right shoelace, the donning of kit in a pre-determined order, the wearing of a lucky mascot or dress item. The term superstition is perhaps more accurately applied to such personal irrationality: the only god visible at the modern Olympics is Mammon.

Social anthropologists have argued that twenty-first century horseracing is similarly beset by ritual, particularly in and around the paddock where the protagonists and their supporters gather before the race.[7] Racing, however, is a sport which appears at first sight to have severed any link with religion at an early stage in its development. Bareback horse races were introduced at the ancient Olympics in 648 BC but were later dropped from the programme, eclipsed as a spectacle by chariot races: it was probably this form of horseracing that was introduced to Britain by the Romans. Yet wherever men own horses, there is a desire to establish which is the fastest and gamble on the contest. It is therefore likely that racing, formal and informal, for pleasure and wagering, took place throughout history but although it soon ceased to have a sacred context, this did not free it from a wider religious philosophy. Until the seventeenth century an understanding of equine health and race training continued to rely on quasi-religious beliefs largely founded on the idea of god-given 'humours' which, in medieval physiology, were also essential elements of the human body. Before the relationship between god and nature altered, allowing the ascendancy of science and reason over blind faith and predetermined abilities, the role of the racehorse trainer was to restore the balance of humours, thus enabling the horse to perform at its best.[8]

A more tenuous connection between racing and religion can be found in the timing of medieval horse races, frequently held on saints' days and holy days. The Italian *palio* sometimes honoured a patron saint, and parish races in Scotland and England were often a feature of seventeenth-century fairs that could trace their origins to a pagan festival or Christian feast.[9] The relationship was largely a product of a bygone religious calendar: holy days, originally set aside for worship in pre-Reformation times which, in post-Restoration Britain, had changed their function and, surviving the opprobrium of church authorities, developed into occasions for secular entertainment.[10] Recent research from the early eighteenth century has shown that 60 per cent of races in Yorkshire, the most significant horseracing region in the country, coincided with fairs and 'holy days', now firmly established in parish consciousness as 'holidays.'[11] A closer association with religion was the continuation into the nineteenth century of festivities centred around St Wilfrid, the patron saint of Ripon, Yorkshire.[12] The races here were an integral part of celebrations which included the parading of an effigy of St Wilfrid: the most important race at Ripon's August meeting is still the Great St Wilfrid Handicap. A more tangential link between horseracing and religion was the birth of steeplechasing in 1752 when two riders are said to have raced a distance of $4^{1}/_{2}$ miles (7 kilometres) over fences between two church steeples in County Cork, Ireland. In general, however, seventeenth and eighteenth-century racing was a secular amusement which seldom occurred on Sundays, the holy day of the Protestant church, emphasising the separation of the sport from religious activities.

For Guttman, the second characteristic of modern sport is equality: contestants should not only be able to compete on equal terms but the contests should also, theoretically, be open to all.[13] This was not the case in former times. Participation in primitive societies was largely dependent on membership of caste or kinship groups while women were excluded from much Greek sport, including the Olympic games, and medieval tournaments were restricted to the nobility. Some Greek and Roman athletic contests were formulated to avoid mismatches, with participants grouped by size, but inequality of conditions, such as pitting men against wild animals, was seen as a positive attraction of Roman gladiatorial combat.[14]

It could be argued that equality of entry to horseracing is an impossible target since the first prerequisite is ownership of a horse and the second, at least for elite racing, is the provision of stake money by each race entrant. Where both conditions pertain, the sport is likely to be dominated by those from higher economic and social groups. Thoroughbred racing in Britain during the early modern period was undoubtedly promoted by royalty and undertaken by aristocratic owners but finance and class were not the sole impediments to participation. Attitudinal barriers were raised against those who were considered undesirable – black balling (vetoing prospective members) was a feature of the exclusive racing societies formed in the eighteenth century such as the Jockey Club and the Royal Caledonian Hunt.[15] Women, with few exceptions, played little or no active part in the sport. On the rare documented occasions when they did, it was as riders and the events provoked largely novelty interest.[16]

Gender was not the sole restriction on competitors. As the sport and the racehorse evolved to encompass shorter races and leaner, younger animals, the necessity of putting up a lightweight jockey began to discriminate against the average male rider. The human element of a racecourse partnership was increasingly drawn from a group of artificially-light hired boys and men; yet, paradoxically, within the chosen few there could be considerable equality. A race such as the Derby required all jockeys to ride at the same weight, 8 stone 7 pounds (54 kilos).[17] To overcome the exclusion of the overweight but enthusiastic owner/rider, a limited number of races specifically for gentlemen carrying 10–14 stone (64–90 kilos) still took place, mostly at meetings sponsored by hunt or racing clubs, but by the early nineteenth century, the racehorse was almost entirely in the hands of the professional. Here was an inverted example of the inequality of access resulting from class which Guttmann admitted was part of modern sport until recent times. He pointed out the disequilibrium between the proficient gentleman amateur and the skilled competitor for whom sport was also livelihood.[18] In this case, the gentlemen did not seek to reject but actively approved of the artisans: they were the means of winning both prestige and prize money. That horseracing displayed strong tendencies towards both professionalism and its ally, commercialism, over two hundred years ago is a subject to which we shall return.

There were further inequalities. The timing of many meetings during the working week helped to ensure an audience drawn largely from the leisured classes. Physical barriers to participation and spectating included the siting of race meetings at private or inaccessible locations: racing at Goodwood took place from 1801 on the estate of the Duke of Richmond while it was said that races were held over different courses on Newmarket Heath to disadvantage those without the means of transport.[19] Others, organised under the auspices of a town council as at Leith (adjacent to Edinburgh), may have been contested by the gentry but were attended en masse by the poor during the eighteenth century. When, in a blatant attempt at gentrification, the racecourse was relocated in 1816 to Musselburgh, some 6 miles (9.5 km) further along the coast, there was a feeling of betrayal amongst 'the folk [who] believed that the races belonged to them.'[20] However, local races of the type which were too lowly to figure in the *Racing Calendar* may have demonstrated greater equality for participants and spectators alike. They frequently took place on public holidays and featured farmers' or tradesmens' horses, competing for simple prizes such as a whip, a saddle or a pair of spurs. But even at this grade of racing, and especially at the small unfashionable country meetings where the prize money was just sufficient to merit inclusion in Weatherbys' volumes, the race conditions were often framed to exclude: horses had to be half-bred, or owned by yeomen or bred within the locality or hunted with a particular pack.

However, some attempts were made to create a level playing field. In addition to the races at even weights already mentioned, others aimed to give smaller horses an equal opportunity to win. For so-called 'give and take' races, a detailed table of weight allowances based on the height of the horse was compiled and published from the outset in Weatherbys' *Racing Calendar*. Furthermore, in one of his infrequent references to horseracing, Guttmann pointed out that the handicapping of racehorses by weight, age and previous performance was an unusual attempt, in eighteenth-century sport, to introduce a measure of equality to competition.[21]

Nevertheless, the overall impression of horseracing at this time was of fragmentation: into elite and low-grade race meetings; handicap, weight-for-age, and races with any number of conditions attached; amateur and professional riders; wealthy owners from the leisured classes with stables full of thoroughbreds and those who worked and owned a horse or two. There was an equality of aim – to organise and win races – but an inequality of means which divided the sport and its participants into discrete zones of competition.

Specialisation of roles, including professionalism, was recognised by Guttmann as a feature of Greek and Roman athletic festivals and successful charioteers earned substantial sums from their victories while jockeys were often paid servants. He went on to note, however, that 'the sports of the medieval and early modern periods were probably a good deal less specialised than those of Roman times.'[22] Dunning, too, showed that folk games such as village football displayed little division of labour amongst players, little distinction between player and spectator and a mixture of play elements – kicking, handling, wrestling – which would later become separated into different games.[23] Horseracing, uniquely different from these mass participant sports, can be further distinguished by early specialisation in animal breeding, diversity of race and sophisticated demarcation of human work roles.

References to specialist 'running horses', ranging from the ninth to the fifteenth centuries, precede the earliest evidence of formal racing. By the time Tregonwell Frampton, the first widely recognised racehorse trainer, became Keeper of the Running Horses to William III in 1695, imported Eastern bloodstock had been used for over half a century to improve the speed and manoevrability of native breeds.[24] A recent authority has even suggested that 'by the end of the century, the racehorse was well on the way to being a specialist whose only roles were to run fast and procreate,' a trend which was set to increase over the next hundred years.[25] The publication of the *General Stud Book* in 1791 confirmed the complex development of the English thoroughbred to date, though recent genetic research has revealed errors in the early entries. It was, nevertheless, a horse bred to be raced.[26]

As already noted, the conditions for races themselves had become increasingly diverse by the early nineteenth century. Matches organised between gentlemen owners and long distance races of around 4 miles (6.5 km) run in heats, which had been the mainstay of British racing for over one hundred years, were supplemented and later overtaken by those ranging from 5 furlongs to 2 miles (1–3 km). Between 1809 and 1839 matches fell from 36 per cent to 7 per cent of all races recorded in the *Racing Calendar*.[27] In 1807, one-third of all races were run over courses of 2 miles, nearly one-quarter over 1 mile or less. With shorter distances and less requirement for stamina, the career of the racehorse could begin earlier: the first race for three-year-olds had been held in 1731 while 1769 had seen the first winning appearance of a two-year-old on the racecourse. The increased popularity of these contests meant that by 1817, nearly 50 per cent of 800 horses racing in Britain were either two or three years old.[28]

The elite racehorse could now boast of its own entourage. In addition to the usual panoply of grooms, stablehands, forage merchants and other trades necessary to support the general horse population, the eighteenth-century racehorse now had a specialist trainer instead of the farrier who had acted as a sort of trainer-cum-vet in the seventeenth century. Although many were employed privately by major owners and have remained largely anonymous, the era of the public trainer had already begun. From the 1760s clusters of public training stables emerged at Epsom downs, Newmarket and several venues in Yorkshire, such as Malton and Middleham.[29] One of the most successful belonged to Robert Robson who sent out seven Derby winners from his Newmarket base in the period 1793 to 1823. 'By the end of the eighteenth century the stable for training horses was a well-developed phenomenon in England, particularly at Newmarket.'[30]

Race riding, as already noted, had also become a specialised occupation with horses normally ridden by lightweight professional jockeys instead of their owners. Frank Buckle whose Classic-winning record was eventually broken by Lester Piggott claimed his twenty-seven successes from 1792 to 1827 and was able to ride at a weight of under 8 stone (51 kilos) throughout his lengthy career. His portrait hangs in the National Horseracing Museum at Newmarket: by the end of the eighteenth century it had become fashionable for jockeys and horses alike to be commemorated on canvas by a number of specialist equine artists such as George Stubbs (1724–1806). There were also specialised roles on the racecourse. The earliest known rules of racing drawn up at Kiplingcotes, Yorkshire in 1619 specify a clerk of the course whose job it was to keep the weights and mend the course. He in turn appointed a man to start the horses. Every race also had to have a judge – frequently several – at the finishing line to determine the winner and places. There were handicappers before the end of the eighteenth century, and annotations of odds on a Newmarket race bill of 1796 clearly demonstrate that betting with bookmakers was taking place.[31] Harry Ogden was alleged to be the first bookmaker to operate on any scale at Newmarket in the 1790s.

Alongside these 'modern' aspects of horseracing, however, were others which continued to display more traditional features. A strict demarcation between contestants and spectators was only enforced by the Jockey Club in 1839. Until then it had been common, certainly at Newmarket, for gentlemen riders to race behind, and sometimes amongst, the main participants, to the confusion of judges and the danger of all. The custom of training racehorses on owners' estates or farms rather than at special stables was certainly maintained in Scotland and probably in several English regions well into the nineteenth century.[32] Reference has also been made to the continued existence of the unsophisticated race meeting at which farmers' horses, hunters and even draught animals took part for paltry prizes. In general, however, elite horseracing in Britain had become an increasingly specialised sport by the 1830s.

One aspect of rationalisation in sport is the development of rules. Obviously any sport would be anarchical without them: Guttmann noted that even primitive sports needed rules. However he argues that the rules of modern sport are qualitatively different in both origin and status.[33] First and foremost, they provide a logical relationship between means and ends: indeed, they *are* the means to an end, stating what has to be done to achieve victory and setting out the constraints within which participants have to operate. The race goes to the swiftest ... unless they have false-started! But additionally, modern sports have rules that are accepted by all within the game and do not differ substantially from place to place.

Perhaps this latter criterion did not apply to early horseracing. Although it was everywhere acknowledged that the winner of the race was the first at the finishing post, all races in the early eighteenth century had their own rules partially determined by local conditions and interests.[34] Before 1800, and even later, most meetings were organised via articles of agreement: legally binding codes of conduct that were signed by participating owners. Each group of race promoters formulated its own articles, including the venue, date and time, financial arrangements, entry procedures, distance and route to be followed, number of heats, types of horse eligible to run, weights to be carried and minimum entry requirement for the race to proceed. Although these often followed a similar pattern, there could be significant differences in the actual regulations put forward. Nevertheless, racing *was* governed by rules. They may not have been universally applied but from the beginning of the early modern period, the manner in which the sport was conducted was subject to written regulation: the racecourse was not a scene of anarchy.

Possibly some local race committees sought early guidance as John Cheny, publisher of the first *Racing Calendar* in 1727, was reportedly asked to include a standard set of articles which could act as a model.[35] It was not until 1751, however, that any general 'Laws of Racing' appeared, in Pond's short-lived *Sporting Kalendar*. Weatherbys' first *Racing Calendar* in 1773 contained a standard format of articles for a match but not till 1797 did it also set out any 'Rules Concerning Horse Racing in General' and these were acknowledged as having been drawn directly from Pond's earlier work.

Guttmann argued that a second major feature of modern rules is a willingness to change them should the need arise. Unlike the rules of sport in primitive societies which were often regarded as god-given and inviolate, those pertaining to modern sport are cultural constructs not divine instructions and as such may be modified. The *Racing Calendar* in the early nineteenth century shows that the Jockey Club, the body that organised racing at Newmarket, amended one or more of its own orders and regulations almost on an annual basis. Perhaps the best example of altering the rules to fit different circumstances is shown in relation to the Royal Plates, a group of races funded by the royal purse and contested at over two dozen racecourses throughout Britain and Ireland. Originally run in the 1730s by older horses as a series of 4-mile (6.5 km) heats under 12 stone weights (76 kilos), they became increasingly unfashionable with the advent of shorter races for younger animals, attracting fewer entrants as the century progressed. In a classic case of bowing to the wind of change, the rules governing the Royal Plates were altered in 1799 to allow younger participants and lower weights. When this failed to have the desired effect, there was a wholesale reduction in the distances from 1833, with many races shortened to 2 miles (3.25 km) and weights lowered to as little as 8 stone 4 pounds (about 53 kilos).[36]

Rationalisation as defined by Guttman was not just a question of rules being set: it also encompassed the application of knowledge in order to improve performance. This had certainly occurred in horseracing well before 1830. Not only did some eighteenth-century trainers stage timed trials to assess the capabilities of their charges, others developed ideas on diet, fluid intake, sweating and purging.[37] So advanced were training methods in horseracing that trainers in the human sports of pedestrianism and pugilism began utilising them as models to improve fitness and endurance.[38] Although breeding theory was not as well documented as training methods, racehorse breeders, possibly influenced by developments in selective breeding in eighteenth-century agriculture, were beginning to use pedigrees as guides to mating, a move assisted by the publication of the *General Stud Book*.

Rule making and enforcement have become closely associated with bureaucratisation. According to Guttmann, a sports bureaucracy performs three main functions: to see that rules and regulations are 'universal'; to facilitate a network of competition from local through to national and international championships; and to ratify records.[39] Here it is doubtful that racing could be regarded as modern within the timeframe being examined. Although the Jockey Club was in control of British thoroughbred flat racing by the late nineteenth century, it had taken decades for it to attain this position. Indeed when it was founded around 1750 it had no pretensions to running a national sport and was just another racing club that organised meetings for the benefit of its members. It had initially appointed a Keeper of the Match Book, a Stakeholder and a Club Secretary, positions consolidated under James Weatherby in 1771. Two years later Weatherby began to publish his *Racing Calendar* which, although primarily concerned with providing information on meetings throughout Britain, also offered a vehicle for Jockey Club pronouncements.

It is possible that by the early nineteenth century the Club was attempting to formalise its influence outside its headquarters at Newmarket. In 1808 the *Racing Calendar* began to publish the results of certain 'Adjudged Cases' already decided by the Jockey Club, perhaps as a guide to local stewards throughout the country, though they also served to draw attention to this function of the Club. In 1816, it published a note stating that 'persons who may be inclined to submit any matters in dispute to the decision of the Stewards of the Jockey Club are at liberty to do so'. For the first time the Club was volunteering to intervene if requested. Yet the number of cases published remained low – a total of eleven in 1826 had only risen to nineteen by 1833 – and most of these came from courses in the south of England. This suggests a limited take-up of the offer to adjudicate. Even as late as 1832 the *Racing Calendar* contained a notice that the Jockey Club Rules and Orders applied only to racing at Newmarket and that it had no authority to extend them to any other racecourse. However, it was noted that 'for the sake of greater uniformity and certainty', it had recommended the adoption of the same rules to the stewards of other races.

Whether the Jockey Club could have enforced any regulations in a country without effective transport and communication systems is debatable. How willing would local stewards and race committees have been to cede power to a distant central authority? Even when Jockey Club approved starters, judges and handicappers were available in the mid-nineteenth century, meetings often continued to appoint their own officials to handle these functions. Up to, and in some instances beyond, the 1830s, regional racing was organised in pockets with local race committees setting their own card of events without regard to Jockey Club wishes. Not till the late nineteenth century, with the introduction of licences for courses, could any meaningful sanctions be used by the Club to back up its demands. Owners too do not appear to have voluntarily accepted Club suggestions. In 1762 the Jockey Club recommended that owners register their colours. Yet by 1794 only thirty-eight appear to have done so out of about three hundred known owners: even in 1833 the figure was just one hundred and fifty from around seven hundred.[40] This was not because they did not have colours to register. Race lists for several meetings in the late eighteenth and early nineteenth centuries, held in the archives of the National Horseracing Museum at Newmarket, note the colours worn by jockeys to identify the horses they were riding, but a check in the *Racing Calendar* shows that very few were 'officially' registered.

However, Guttmann credited both Greek and Roman sport with 'a nascent form of sports bureaucracy' in that they elected officials and administered athletic competitions.[41] Judged by these criteria, British horseracing had undoubtedly embarked on a modernising path by the end of the eighteenth century, as already noted under specialisation. As for the two other functional roles identified by Guttman for a modern sports bureaucracy – the establishment of a hierarchy of competition at a national and international level and the ratification of records – neither had been taken up by any racing authority in 1830 (or in 1930, for that matter!)[42] Not until the development of European Pattern racing in 1971 was any attempt made to establish a system of international competition through which participants could gain a formal place in racing's meritocracy. Some races had earlier been accepted as tests of the best British horses but the Jockey Club had no role to play in this, other than instigating two of the five Classic three-year-old races at its Newmarket base. Even these leading races were not international by the 1830s: what gave racing an international dimension in this period was the flow of bloodstock between nations and sometimes continents. Five English Derby winners were exported to the United States between 1780 and 1799; others were sent to Prussia, France and Russia between 1821 and 1830.[43] However, these transactions were the product of unregulated private enterprise and owed nothing to any bureaucratic structures in racing.

Guttmann asserted that 'modern sports are characterised by the almost inevitable tendency to transform every athletic feat into one that can be measured and quantified.'[44] Quantification has long been a feature of British horseracing. Distances to be run and weights to be carried were a necessary part of the sport and were declared in all articles. However, what Guttmann meant by quantification was the measuring of achievement, and little of this is apparent within horseracing before 1830. Winning margins, for example, were not formally recorded in the *Racing Calendar* until 1842. Given the importance of commercial factors in racing, it is perhaps less surprising to find lists of winners printed there from the outset, enumerating the prizes won by each animal. A separate list gave the winners of all Royal Plates but no attempt was made to rank any horse by stakes won. They were arranged alphabetically according to their sire, with wins totalled but not winnings. Thus it is fairly easy to see which stallion had sired most winners in a season but not which racehorse had achieved the most wins or financial reward.

Guttmann also maintained that the combination of 'the impulse to quantification, with the desire to win, to excel, to be the best' resulted in the concept of the record.[45] Although the quest for records follows on from quantification in many sports, this is far less the case in horseracing where records are dependent not only on the quality of the horse itself but also the skills, tactics and ability of the jockey, and crucially on the state of the going. Firm ground produces record times, waterlogged courses don't! What people remember about racing are the horses, and not what times they did but what rivals they beat (although the tendency to ignore speed may be less pronounced in America where standardised tracks have led to sectional timing and more readily comparable statistics). The short career of a racehorse, sometimes as little as two years, combined with the age restrictions of many top races – the Classics, for example, may only be won once, in a horse's three-year-old season – are not conducive to record setting. Only when the horse goes to stud does measurement become an issue but even the concept of leading stallion did not include place money won by its offspring: to be second in a major race did not improve the quantitative standing of the parent. As for human effort, the British champion jockey title was not awarded until 1848 (although riding the most winners in a season does not necessarily infer that the recipient is the best jockey). No account is taken of success rates or stakes won – or the quality of horses ridden! No owners' or trainers' championships existed before the late nineteenth century, but when they did emerge they were based on prize money won, perhaps a better measure of the quality of achievement.

Guttmann summed up his original findings in a table, reproduced below, to which we have added horseracing. Disappointingly, this would appear to indicate that British racing was no more advanced than sport in Greek and Roman times. While it undoubtedly operated in a secular environment and was

A Modern Sport? [151

already highly specialised, it was only partially rationalised and bureaucratised according to Guttman's criteria and failed almost entirely to meet his conditions for quantification and records. In terms of equality, there was also a long way to go. It could be argued, however, that equality is an impossible aim given the financial cost of the sport: horseracing is scarcely more equal in 2003 in terms of access than it was in 1803.

Perhaps the next stage is to consider whether Guttman has in fact selected appropriate yardsticks by which to measure the modernity of sports, particularly horseracing, which does not sit easily with his definitions. It has to be questioned whether the criteria laid down by Guttmann are wholly pertinent to such a unique sport: or perhaps any sport? Although his model has become the accepted baseline for sports historians, even by those who argue from a different perspective, it has not been without its detractors.[46] The retrospective sessions at the NASSH conference were not merely celebratory: strong criticism was also made of Guttmann's assumptions and methodology. Yet even such a trenchant critic as Douglas Booth, who queried Guttmann's relative disregard of class and political economy, acknowledged that the book still 'offers scholars the most complete list of the structural characteristics of modern sport' and argued that 'no one has seriously challenged or improved on that list.'[47]

The Characteristics of Sports in Various Ages (adapted from Guttmann)						
	Primitive Sports	Greek Sports	Roman Sports	Medieval Sports	Modern Sports	Horseracing before 1839
Secularism	Yes & No	Yes & No	Yes & No	Yes & No	Yes	Yes
Equality	No	Yes & No	Yes & No	No	Yes	Yes & No
Specialisation	No	Yes	Yes	No	Yes	Yes
Rationalisation	No	Yes	Yes	No	Yes	Yes & No
Bureaucracy	No	Yes & No	Yes	No	Yes	Yes & No
Quantification	No	No	Yes & No	No	Yes	No
Records	No	No	No	No	Yes	No

This is not entirely true. Melvin Adelman, for one, has questioned the wholesale acceptance of Guttmann's concepts.

In *A Sporting Time: New York City and the Rise of Modern Athletics 1820–70*, he omitted secularism and equality, compacted quantification (re-titled statistics) with records, and introduced the notion of public information as well as modifying some of the conceptual definitions of Guttmann. The characteristics of modern ideal sporting types as outlined by Adelman were sixfold.[48] First, there should be formal organisation, institutionally differentiated at local, regional and national level. Second, formal, standardised and written rules should be rationally worked out and legitimated by organisational means. Third, national and international competitions should provide an opportunity for participants to establish more than local reputations. Fourth, he looked for high role differentiation with strict distinctions between playing and spectating and the emergence of specialists, some of whom would be professionals. Fifth came the wide provision of public information with regular reports in the press and the publication of playing manuals and other guides to the sport. Finally statistics and records should be kept and published on a regular basis with records of achievement sanctioned by national associations.

Adelman's removal of equality from the criteria is obviously beneficial in any assessment of racing's modernity and his new concept of public information may be more directly relevant. British horseracing was certainly the subject of much public report and scrutiny. Advertisements for meetings and details of the results featured extensively in the press and sporting magazines. Local entrepreneurs sold lists of runners to the public, precursors of the racecards that developed in the mid-nineteenth century. More generally, information was available in the unbroken series of racing calendars published from 1727. The other major source of information in British horseracing, the *General Stud Book*, also had a long history: indeed the British thoroughbred racehorse has the best-documented genealogy of any species.

Under Adelman's framework British horseracing may be regarded as more modern by the 1830s than is suggested by an application of Guttmann's original concepts. However, both Guttmann and to a lesser extent Adelman fail to deal adequately with two major aspects of sport which, it can be argued, demonstrate highly modernistic tendencies: professionalism and commercialism. The time commitment involved in both specialisation and professionalism led Guttmann to suggest that 'to an extent, they are the same thing' while he discussed commercialism in sport mainly as a twentieth-century phenomenon.[49] Presumably these were also the issues at the forefront of his thoughts when he referred to sporting activities 'partly pursued for their own sake, partly for other ends which are equally secular', though he failed to elaborate on the subject.[50]

Horseracing embraced both of these interrelated features well before the 1830s. As we have seen, professional jockeys riding for hire were commonplace on the turf before the end of the eighteenth century; so were those who trained thoroughbred racing stock for a living. It can be suggested that many owners also exhibited a professional attitude in that they treated racing as a serious pastime, spending not only money on breeding, training and racing horses but devoting considerable time and energy to planning their racing and breeding careers.

Although it may not be seen as a necessary distinguishing characteristic, commercialism had been a key driving force behind the shaping of sport in the eighteenth century. While entry to a race meeting was free for most spectators, considerable numbers sought a better vantage point or more social exclusivity by paying for the use of a grandstand. Substantial constructions of two, three or even four storeys were erected at York in 1754, Doncaster in 1779, Ascot in 1821 and Epsom in 1830. Even the ordinary spectator was subject to commercial factors at the racecourse, either when purchasing food and drink at the refreshment booths or risking money at the evens/odds tables (an early form of roulette). Other sports also involved cash transactions, particularly those promoted by publicans with the aim of attracting a drinking clientele, but it was in the scale of its association with moneymaking that horseracing was half a century ahead of other sporting activities. Within racing itself it can be argued that there was a far greater focus on making money – not necessarily profit maximisation – than in most other sports. Although some aristocrats and landed gentlemen bred horses in the hope of winning a major race, other breeders, especially those who owned reputable stallions, were in it for commercial gain as is apparent from their advertisements in the *Racing Calendar* and other publications.

Elements of both professionalism and commercialism can be found much earlier in sport than the eighteenth century, but this did not lessen the argument that they are associated with modernisation. Guttmann himself did not postulate a progressive theory of sports history. Although he saw Greek sport as substantially more advanced than primitive sport and Roman sport as slightly more advance than Greek because of its fuller adoption of bureaucracy and acceptance of quantification, much medieval sport had, in his opinion, lapsed back to the level found in primitive society. It should also be noted that an association with gambling complicates any discussion of the turf. Many well-established sports of the late eighteenth and early nineteenth centuries, not just horseracing, in fact owe their development to patronage by gamblers, among them most brutal animal sports, pedestrianism, prize fighting and cricket. Yet Guttmann's tome contains only three references to gambling, none of them in the context of his conceptual framework.

British horseracing, by any realistic measurement, had become 'modern' by the 1830s, although this was most obvious at the elite level. Away from Newmarket, York and other major centres of the sport, some forms of racing continued as they had for many decades, not unaffected by changes in society and sport, but clinging to the ways of the traditionalist rather than following the path of the moderniser. Whether the co-existence of races for farmers' horses with those for thoroughbreds or the continued survival of owner-riders and owner-trainers outside the major venues undermines any talk of modernisation is a moot point. Here Guttmann's hypothesis is confusing. His framework apparently does not allow for both 'continuity' *and* 'change' within a modernised sport. All but one of his characteristics – that of records – can be found in Roman sports and only that aspect and quantification are missing in the earlier Greek sports. He accepts that in those periods a 'yes and no' situation can pertain in several areas: only for modern sports does he insist that all features must unequivocally exist in an undiluted form. Hence modern sport cannot simultaneously have and not have some of his characteristics, though he still acknowledges that much of it has incorporated inequalities based on race, class and gender.51 The explanation of this seemingly contradictory position lies in the fact that Guttmann's typology was designed as a classic

Weberian 'ideal-type' schema. As Guttmann himself says, these are not intended to be direct statements about the real world but attempts to achieve conceptual clarity in order to assess the observed differences between the ideal and the actual.52 Whether any sport at any time could fully meet his criteria is debatable.

Bibliography

ADELMAN 1986
MELVIN L ADELMAN, *A sporting time: New York City and the rise of modern athletics 1820–70*, University of Illinois Press, Urbana.

BOOTH 2001
DOUGLAS BOOTH, *From ritual to record: Allen Guttmann's insights into modernization and modernity*, <<Sport History Review>>, 32.1, 2001, pp.19–27.

BURNETT 1998
JOHN BURNETT, *The sites and landscapes of horse racing in Scotland before 1860*, <<The Sports Historian>>18.1, 1998, pp.55–75.

BURNETT 2000
JOHN BURNETT, *Riot, revelry and rout: sport in lowland Scotland before 1860*, Tuckwell, East Linton.

CASSIDY 2002
REBECCA CASSIDY, *The sport of kings: kinship, class and thoroughbred breeding in Newmarket*, Cambridge University Press, Cambridge.

GUTTMANN 1978
ALLEN GUTTMANN, *From ritual to record: the nature of modern sports*, Columbia University Press, New York.

GUTTMANN 1986
ALLEN GUTTMANN, *Sports spectators*, Columbia University Press, New York.

GUTTMAN 1996

ALLEN GUTTMANN, *Ritual* in *Encyclopedia of world sport* edited by DAVID LEVINSON and KAREN CHRISTENSEN, ABC-CLIO, Santa Barbara, (3 vols.), pp.799–803.

GUTTMANN 2003
ALLEN GUTTMANN, *Ideal types and historical variation,* in *The essence of sport* edited by VERNON MØLLER and JOHN NAURIGHT, University Press of Southern Denmark, Odense, pp. 129–136.

HILL-CUNNINGHAM 2002
EMMELINE HILL and PATRICK CUNNINGHAM, *History and integrity of thoroughbred dam lines revealed in equine mt variation,* <<Animal Genetics>>, 33.4, 2002, pp.287–294.

HUGGINS 1996
MIKE HUGGINS, *Nineteenth-century racehorse stables in their rural setting: a social and economic study,* <<Rural History>>, 7.2, 1996, pp.177–190.

HUGGINS 2000
MIKE HUGGINS, *Flat racing and British society 1790–1914: a social and economic history,* Cass, London.

KAY 2000
JOYCE KAY, *Closing the stable door and the public purse: the rise and fall of the Royal Plates,* <<The Sports Historian>>20.1, 2000, pp.18–32.

KAY 2002
JOYCE KAY, *The actress, the politician and the brigadier: British horseracing through the pages of Weatherby's Racing Calendar* in *Proceedings of the 5th international CESH congress,* edited by THERESA GONZALEZ AJA, Madrid, pp. 367–375.

MAGDALINSKI-CHANDLER 2002
TARA MAGDALINSKI and TIMOTHY CHANDLER, *With god on their side: sport in the service of religion,* Routledge, London.

MALCOLMSON 1973

R.W. MALCOLMSON, *Popular recreations in English society 1700–1850*, Cambridge University Press, Cambridge.

MEWETT 2002
PETER G MEWETT, *From horses to humans: species crossovers in the origin of modern sports training*, <<Sport History Review>>, 33.2, 2002, pp.95–120.

MIDDLETON-VAMPLEW 1998
IRIS MIDDLETON and WRAY VAMPLEW, *Sport and the English leisure calendar: horse-racing in early eighteenth-century Yorkshire*, <<Ludica>>, 4,1998, pp.65–82.

MIDDLETON 2000
IRIS MIDDLETON, *The developing pattern of horse racing in Yorkshire 1700–1749: an analysis of the people and places*, Ph.D. thesis De Montfort University.

MORTIMER 1978
ROGER MORTIMER and others, *Biographical encyclopaedia of British flat racing*, Macdonald and Jane's, London.

PARASCHAK 2001
VICTORIA PARASCHAK, *Introduction*, <<Sport History Review>>, 32.1, 2001, p.1.

PRIOR 1926
C. W. PRIOR, *The history of the Racing Calendar and Stud Book*, Sporting Life, London.

TYRREL 1989
JOHN TYRREL, *Racecourses on the flat*, Crowood Press, Marlborough.

VAMPLEW 1976
WRAY VAMPLEW, *The turf: a social and economic history of horse racing*, Allen Lane, London.

WEATHERBY 1773–1839
JAMES WEATHERBY, *The Racing Calendar*, London.

References

1. GUTTMANN 2003, p.139 now says that if he were to reformulate his views he would probably consider specialisation and bureaucracy as sub-categories of rationalisation, but this does not change the overall conceptual argument of his modernisation thesis.
2. GUTTMANN 1978, p.7.
3. HUGGINS 2000, p.119.
4. GUTTMANN 1978, p.26.
5. GUTTMANN 1996, p.799.
6. MAGDALINSKI & CHANDLER 2002, p.2.
7. CASSIDY 2002, p.57.
8. MEWETT 2002, p.101.
9. BURNETT 2000, p.111.
10. MALCOLMSON 1973, pp. 5–6.
11. MIDDLETON & VAMPLEW 1998, p.69.
12. HUGGINS 2000, p.123.
13. GUTTMAN 1978, p.26.
14. GUTTMAN 1978, p.28.
15. VAMPLEW 1976, p.77; NMS.
16. National Horseracing Museum: York race bill 1804; TYRREL 1989, pp.80–82.
17. This type of race, at even weights, became increasingly popular, although an allowance of several pounds was always made for fillies. By 1807 nearly half of the contests at some race meetings were framed in this way.
18. GUTTMANN 1978, p.31.
19. VAMPLEW 1976, p.30.
20. BURNETT 2000, pp.105–108.
21. GUTTMANN 1986, p.63.
22. GUTTMANN 1978, p.37.
23. GUTTMANN 1978, p.38.
24. PRIOR 1926, pp.13–14.
25. BURNETT 2000, p.104.
26. HILL and CUNNINGHAM 2002, pp.287–294.
27. HUGGINS 2000, p.35.
28. HUGGINS 2000, p.33.
29. HUGGINS 1996, p.178.
30. BURNETT 1998, p.56.
31. National Horseracing Museum: Newmarket race bill, 1796.
32. BURNETT 1998, p.56.

33. GUTTMANN 1978, p.40.
34. MIDDLETON 2000, pp. 60–68.
35. MIDDLETON 2000, p.26.
36. KAY 2000, pp.20–21.
37. MIDDLETON 2000, p.23; MEWETT 2002, pp.103–108.
38. MEWETT 2002, p.98.
39. GUTTMANN 1978, p.47.
40. KAY 2002, p.371.
41. GUTTMANN 1978, p.45.
42. GUTTMANN 1978, p.47.
43. MORTIMER 1978, p.170.
44. GUTTMANN 1978, p.47.
45. GUTTMANN 1978, p.51.
46. PARASCHAK 2001, p.1.
47. BOOTH 2001, p.25.
48. ADELMAN 1986, p.6.
49. GUTTMANN 1978, p.39, p.77.
50. GUTTMANN 1978, p,26.
51. GUTTMANN 1978, pp. 32–35.
52. GUTTMANN 1978, pp. 32–35.

Women to the Fore: Gender Accommodation and Resistance at the British Golf Club Before 1914[1]

Introduction

In the four decades before the First World War golf was one of the fastest growing recreational activities in Britain. From less than 100 clubs in the 1870s the total rose to almost 3,000 by 1914 with an estimated aggregate membership of over 350,000 golfers. Whilst golf was not a sport of courage and overt masculinity like cricket, football and rugby it was still framed as a male-dominant activity. Early female golfers faced ridicule and restriction, though, as this infers, the sport was not gender exclusive. Indeed significant numbers of middle-class women played the game either within the 'ladies' section' of male clubs or often at clubs developed specifically for female participants. In 1900 63 clubs were affiliated to the Ladies' Golf Union [LGU]; by 1911 there were 400 clubs with 50,000 members; and for 1914 the *LGU Year Book* records 548 clubs suggesting perhaps over 60,000 female golfers, a significant proportion of all those playing the game at club level.[2] As with men, the popularity of golf participation had increased with the introduction of the rubber-cored ball to Britain in 1901, a technological breakthrough that offered golfers greater distance to their drives, most iron shots and even topped efforts.[3] Yet the role of women in golf and golf clubs has been marginalized by historians who, like contemporary male golfers, have seen them as inferior players by virtue of their lesser strength and perceived emotional fragility.[4]

The aim of this article is to pull women in from the periphery and show that they had a significant role in the organisation, promotion and development of golf. It will also look at two other groups of women at the golf club, those of a lower social class to the members who found employment as cooks, cleaners and even caddies, and those who exhibited hostility to the clubs as part of militant suffragette activity. The paper will provide evidence on gender power relationships between male and female golfers, employers and employees, and suffragettes and the political establishment.

Motivations

As with male players golf for women was mainly a middle-class pursuit: the costs incurred for equipment and subscriptions saw to this. A first-class woman golfer could have been spending up to £100 a year and even an ordinary player would lay out around £30, no small sum when the average level of full-time earnings was 28 shillings a week.[5] Coupled with the opportunities for midweek play, this meant that women's golf was a relatively exclusive game for females of a certain socio-economic class. Social barriers could also be erected as at Burbage where a shopkeeper was informed that she was ineligible for membership but an ordinary member's subscription would cover 'any governess in charge of a member's children'.[6]

One journal aimed at a middle-class female readership maintained that golf was 'an excellent means of combining fresh air, exercise and society.'[7] This summed up the situation for most women golfers. They saw golf as a gentle form of healthy exercise that required skill rather than force and which allowed time on and off the course for social interaction. Some, satirised by a male correspondent to *Golf Illustrated*, took up the game because 'Mrs So-and-so plays and the golf course is delightful.'[8] Even Blanche Martin, the first treasurer of the LGU, identified a 'large army of lesser golfers ... frivolous and unpromising' who played simply to keep up their social reputation and came up 'to the links bedecked in feathers and ribbons, and their feeble expletives, as they ineffectively waggle a club of whose name and nature they are totally ignorant, can be heard on every ladies' course wherever the game is established.'[9] Yet, as another supporter of women's golf acknowledged, 'were it not for this burning desire ... to be in fashion, it would be financially impossible to keep our golf clubs going. Quite sixty per cent of the members support our club only because it is the correct thing to do. So they fill their niche in the general scheme of things, pay their subscriptions, wear fascinating golf costumes ... please themselves, and do comparatively little harm.'[10]

Golf, unlike many sports, offered the possibility of mixed gender participation. For a few this might have romantic connotations. For a greater number it provided an opportunity for a family or married couple to share recreation together as at Edinburgh Ladies' where sons, daughters and male 'associates' were welcomed as members and mixed foursomes were included amongst the numerous competitions.[11] Some clubs afforded female relatives special rates as at Littlehampton where wives, daughters and sisters of members were allowed to play for 2s 6d a week or 10s 6d annually.[12] The Lundin Ladies' Golf Club in Fife was particularly family friendly, being open to ladies, 'gentlemen associates' and children over seven, for whom it organised competitions during the summer holidays when the local village became a popular resort for families from elsewhere in Scotland.[13] Even if they played without males, golf offered female family members an opportunity to socialise together. Judging from the addresses, the membership register at Wirral Ladies in 1895 included at least 9 mother and daughter combinations and an additional 19 sets of sisters. At Stanmore, a total female membership of 173 between 1907 and 1909 included 78 married women, eleven mothers and daughters and nine groups of sisters.[14] Although the married cohort were mainly wives of club members, opportunities to play together on the main course were restricted to Tuesdays until 1911 when mixed foursomes were introduced as an experiment at quiet times at the weekend.[15] These figures do not account for all female players: a considerable number (at least 25%) of unmarried women had no obvious relatives at the club. Who they were and how they financed their membership remain unresearched issues.

Clubs of Their Own

Whilst the social golfers might 'vie with each other in the excellence of their tea-cakes', others sought competition on the course 'and played in a style which some gentlemen themselves might well have tried to emulate.'[16] For this substantial minority golf was a serious sport but one of separate and often unequal development. There were no followers of the Barnehurst Golf Club model in which men and women had the same rights of membership, equal use of the links, and similar access to the clubhouse where certain rooms were reserved exclusively for each sex. Situated near London on Bexley Heath, the course was unique as it had been designed by James Braid, the professional and Open Champion of 1901, as a gift from Christopher Gray to his wife. Yet although four years on from its inception a sporting journal noted that 'the experiment of the entente cordiale between the sexes at golf had proved a brilliant success at Barnehurst',[17] it seems that no other clubs copied the idea.

Instead a substantial number of female golfers belonged to clubs specifically organised for women. The first properly constituted ladies' golf club was at St Andrews in 1867, soon followed by one at Westward Ho! in Devon. Both were established by male golfers for their female relatives and neither possessed a full-length course. That at St Andrews was little more than a long putting course; the other had holes between 50 and 120 yards, significantly less than on the parent course on which the men played.[18]

Most women golfers, however, became members of what was often labelled a ladies' club but which was in reality a 'ladies' section' within a parent club. Most of the newer clubs of the 1890s onwards had allowed women membership from their foundation but they moved to form separate ladies' sections [or even clubs] when numbers increased.[19] South Staffordshire typified the experience: when their female numbers rose from an initial 15 in 1892 to 65 four years later a separate nine-hole course was laid out for their exclusive use.[20]

Whether they were labelled members of a branch, as at Folkestone Ladies', Bexhill, and Hastings & St Leonards, or 'associate members', as were the women at Heswall Golf Club in Cheshire, they were subject to restrictions on when they could play. Usually the course was solely for men on competition days and on Saturdays either all or part of the day. Additional restrictions at some clubs included not being able to play on Bank Holidays as at Chester and Leicestershire Ladies' or on Thursday half holidays at Blairgowrie.[21] Even when they shared playing times with males female golfers were expected to give way to men on the course. When women were allowed to play at Dunbar one of the first rules was that 'they shall interfere as little as possible with the gentlemen players and allow them to pass when called upon'.[22]

The objections to women centred around slow play, attributable to them taking more strokes due to the lesser distances that they hit the ball, and their inadequacy in dealing with bunkers and other hazards. One way round the problem was to develop separate playing facilities for men and women. At Dunbar ladies were provided with a short course of 12 holes as there were so many women 'causing delay and inconvenience to members'; at Beverley and East Riding Golf Club in East Humberside a proposal was made in 1889 that ladies 'form a ground of their own' on which they would have unrestricted use of their course; and at Formby, although ladies had been members of the Formby Golf Club from its inception in 1884 (paying only half the men's subscription), with membership booming and changes made to lengthen the course the gentlemen decided that 'the women should have a course of their own'.[23] What is not clear is the extent to which clubs were formed at the initiative of women rather than at the behest of men. Lady members at Seaford near Eastbourne formed their own club in 1887 and played on a nine-hole course as times were restricted for them on the main course and Brighton and Hove Ladies' established their own club in 1891, two years after the men, and also developed their own nine-hole course.[24]

Female social golfers might have preferred such an arrangement.[25] Many men certainly did. Scottish High Court judge, Lord Wellwood, did not wish to share his course with women. He accepted that 'if they chose to play when the male golfers are feeding or resting no one can object. But at other times ... they are in the way'. He was not alone in his views. As one female golfer acknowledged 'gentlemen feel the presence of women on the links to be irksome we know and that is why so many ladies' links are being formed, for it is embarrassing for women to feel themselves in the way.'[26]

The pattern of differentiated courses for women that had begun at St Andrews and Westward Ho! continued at least up to 1914. Theirs tended to be of nine holes (eighteen was often seen as too tiring), of much less yardage than those of men, and without serious hazards.[27] This did not suit the better female players who wished to play challenging golf. The club course then became contested terrain. As Horace Hutchinson noted in respect of the incursion on his own links: 'We used to hear at first: "It's absurd, these ladies not sticking to their own course; they can't drive far enough to be able to appreciate the long course." But then it very soon became evident that they could play better than a large number of the male members of the club, which rather knocked the bottom out of the argument.'[28]

The issue then became one of distinguishing between female social golfers and the more serious women players.[29] What tended to happen was that many clubs allowed women the privilege of playing over the men's course perhaps on one specified day a week but allowed greater access to those with low handicaps, thus keeping off the links 'the inefficient lady players who would be apt to block the green and whose right place is on their own course, while it freely admits those who are capable of appreciating the blessing of the long course.'[30] An example of such quality control was at Bath where members of the Bath Ladies were allowed to play on the gentlemen's course if their handicaps were 14 or under. Interestingly at Stanmore and Minchinhampton, both with nine-hole ladies' courses, important matches for women were played over the men's course.[31] Nevertheless these women, like any that used the men's course, played off advanced tees so as to shorten the length of the round, a device that reinforced the notion of golf as masculine.

There was less compromise off the course. At Beverley and East Riding the women were allowed to rent a room in the clubhouse but had their refreshments served through a hatch. Whilst Douglas Park allowed women to use the men's dining room for lunch and tea [though only during designated 'ladies' hours'], Dunbar was more typical in not admitting them to the clubhouse at all.[32] Even the most liberal clubs drew the line at letting women have equal rights in the clubhouse. At Littlestone, one of the very few clubs where women and men shared unrestricted use of the course, they were only allowed in by special invitation at Christmas and could not enter by the front door. Indeed on one occasion when a group of visiting women found the ladies' clubhouse locked they were refused permission to dine in the men's clubhouse and had to eat outside on the balcony despite driving wind and rain.[33]

The solution adopted by several women's clubs was to build their own premises. As with those of men they varied in their level of sophistication. Within the same county, for example, they ranged from Hoylake Ladies' GC's 'little shanty that did not even seem to stand straight on its own little particular sandhill' to West Lancashire's 'bright airy sanctum, arrayed in lace curtains and striped sunblinds and dainty furnishings ... the hall and entertaining rooms are both lofty and commodious and the kitchen is, as it should be, the best room in the house and shining brilliantly with copper and brass.'[34] It is not clear where the money came from to build such premises. At Seaford and Kilmacolm the men loaned the women sufficient money. Presumably, as at Sutton Coldfield, this was repaid via fundraising events such as theatricals, a rise in subscription fees and donations from the members.[35]

Like the clubhouse, power too was generally not for sharing. Purley Downs was a rarity in that women could become full members with equal access to the course but there was a limit set of a dozen only and they still had no voting rights as was the case at almost every club throughout Britain. Most were like South Beds where lady members were not admitted to the AGM but were able to join the men for a social afterwards. At Braemar, most unusually, they were allowed to attend and vote at general meetings, but they were not allowed to hold office.[36]

Even when men helped to establish separate clubs or branches for women, there was sometimes a reluctance to devolve power to the female offshoots. Clearly, as was openly specified at Douglas Park and implicitly understood elsewhere, 'they shall have no voice in the management of the club' but even the right to make decisions within their own section was often curtailed. The Ladies' Committee at Stanmore had no power to confirm new female members who could be elected directly by the men. At Eastbourne Ladies the committee had no representation of ladies and was run by five gentlemen, with a Secretary and President who were also male. At least, unlike at Craigmillar Park in Edinburgh, the women do not seem to have been relegated to a Tea Committee! Another Scottish club, Edinburgh

Ladies, initially had a male President, Secretary and both Vice-Captains, and sixteen of the twenty committee positions went to men. At Rochdale, ladies were allowed to elect their own captain, secretary, treasurer and committee but all decisions had to be approved by the exclusively male main club committee.[37] Of course this followed the political thinking of the time with women often denied a say in the running of anything, except the household.

There was some change in the relative status of women at several clubs before the First World War. Until 1913 women at the Blackburn club could not play on Saturdays or after 1.00 pm on Thursdays but thereafter they were allowed to play until noon on Saturdays when there was no male competition being held and on Thursday afternoons before 3.00 pm. Similarly at Sutton Coldfield a previous ban on Saturday play for women gave way to a restriction only after midday. Off the links Dunbar had agreed to provide accommodation for ladies in the south club room and men were to use it only if accompanying a lady and by 1913 Edinburgh Ladies had reduced its committee to thirteen but expanded the female representation to six.[38]

Nor were restrictions unilateral. Although – perhaps because – women faced exclusionary policies from male club members, they were prepared to introduce their own restrictions. At Minchinhampton in 1906, when women were prohibited from playing on the men's course at certain hours, the response was a directive to the gentlemen that 'no men (whether with or without a lady) to commence play on the ladies' links between … etc'!̓[39] Yet the ladies' clubs did not adopt full exclusionary policies towards men. At Lundin Links, for example, perhaps in a move to promote mixed gender social golf, gentlemen 'were allowed to play [on the women's course] only when accompanying ladies.' Hoylake Ladies established their club in 1895 and allowed male relatives to become 'associate members' at special rates of £6 6s entrance fee and an annual subscription of £2.[40] Possibly the financial motive was imperative in this and similar cases. Ladies' clubs, like those of men, needed money to cover operating costs.

Despite being physically restricted to lesser facilities on and off the course, symbolically relegated to the 'ladies' section', and having little or no voice in parent club affairs, women's golf was an expanding sport at both recreational and elite level. A contributory factor was that, although men sometimes continued to intervene in the ladies' clubs and sections, sufficient women came forward to take on the necessary administrative and organisational tasks required to run over 500 ladies' clubs and, as one grudging critic acknowledged, 'the ladies show a very marked capability for managing their own golfing affairs.'[41]

Wider Organisation

Some of these female administrators made their mark beyond the confines of their own clubs as women's golf progressed beyond men's in two organisational respects, a representative national body and the development of a standardised system of handicapping, two things that did not appear in men's golf till more than a decade later.[42] The initiative came from Issette Pearson who had earlier led the revival of Wimbledon Ladies' Golf Club in the late 1880s. This time she proposed setting up a Ladies' Golf Union. She felt that a national body was required to bring some regulation and organisation to the game. A governing body could offer advice to women golfers, suggest solutions to problems within clubs, and deal with the anomalies of handicaps. It was Miss Pearson's belief that the LGU would give women's golf more focus. Women would be kept informed about who was playing the game, where it was being played and what opportunities were available for them to compete nationally, thus hopefully raising the standards of play.

Her decision to circulate all the known ladies' golf clubs in Britain and call all those who might be interested to a preliminary meeting in London at the Grand Hotel, Northumberland Avenue on 19 April 1893 significantly coincided with the beginning of the London season when many golf club members would be in town. Clubs expressing an interest sent along delegates with fifteen English clubs and one Scottish club represented.[43]

Issette Pearson sought the advice and support of Laidlaw Purves, one of the leading players from the Wimbledon Club, to assist with the initial organisation of the meeting. Purves was sympathetic with the objectives of the ladies as he had tried unsuccessfully to establish a similar golfing association for men. He gave his backing to the scheme paying tribute to the women present at the meeting and indicating that their presence signified 'the welfare of present and future golfers, which had not been evinced to the majority of the other sex'.[44] The meeting also received the support of a society magazine, the *Gentlewoman*, which reported the instigation of the LGU as 'a much needed movement for lady golfers.'[45]

The idea of the LGU was not to 'dictate' to affiliated clubs how they should be run but to 'encourage a universality of aims' which would, it was hoped, 'increase the sense of comradeship and sportsmanship'.[46] Clubs which affiliated to the Union would have the opportunity of addressing their problems directly to this body which would give women golfers representation. The purpose and objectives of the LGU were: to promote the interests of the game of golf; to obtain a uniformity of the rules of the game by establishing a representative legislative authority; to establish a uniform system of handicapping; to act as a tribunal and court of reference on points of uncertainty; and to arrange an annual championship competition and to obtain funds necessary for that purpose. In contrast to men's golf which suffered from 'an oligarchy of each local club ruling over its individual members, and a great oligarchy of an ancient and venerable club ruling over the golfing world', the LGU would provide an opportunity for all clubs to vote on issues.[47]

All affiliated clubs were to submit their local rules and bye-laws to the executive council in order that the Union could advise on those which were deemed unnecessary or contrary to the laws of golf. Sometimes in open competitions or inter-club matches difficulties of interpretation had arisen and it was considered that an impartial body could be a point of reference for club secretaries if assistance was necessary.[48]

It was agreed at the preliminary meeting that the Union would be run by an executive of office bearers, consisting of four vice-presidents, a treasurer, a secretary and a council of delegates. Although the LGU was willing to develop women's golf on separate lines from men, they drew on the expertise of men from the golf world. Initially all four vice-presidents were males from different parts of the country and not till 1908 was Lady Alice Stanley appointed as the first female vice-president. That said, one researcher who has read the Minutes of the LGU argues that male influence on decision-making was minimal.[49]

As part of its objective to raise golfing standards the LGU felt that a national championship open to all female golfers would bring focus to women's golf and give the best players the opportunity to compete against each other. The women of St Anne's Golf Club in Lancashire had already announced in April 1893 (prior to the formation of the LGU) that they were considering running an 'open' competition and that they had received contributions from other clubs towards the purchase of a fifty-guinea challenge cup. St Anne's and the LGU combined their efforts. The newly-formed LGU agreed to organize the national championship and accepted the offer made by St Anne's to use its course. This club had a reputation of 'treating its female members with fairness' which indicated that they could rely on assistance from the male members of the club.[50] Issette Pearson, with the assistance of Laidlaw Purves and the LGU committee, proceeded to organise the event. Some male golfers were sceptical about women's competence in organising let alone playing in a major championship. Among them was Horace Hutchison, a British Amateur champion, who predicted in a letter in April 1893, that there would be no more than one such championship.

> "They will never go through *one* Ladies' Championship with credit. Tears will bedew, if wigs do not bestrew, the green. Constitutionally and physically women are unfitted for golf. They will never last through two rounds of a long course in a day. Nor can they hope to defy the wind and weather encountered on our best links even in spring and summer. Temperamentally the strain will be too great for them. The first Ladies' Championship will be the last unless I and others are greatly mistaken."[51]

He was decidedly wrong and sporting enough to concede so, to the extent of becoming a Vice-President of the LGU in 1901.

In a little under two months after the inaugural meeting in April 1893 to form the Union, all the necessary arrangements for the Ladies' Championship to take place between the 13th and 15th June 1893 had been made. This inaugural national championship marked the beginning of women's golf as a serious sport.[52] In 1893 38 women played matches twice round the nine-hole course at St Anne's but from 1894 the championship was played on men's courses. In 1897 107 entrants challenged the seaside links at Gullane and in 1914 a record 166 women played at Hunstanton. Perhaps the most significant championship was that of 1908, later described by LGU official Mabel Stringer as 'epoch-making', for it was held in front of several thousand spectators at the Old Course in St Andrews, the traditional home of (men's) golf. The Royal & Ancient even relaxed its rules to allow the competitors into the club premises to view trophies.[53]

Another major achievement of the LGU was the establishment of a national system of handicapping. At the end of the nineteenth century each club calculated handicaps by its own methods and based on conditions at its own course, usually giving the best player scratch and ranking the others relative to that player. Some used best performances, others looked to the average. This caused confusion and even friction in inter-club or open meetings. The LGU introduced more consistency by persuading clubs to accept an agreed method of calculating par against which a handicap could be struck on the basis of two scores on a prize or medal day (i.e. in competitive not recreational golf). While not insisting that member clubs adopted its system of handicapping, tactically the LGU enhanced its position by donating silver medals for competition at every club that did take it up.[54] Within a decade the LGU's methodology had become widely accepted and provided a reasonably reliable indicator of the quality of players from club to club. In 1897 four volunteer LGU handicap managers were at work; by 1905 this had risen to 15. Such was the success of the handicap system that it became extensively adopted by female clubs in both Australia and New Zealand.[55]

The publication of a handbook from 1894 was also a pioneering golfing venture by women. It was issued free to affiliated clubs by the LGU to provide an official point of reference but was also available for sale to individuals and other clubs. However sales did not cover costs and, despite sponsorship first from the *Gentlewoman* magazine and then from the Golf Agency (who insisted on more advertising), the *Handbook* struggled for viability. The situation improved from 1906 when Miss Pearson, who remained Hon. Secretary of the LGU till 1921, brought in the idea that affiliated clubs should be compelled to purchase copies, the numbers required to be in proportion to membership.[56]

Whilst appreciative of the social golfer the LGU was aimed at the competitive golfer. That they hit the target was indicated in a comment in *Ladies' Field* in 1908 that 'Ladies have improved their game in leaps and bounds. The improvement is due to the inauguration of a Ladies' Open Championship and other open meetings and competitions encouraged by the LGU.'[57] Those other competitions included home internationals which by the early 1900s had become a regular feature in the women's golfing calendar.

Club Servants

One reason why middle-class women had the time to play golf or become administrators at club level and beyond was that some other tasks were undertaken by their household servants. Servants were also in attendance at the golf club to help the middle-class players replicate a leisured life-style within the clubhouse.

Golf clubs were not just sporting enterprises, they were also local businesses that employed people both on and off the course. The clubhouse was where women found jobs in catering and hospitality which were important for revenue raising or member satisfaction. Being a club-mistress at a top club could be like running a hotel (though under committee instruction) but at a smaller one it could be a grandiose title for a combination of tea dispenser, cleaner and washerwoman, as at Torwoodlee where Mrs Crombie was expected to clean the clubhouse and lavatories and keep the floor properly washed. Such jobs often came as a package deal when a husband was offered a greenkeeping or caretaking position. This was standard practice at Blackburn where four married couples were employed between 1895 and 1914. Other club-mistresses were independent female entrepreneurs who operated catering on a retainer plus profits system, a similar procedure to how most club golf professionals ran their shops. A few took on additional tasks. At Douglas Park Miss Christian Morrison agreed to clean the ladies' clubhouse for an extra 1s 9d a month and between July and September she was paid an additional 2s 6d a week for assisting in the bar and dining room. As well as being caretaker at Beverley and East Riding, Mrs Smith also acted as a caddie-mistress.[58] However, she employed no female caddies.

Women as cooks or cleaners raised no issues at golf clubs, not so females carrying golf bags for members. Some clubs, such as

Reigate Heath in 1902 specifically banned their employment.[59] Others operated an unwritten discriminatory policy. Yet there were exceptions. The first mention of regular girl caddies seems to have been at Guernsey in 1890, though one golf historian claims that girls replaced striking male caddies for six weeks at Gullane in Scotland around 1870. From about 1890 too, four years after the club was founded, Lytham and St Annes employed girls, though they had to be over fourteen and could carry only for lady members. By 1897, however, they could caddy for men and at the Autumn meeting that year girl caddies outnumbered boys. Girls were also caddying at Newquay in 1901 and at Huntercombe in Oxfordshire and several Yorkshire courses prior to the First World War. Nevertheless they were uncommon enough for comments to be made in *Golf Illustrated* about the fashion for girl caddies at some continental clubs.[60] Women caddies were even rarer. At Royal Ashdown, Mrs Mitchell, from the family that produced Abe Mitchell the professional golfer, carried from the turn of the century, initially because she lived close to the professional's shop and helped out when there was a shortage, and at Westward Ho! Mrs Williams became a first-class caddy in 1910. Bernard Darwin, the golf writer, also recalled a Mary Davina, who carried clubs at Aberdovey in Mid-Wales and champion Midlands' golfer Lily Moore had a female caddie.[61] It is significant that neither girl nor women caddies are mentioned in a major inquiry into the social and economic condition of caddies conducted in 1912.[62]

That caddies were predominantly male owes more to social mores than the requirements of the job. Possibly carrying a bag of clubs around the course was seen as being too heavy work for women, but many members of clubs had no hesitation in employing children as caddies or females for hard domestic work in their households. Nor did the Secretary of Copt Heath resile from paying two women at 1s 9d a day to pick stones from the fairway.[63] More likely it was the perceived disreputable nature of those who caddied, particularly adult males, and a desire to keep females protected from their influence.[64]

Unlike their male counterparts there was no chance of a female caddie advancing to green-keeper or golf professional. This would have involved an apprenticeship (assistantship) to an existing professional in which the art of club-making would be taught and this was exclusively for males.⁶⁵ Indeed there does not appear to have been a female assistant in British golf until the 1930s when Sydney Wingate appointed his sister Poppy to help him at Temple Newsham. That said, there were at least two women golf teachers. Mrs Gordon Robertson in 1905 became an instructor specifically for female players. By 1908 she claimed to have given over 2,000 lessons, mainly at the Prince's (Mitcham) and West Middlesex clubs but also on a peripatetic basis when requested by other clubs. Additionally in 1911 Sunningdale Ladies employed Lily Freemantle, daughter of a male professional.⁶⁶

Suffragettes

A male commentator writing in 1913 reckoned that 'women on the links have made greater strides than in any other section of womanhood.'⁶⁷ Certainly they had made more progress there than in the struggle for the franchise, though, except at the few fully independent ladies' clubs, voting rights for women at golf clubs mirrored those in society at large. Nearly forty years of campaigning had brought female suffragists no closer to achieving their political aims. Although the founding of the more militant Women's Social and Political Union (WSPU) by Emmeline Pankhurst in 1903 had led to demonstrations, publicity stunts and an escalating level of disorderly behaviour, culminating in prison sentences and hunger strikes, an all-male parliament still refused to grant women the vote.

In January 1913 the WSPU embarked on its most serious campaign of violence, prompted by the failure of the latest franchise bill, with Mrs Pankhurst declaring that members of the organisation intended to inflict widespread damage against property. For the next eighteen months private houses, public buildings, postal services and transport throughout Britain were burned down, bombed, disrupted and destroyed.⁶⁸ Sports venues such as racecourses, cricket grounds and football stadiums were subject to arson attacks, bowling greens and tennis courts were hacked up, boat houses and billiard rooms damaged. The sportsmen who suffered the greatest inconvenience, however, were golfers.

Golf courses – vast, semi-rural and difficult to protect from intruders – were easy prey to suffragettes toting trowels and bottles of corrosive fluid. Although fires were sometimes started at clubhouses the most common atrocity was cutting or digging up the turf and throwing acid around the greens. Sometimes VW or Votes for Women were carved or etched on the ground. Unlike grandstand saboteurs, few perpetrators of acid attacks were ever caught; they took advantage of quiet locations under cover of darkness.[69] But ease of access was not the main reason why golf was singled out for attention. Although this paper has shown that large numbers of women played the game golf clubs were targeted because suffragettes apparently saw them as the haunts of male chauvinists and of figures of authority who could change society.[70] This is the likeliest explanation: during the Edwardian era golf had become the favoured pastime of many Liberal MPs whose party dominated British politics in the period 1906–14 and whose leaders were implacably opposed to female suffrage.

The Prime Minister and several of his Cabinet colleagues had in fact been subjected to suffragette abuse on the golf course for years. As early as 1909, Asquith and Home Secretary Herbert Gladstone had been cornered by three determined young members of the WSPU while playing in Kent. A report on the incident commented that 'the Suffragette harpies' were ever on the track of the Prime Minister. But it was on the links of north-east Scotland where Asquith passed many days during the summer Parliamentary recess that most incidents occurred. He was verbally assaulted by a Mrs Cruikshank while playing at Aboyne near Balmoral in August 1912. A few weeks later he and Reginald McKenna, the current Home Secretary, were set upon by two women at the Royal Dornoch course. And in a much publicised incident a year later he and his daughter were attacked on the 17th green of the Moray Golf Club at Lossiemouth by two women who allegedly seized his arms, knocked his hat off, tugged his hair and shouted abuse.[71]

The attitude of the golfing community to these acts of violence against persons and property can be followed privately in the minutes of individual golf clubs and publicly in the national press. In 1913 the *Sunday Times* warned suffragettes not to alienate golfers as they were a large and influential class.[72] Mrs Pankhurst responded to widespread condemnation by announcing that, 'We are not fighting you because you play golf. We are not fighting you at all but trying to stir you up.'[73] In this she undoubtedly succeeded. According to Constance Rover, an early historian of the women's suffrage movement, 'the activities which enraged the public most were the setting fire to the contents of pillar boxes and damage to golf courses.'[74]

During February and March that year a war of words took place in the pages of *Golf Illustrated* as supporters and detractors of the suffrage movement tried to put across their opinions. These frequently took the form of verses, stirring or scathing according to the author's stance, or cartoons ridiculing the tactics of the suffragettes. The female editor of the 'Woman's Golf' section felt sure that no golfers were amongst the 'scratchers and scrapers' as 'golfing instinct would somehow come before political hysteria.'[75] A report from St Andrews suggested that any suffragette damage to the Old Course should result in the offenders being ducked in the Swilken Burn.[76] As for the perpetrators of the crimes they seemed to rejoice in the outcome of their deeds. Hannah Mitchell, a member of the WSPU, later wrote that 'there did seem something to laugh at in the idea of the plus-foured MP toddling along to his favourite golf links, to find, cut in the sacred sward, the terrible slogan, "Votes for Women".'[77] This statement seems to reinforce the notion that suffragettes were more intent in getting their message across to golfing politicians than in upsetting ordinary club members.

Although 'the tearing of the greens' was widely reported in the press, it is in privately published individual club histories that much new material has come to light. During 1913 committees can be seen wrestling with awkward and potentially expensive problems. Decisions had to be taken about whether or not to insure against suffrage atrocities and whether to set aside extra funds to pay for guarding the greens. After underwriters at Lloyds had begun to offer policies specifically to protect golf clubs, the modest and the prestigious took advantage of this service, from Denham in Buckinghamshire to the Old and New Courses at St Andrews, the latter insured for £1,000 against damage.[78] Two hundred watchers were enrolled to guard the Fife greens day and night before the Amateur Championship in May and Boy Scouts patrolled the links at Lytham ahead of the Open.[79] At a less exalted level, the greenkeeper at the Royal County Down Golf Club was awarded £2 'for his attention to the greens from attacks by the suffragettes' while Rye Golf Club provided guards to escort competitors threatened with violence during the Bar Golfing Society visit to the course.[80]

A further, and largely unrecorded, aspect of the WSPU campaign against golf concerns female suffragists who played the game. It would be misleading to think of all suffrage activists as blinkered idealists, dedicated to 'The Cause' and lacking other interests. On the contrary, many rank-and-file members – and a few leaders – of both militant and non-militant societies enjoyed sport, and golf was as popular amongst suffrage women as it was with many Edwardian ladies.[81] The dilemmas for these golfers were whether to condone militant tactics and, if so, how to support the campaign while ensuring that acid-wielding suffragettes avoided their own club. The ladies' section at Woking was convinced that the 'Destroying Angel' had passed over them because several prominent suffragettes, who had the ear of Mrs Pankhurst, were members.[82] Tensions between male and female golfers as a result of suffrage 'outrages' only diminished when militancy was halted on the outbreak of war.

Conclusions

The suffrage movement was part of a wider shift in women's attitudes and behaviours, certainly among the middle class. Part of the phenomenon was a growing involvement in sport. *Punch* printed many misogynist cartoons about women in sport, parodying them as inept participants. However, the very fact that it did so for over a decade could suggest that women were persistent in their efforts to play sport.[83] For women, golf clubs in particular were an enclave outside the home where they had the opportunity to experience not only fresh air, exercise, relaxation and enjoyment but also competition.

Although some detractors remained, generally by 1914 women golfers had been accepted both on and off the links. As Mabel Stringer, a member of the LGU executive, put it in regard to the 1908 Ladies Championship, 'men who came to scoff stayed to watch'. Women golfers began to feature in advertisements aimed not just at women or even at golfers: for example to extol the benefits of Bovril for 'health, strength and beauty' and Elliman's embrocation for 'aches and bruises'.[84]

In playing golf women were not really threatening the male golf world. A few choleric colonels might be aghast at the thought of women hacking around the links but generally women were accepted at most clubs, though usually under conditions laid down by the committee, all of whom would be males. Although there were significant exceptions, at club level women tended to accept their subordinate role with its restrictions on playing times, separate shorter and less challenging courses, and lack of decision-making power. Indeed many social players might have preferred such a situation. There was certainly no consideration of undermining class relationships which were replicated in golf with servants being employed to cater to the on and off-course needs of middle-class golfers.

Women's golf, particularly that of the 'ladies' section', developed separately but not fully independently from men. Women faced restricted access to clubhouse facilities, usually had no vote at the AGM, and generally were not represented on the main club committee. This discrimination was reflected in a difference in entry fees and in the cost of subscriptions between men and women. It was, however, in the financial interests of the men to have a thriving ladies section as, despite these lower subscriptions, they made a contribution to the club's coffers via purchases at the professional's shops, payment for lessons, hiring of caddies, and, when allowed, using the clubhouse for meals and refreshments. Yet discrimination and segregation generally came by consent and, despite the restrictions, the number of female players continued to increase.

Women who had demonstrated their ability to organise domestically did the same when it came to forming and running their own local golf clubs. At a wider organisational level women were to the fore. The establishment of the LGU (in advance of a similar organisation for men) with the consequent inauguration of an open championship, the introduction of home international matches, and the development of a national handicapping system (again in advance of men) did much to raise the standard of women's golf. The LGU not only showed that women could create and run a national organisation, but had an important role in demonstrating that women could be serious golfers.

References

1. Some of the evidence here is drawn from a Leverhulme-funded grant to investigate the Emergence of the Golf Club as a British Social

Institution before 1914.

2. *LGU Year Books*, London 1900, 1914; M. Stringer, 'Women's Golf in 1911', *Golfing* 28 December 1911.

3. W. Vamplew, 'Sporting Innovation: The American Invasion of the British Turf and Links 1895–1905, *Sport History Review*, 2004, 35.2, p. 126.

4. Two exceptions, but unpublished, are H. Pearson, 'The Ladies' Section: The Development and Popular Perceptions of Ladies' Golf in Britain 1890–1914', M.A. Hons dissertation, Economic History Department, University of Edinburgh, 2002 and J. George, 'Women and Golf in Scotland', Ph.D., Scottish Studies, University of Edinburgh, 2003.

5. F. G. Aflalo, *The Cost of Sport*, London, p. 285; C. Lindsay, 'A Century of Labour Market Change: 1900 to 2000', *Labour Market Trends*, March 2003, p. 141.

6. M. Mortimer, *The Spirit of Cavendish Golf Club with Burbage Ladies' Golf Club 1899–1999*, Grant, Worcestershire, 2000, p. 7, p. 9.

7. *Ladies Field*, 25 February 1899, p. 493.

8. *Golf Illustrated*, 29 December 1899, p. 24.

9. B. Martin, 'On Lady Golfers', *The Annual of the Ladies' Golf Union* (1893–94), p. 24.

10. E. M. Boys and L. Mackern, *Our Lady of the Green*, Lawrence, London, 1899 p. 24.

11. The *LGU Official Year Book*, London, 1914, pp. 419–421.

12. R. Milton, *A History of Ladies Golf in Sussex*, Sussex County Ladies' Golf Association, Brighton, p. 78.

13. A. Elliot, *Lundin Ladies' Golf Club 1891–1991*, Artigraff, Buckhaven, 1991, p. 4, p. 20.

14. B. Lloyd, *Wirral Ladies: A Centennial Portrait*, Grant, Droitwich, 1993, p. 7; Holt, *Stanmore*, p. 83.

15. R. Holt, *Stanmore Golf Club 1883–1993*, Club, Stanmore, 1993, p. 84.

16. J. Kerr, *The Golf Book of East Lothian*, Constable, Edinburgh, 1896, p. 294, p. 133.

17. *The Bystander*, 15 March 1905.

18. Pearson, 'Ladies' Section', p. 12; E. J. Davies and G. W. Brown, *The Royal North Devon Golf Club 1864–1989*, Club, Westward Ho!, 1989, p. 35.

19. Of a sample of 43 separate ladies clubs in England in 1913 three had no male equivalent. Of the others none were formed

simultaneously with a man's club though 8 followed within a year. A further 17 came within 5 years but 15 took longer than this. There was a different pattern in Scotland, perhaps owing something to the earlier development of the game there. Although again there were three clubs with no male equivalent, 16 of the 18 in a Scottish sample had a lag of over 6 years. (based on data in *Nisbet's Golf Guide and Year Book*, Nisbet, London, 1913)

20. T. Boliver, *South Staffordshire Golf Club 1892–1992*, Club, Wolverhampton, 1992, pp. 11,15.

21. *Nisbet's Year Book*, 1913, p. 86, p. 213; A. McIntosh, *Blairgowrie Golf Club 1889–1989*, Club, Blairgowrie, 1989, p.14.

22. J. H. Legge, *Dunbar Ladies' Golf Club: The First 100 Years*, Club, Dunbar, 1994, p. 2.

23. B. Ironside, *Dunbar Golf Club: A Short History*, Club, Dunbar, 1977, p.14; J. M. G. Ward, *One Hundred Years of Golf On Westwood*, Coxton, Beverley, 1990, p. 67; P. Davis, *Formby Ladies' Golf Club: A History of the Club*, Club, Formby, 1996, p. 10.

24. Milton, *Ladies Golf in Sussex*, p. 81, p. 75.

25. At Purley Downs women could become full members but most opted for associate membership with its playing restrictions and lower fees. H. Sagar, *A History of Purley Downs Golf Club*, Club, Purley Downs, 1983, p. 75.

26. Lord Wellwood, 'General Remarks on the Game' in H. G. Hutchinson (ed), *Golf*, Longmans Green, London, 1892, p. 47; *Gentlewoman*, 7 March 1891.

27. A. M. Starkie-Bence, 'Golf' in Frances E. Slaughter (ed.), *The Sportswoman's Library*, Constable, London, 1898, vol I, pp. 260–267. Of a sample from Nisbet of 29 women's clubs with a separate course 25 possessed 9 holes or less]

28. Hutchinson, *Book of Golf*, p. 71.

29. This begs the question of how many men were merely 'social' golfers. They cannot all have been competent and serious.

30. Hutchinson, *Book of Golf*, p. 73.

31. *Nisbet's Year Book*, 1913, p. 30, p. 264.

32. Ward, *One Hundred Years*, p. 70; J. O. MacCabe, *The First Eighty Years: Douglas Park Golf Club*, Club, Douglas Park, 1982, p. 68; Ironside, *Dunbar*, p. 16.

33. M. Stringer, *Golfing Reminiscences*, Mills & Boon, London, 1924, p. 14, p. 24; *Ladies Field*, 23 October 1909, p. 546.

34. Stringer, *Reminiscences*, pp. 22–23.

35. J. Walsh, *Seaford Golf Club: A History*, Lindel, Seaford, 1986,p. 82; G. Laidlaw & D. Masson, *A Very Pleasant Golfing Place: A Centenary History of the Kilmacolm Golf Club*, Club, Kilmacolm, 1991, p. 92, p. 97; D. Hoskinson, *Sutton Coldfield Ladies' Golf Club 1892–1992*, Grant, Worcestershire, 1992, pp. 3–5.
36. Sagar, *Purley Downs*, p. 75; J. A. Kingham, *South Beds Golf Club. The First 100 Years 1892–1992*, Club, Luton, 1992, p. 39; E. M. Soulsby, *Braemar Golf Club: The Story of the First 100 Years*, Club, Braemar, 2002, p. 16.
37. MacCabe, *Douglas Park*, p. 66; Holt, *Stanmore*, p. 83; Milton, *Ladies Golf in Sussex*, p. 4; W. Russell, *A History of Craigmillar Park Golf Club 1895–1995*, John Donald, Edinburgh, 1995, p. 3; *LGU Annual*, 1897, p. 120; E. Deasy, *Rochdale Golf Club 1888–1988*, Club, Rochdale, 1987, p. 35.
38. R. B. Smith, *Blackburn Golf Club 100 Years 1894–1994*, Club, Blackburn, 1993, pp. 18–19; D. Hoskinson, *Sutton Coldfield Ladies' Golf Club 1892–1992*, Grant, Worcestershire, 1992, p. 11, p. 52; Ironside, *Dunbar*, p. 19; *LGU Annual*, 1897, p. 120.
39. D. Martin, *Minchinhampton Golf Club Centenary History 1889–1989*, Club, Minchinhampton, 1989, p. 118.
40. *Nisbet's*, 1906, p. 316; *LGU Year Book 1906*, pp. 475–9; Elliot, *Lundin Ladies*, p. 4.
41. *Golf*, 11 August 1905, p. 314.
42. Irish men had formed a Union in 1891 but there was no Welsh Union till 1895 or Scottish till 1920 and an English one was not formed till 1924. The handicapping scheme prepared by the British Golf Union Joint Advisory Committee did not become operational until March 1926 (*Golfers Handbook*, Glasgow, 1954, p. 123).
43. R. Cossey, *Golfing Ladies: Five Centuries of Golf in Great Britain and Northern Ireland*, Orbis, London, 1984, p. 24.
44. Boys and Mackern, *Lady of the Green*, p. 14.
45. *The Gentlewoman*, 29 April 1893. This journal promoted sport and especially golf for women producing a golfing supplement, *The Golfing Gentlewoman* between 1914 and 1916.
46. Boys and Mackern, *Lady of the Green*, p. 16.
47. *Annual Report of LGU*, 1893, p. 38.
48. Cossey, *Golfing Ladies*, p. 27.
49. Pearson, 'Ladies' Section', p. 28.
50. M. Crane, *The Story of Ladies' Golf*, Stanley Paul, London, p. 18.
51. Cited in Stringer, *Reminiscences*, p.13.

52. Officially known as the Ladies' British Open Amateur Championship but generally referred to as the Ladies' Championship.
53. Stringer, *Reminiscences*, p. 25; M. E. Stringer, 'Ladies' Golf in the Spring of 1908', *Badminton Magazine*, 1908, 27, p. 45.
54. Starkie Bence, 'Golf', p. 327.
55. Cossey, *Golfing Ladies*, pp. 46–49; Stringer, 'Ladies' Golf', p. 48.
56. Cossey *Golfing Ladies*, pp. 30–31.
57. *The Ladies' Field*, 16 May 1908, p. 675.
58. Anon. *Torwoodlee 1895–1995 Centenary*, Club, Torwoodlee, 1995, p. 9; Smith, *Blackburn*, p. 13, p. 15, pp. 23–24; McMillan, *Douglas Park*, p. 113; Ward, *One Hundred Years of Golf*, p. 31, p. 35.
59. C. Sheldon, *Reigate Heath and its Golf Club*, Straker, London, 1982, p. 43.
60. D. Stirk, *'Carry Your Bag, Sir?'*, Witherby, London, 1989, pp. 112–113, 115; J. Adams, *Huntercombe Golf Club 1900–1983*, Higgs, Henley-on-Thames, 1984, p. 19; *Golf Illustrated*, 25 July, 4 July, 24 October 1913; 13 March, 31 July 1914.
61. Stirk, *Carry Your Bag*, pp. 114–5; 44; *Times*, 5 September 1919; D. Cadney, *The Story of Olton Golf Club*, Grant, Worcestershire, 1991, p. 58.
62. Agenda Club, *The Rough and the Fairway: An Enquiry by the Agenda Club into the Problem of the Golf Caddie*, Heinemann, London 1912.
63. V. Summers, *Copt Heath Golf Club to 1990*, Club, Birmingham, 1990, p. 120.
64. Agenda Club, *Rough and Fairway*, p. 9.
65. W. Vamplew, 'Exploited Labour or Successful Workingmen: Golf Professionals and Professional Golfers in Britain before 1914', *Economic History Review* (forthcoming).
66. R. Holt, P. Lewis and W. Vamplew, *The Professional Golfers' Association 1901–2001*, Grant, Worcestershire, 2002, p.54; Stringer, 'Ladies Golf', p. 50; J. Lowerson 'Golf' in T. Mason *Sport in Britain*, Cambridge U. P., Cambridge, 1989, p. 206; A. Jackson, *The British Professional Golfers 1887–1930: A Register*, Grant, Worcestershire, 1994, p. 32.
67. *Ladies' Golf*, April 1913, II, p.38.
68. A. Rosen, *Rise Up, Women! The Militant Campaign of the WSPU, 1903–1914*, Routledge & Kegan Paul, London, 1974, p. 188.
69. The substantial drop in the number of golf course incidents during the summer of 1913 may be partly explained by the long daylight hours
70. J. Connelly, *A Temple of Golf: The History of Woking Golf Club*,

1893–1993, Club, Woking, 1993, p. 104.

71. D. Hamilton, *Golf: Scotland's Game*, Partick Press, Kilmalcolm, 1998, p.228; *Golf Illustrated*, 17 September 1909; E. Crawford, *The Women's Suffrage Movement: A Reference Guide 1866–1928*, UCL Press, London, 2000, p. 296; L. Leneman, *A Guid Cause; The Women's Suffrage Movement in Scotland*, Aberdeen U. P. Aberdeen, 1991, p. 116, p. 155; J. McConachie, *The Moray Club at Lossiemouth, 1889–1989*, Club, Lossiemouth, 1988, pp. 27–8.

72. *Sunday Times*, 14 February 1913.

73. *Golf Illustrated*, 21 February 1913.

74. C. Rover, *Women's Suffrage and Party Politics in Britain 1866–1914*, Routledge & Kegan Paul, London, 1967, p. 82.

75. *Golf Illustrated*, 21 February 1913.

76. *Golf Illustrated*, 28 February 1913.

77. G. Mitchell (ed), *The Hard Way Up: the Autobiography of Hannah Mitchell*, Faber, London, 1977, p.176.

78. M. Melford and B. Fenning, *Denham Described: A History of Denham Golf Club 1910–1992*, Grant, Droitwich, 1992, p.14; Minutes of Royal & Ancient Golf Club, 5 March 1913.

79. *Golf Illustrated*, 16 May 1913; E. A. Nickson, *The Lytham Century. A History of Royal Lytham & St Annes Golf Club 1886–1986*, Author, Lytham, 1986, p. 115.

80. H. McCaw and B. Henderson, *Royal County Down Golf Club: the First Century*, Club, County Down, 1988, p. 47; D. Vidler, *Rye Golf Club: the First 90 Years*, Club, Rye, 1984, p. 53.

81. A.J.R., *The Suffrage Annual and Women's Who's Who*, Stanley Paul, London, 1913. Of 176 women who listed a sport amongst their recreations, 32 (including 8 members of the WSPU) mentioned golf, the highest number after walking and cycling. For a fuller analysis see J. Kay, '"No Time for Recreations till the Vote is Won"? Suffrage Activists and Leisure in Edwardian Britain', *Women's History Review* (forthcoming).

82. Connelly, *Temple of Golf*, p. 106.

83. M. Constanzo, '"One Can't Shake Off the Women": Images of Sport and Gender in *Punch*, 1901–10', *International Journal of the History of Sport* 19.1, 2002, pp. 31–56.

84. Stringer, *Reminiscences*, p. 45; Pearson, 'Ladies' Section', p. 48.

The Rough and the Fairway: Processes and Problems in Ryder Cup Team Selection 1927–2006[1]

Introduction

Competed for by European and American golfers, the Ryder Cup is unusual in professional sport as the participants play without financial reward using a team format in a game normally associated at the their level with individual rivalry. This paper will outline the history of the competition, examine implications of the selection policies and procedures and discuss the issue of identity, particularly when the non-American opposition switched from being British to European. It will also add to the relatively sparse coverage of golf in academic literature. What has been written has focused on the gender divide,[2] the economics of the sport[3] and, more recently, the environment.[4] The Ryder Cup itself, whilst the subject of several popular works, has had only one academic article devoted to it on this side of the Atlantic.[5]

Most academic work on selection has centred on the politics of exclusion via segregation or discrimination, as in apartheid South Africa, or in the political use of discriminatory quotas, as in the same country post apartheid.[6] There is, however, an emerging debate in sports law on selection policies for teams as human rights legislation and a growing litigious tendency among athletes has encouraged sports associations to formally publish their selection policies and appeal procedures.[7] Even in a minority, relatively non-commercial sport such as orienteering the ruling body has acknowledged that this had to be done as 'selection is the most visible expression of the way in which we conduct our affairs; because of its wide reaching effects on athletes' careers and their confidence in the system; and because of the associated legal implications.'[8]

Much more academic literature exists on 'national' identity in sport though even here both the British and the European dimension have been relatively neglected. When looking at Britain a recent collection of essays on sport and national identity concentrated on English football, Welsh rugby, Scottish football and rugby, and football in the Republic of Ireland, eschewing any real consideration of British teams.[9] The concept of a European identity above a national one has been seen as a political not a sporting issue and hardly features in academic sports literature.[10]

Background

The Ryder Cup owes its existence to the ill-health of a middle-aged English seed merchant. Advised by a friend to take up golf as an antidote to stress, Samuel Ryder became addicted to the game.[11] His passion for the sport led to him appointing Abe Mitchell, a leading British professional, as his personal golf tutor in 1925; this was a sinecure designed to allow Mitchell time to practise and compete effectively against the Americans who were beginning to dominate the Open Championship.[12] Ryder had a high regard for professional golfers and sponsored matches and even tournaments to assist their development.[13]

His patriotism and love of golf came together in an offer to award a trophy for an international match between representatives of the British and American Professional Golf Associations (PGAs), the two leading groups of golfers in the world. He had already funded a similar match at Wentworth in 1926 between British and American professionals prior to the latter playing the qualifying rounds for that year's Open.[14] Two years earlier he had sponsored a 72–hole fourball match between two Americans and two British players, one of them Abe Mitchell, and in 1925 he paid for a singles match between Mitchell and Jim Barnes, an Englishman who had emigrated to the States.[15] The competition for the Ryder Cup itself, a 100–guinea gold trophy with the figure of Abe Mitchell on top, began at the Worcester Country Club, Massachusetts in June 1927 when the hosts trounced their visitors $9^1/_2 - 2^1/_2$.

The initial Deed of Trust by which Ryder donated the trophy had stated that the Cup should be played for on an annual basis, though this idea was quickly shelved and the competition became biennial, alternating with the Walker Cup for amateur golfers. In the six contests before the Second World War the home team triumphed on five occasions but the American victory at Southport in the last pre-war match was a portent of their coming domination. The first post-war match, held in Portland, Oregon, was a humiliating defeat for the British team by 11–1. Reminiscent of the mock obituary that created the Ashes in cricket sixty years before, one journalist wrote that 'Here, on November 2 1947, died British golf'.[16] There was no resurrection. From 1947 to 1983 Britain gained a solitary victory, at Lindrick in 1957, which brought a CBE for captain Dai Rees but no real change in the trend of match results. In 1975 after the Americans had won 8 of the last 9 matches and tied the other, Michael McDonnell, the *Daily Mail* golf correspondent, summed up popular opinion when he proclaimed 'the Ryder Cup passed away again yesterday. Not for just another two years but almost certainly for ever. There is no further point to this charade.'[17] American players were becoming uninterested; more significantly so was American television.

Following another British defeat on home ground at Lytham in 1977, golfing folklore has it that overtures from American golfing legend Jack Nicklaus to Lord Derby, President of the British PGA, led to an expansion of the British team to include players from elsewhere. Ten years earlier Bob Creasey of the United States PGA had sent a letter to the British PGA Executive requesting that the team be enlarged to include the Commonwealth countries but, mindful of possible political difficulties and a lessened audience at the next match, a decision was put off until after the 1969 event at Birkdale. This resulted in a conceded tie and the idea was shelved.[18] Nicklaus had offered the suggestion of an alliance of English-speaking countries as another alternative but the way forward was European-focused with the new political alignments and golfing logic coming together. In the late 1960s a European golf circuit developed which began to attract top players. In 1970 the French Open was included in the Order of Merit for Ryder Cup points and a year later the British and European tours were merged, essentially because it was believed that the British sponsorship market had reached its limit. This provided an opportunity for European and British players to compete regularly at the highest level.

Moreover in 1975 the European Tour Players Division split from the PGA itself making the British tournament players' links with their European counterparts stronger.[19]

Introducing European players was not an immediate panacea. In 1979 two Spaniards justified the European nomenclature but the result was still a defeat. Two years later at Walton Heath the Europeans, this time with a German and a Spaniard, were thrashed $18^1/_2$ to $9^1/_2$: in mitigation their opponents were regarded as one of the strongest American teams ever as all but one of its members either had won or were to win a Major. Nor was it a case of third time lucky, though the American win in 1983 was by the narrowest of margins. Then came a reversal of fortunes. The most European team to that date, with four Spanish players and a German, gained a win at the Belfry in 1985, the date, according to team captain Tony Jacklin, that 'European golf came of age'.[20] This was followed by the first-ever Ryder Cup victory on an American course at Muirfield Village in 1987 before the cup was retained with a tie at the Belfry in 1989. The growing vigour of the European tour, aided perhaps by an expansion of prizemoney and no gaps in the weekly schedule of events, had strengthened the depth of the team. The match is no longer predictable: indeed the Europeans have won the last three, though this is still far from the earlier winning streaks of the Americans.

Selection

Findlay and Corbett have pointed out that many selection decisions in representative sport are technically complex with policies relating to eligibility, selection and appeals written by people not skilled in drafting legislation. This can result in criteria that are 'vague, incomplete, contradictory and even silent on critical points'.[21] The Ryder Cup was no exception.[22]

The Deed of Trust for the Cup stipulated that players would be selected solely by their respective PGAs. Hence the 1926 match is regarded as a precursor to the Ryder Cup and not the first match as the American team on that occasion was selected by one of their players, Walter Hagen. What the Deed did not do was place any restrictions on how the teams were to be selected; in particular it set no birth or residential qualifications. For the 1927 and 1929 matches the Americans decided that their players should be native-born and resident in the United States thus ruling out stars such as Scotsman Tommy Armour and English emigrant Jim Barnes. The British PGA did not operate such restrictions, allowing them to play Aubrey Boomer who was a professional in France at the time. After discussion, a revised Deed of Trust was agreed which stipulated that the American practice was to be followed; thereafter Boomer, as well as Percy Alliss, a professional in Berlin, became ineligible.

Further conditions imposed on the British team by the PGA deprived it of one of its best players, Henry Cotton.[23] But according to his biographer,

> The root cause of this situation was a conflict which was to bedevil
> Ryder Cup selection for years to come: whether selection to the team
> was to be an honour conferred by the Professional Golfers' Association
> for loyal and meritorious service or whether it should be a process of
> choosing the team most likely to win the trophy.[24]

Fifty years later, Robert Green, Assistant Editor of *Golf World*, indicated that little had changed. Top European golfers who regularly competed on the American circuit, such as Nick Faldo and Seve Ballesteros, were deemed ineligible, leaving a team partially composed of lesser lights to contest the event. He echoed the earlier view: 'a place in the team should not be seen as a reward for loyalty to the European circuit.'[25] Two years later Dobereiner re-iterated this position. He complained that the system for Ryder Cup selection was for plodders – 'players who have scraped into the side by virtue of playing every tournament and racking up enough points from consistent finishes.'[26] The players themselves, however, preferred the more objective selection conferred by a money list or order of merit to the subjective committee or captain's decision, in which favouritism or bias might play a part.

Before any team could be chosen it was necessary to select the selectors, and this in itself could be a controversial issue. Although the first Ryder Cup selection committee consisted of the famous playing triumvirate of Vardon, Braid and Taylor, most of those during the thirties were composed of five or six members of the PGA Executive Committee, normally the chairman, captain and secretaries of at least two regional committees. The immediate post-war years saw increasing friction between the regions, perhaps indicating the growing prestige and publicity surrounding the event – by 1953 the BBC had even expressed an interest in televising it. 1949 had seen nine nominations for four committee places. 1951 saw disputes between the major regional sections, each keen to have the privilege of a member on the selection committee. By 1953 open warfare had broken out; such heated discussions took place concerning the non-appointment of a representative from the northern section that the chairman had to appeal for unity. The issue was resolved only when it became apparent that the captain of the Association was currently a northern section member.[27] After such an unseemly episode, the PGA tournament committee took over the duties of Ryder Cup selection.

Who formed that committee continued to be a thorny issue. In 1963 five tournament committee members plus the Ryder Cup Captain had the power to co-opt yet more selectors; by 1967 there was a selection committee of six plus the Ryder Cup Captain. For the next decade the selectors were reduced to three, usually the present and a past Ryder Cup Captain, together with the leader in the Order of Merit. But even then there was no consistency. In 1969 and 1973 the past Captain was the immediate predecessor, in 1971 it was any previous Captain, in 1975 there was no stipulation about past captaincy and only two selectors were deemed necessary. Such a restricted choice still led to indecision: the Ryder Cup Captain and the leading player in the Order of Merit was later amended to the Captain and 'any additional persons he wishes to nominate.'[28] By 1981, the situation resembled that of twenty years earlier, except the six selectors were chosen from the European Tour Board of Management Committee. This, it must be remembered, was merely to choose those entrusted with the power to select a team of twelve golfers.

Several methods of choosing players had been tried over the previous three decades: short lists of up to 30, trial matches, and automatic selection for the winners of major events had all formed part of the process. Final decision making, however, was by committee 'after discussion', sometimes 'after considerable discussion' although the first five or six names on the team sheet were often unanimous. The first instances of both 'player power' and automatic selection from an objective list occurred in 1955. A tournament committee of four was ultimately responsible for the decision but the initial choice was based on the seven leading players in the averages, who in turn assisted in choosing the remaining three. A Ryder Cup points system was instituted at the end of that year and the top ten players in July 1957 formed the team, thereby diminishing the power of selectors. By 1959, a version of the 1955 system was back in place and these two methods – automatic selection from a list, or a hybrid 'list plus selection by committee' – held sway until the 1980s.

In 1971 Captain Eric Brown expressed a preference for greater personal selection instead of an automatic list and was reminded by fellow committee members that this 'went completely against what the Tournament Committee appeared to have in mind.'[29] After several proposals and voting, he won the day, although the Tournament Committee later expressed disappointment that its unanimous recommendation for selection had been rejected. In 1981, it was suggested that the views of the team captain far outweighed those of his co-selectors, enabling him to exclude players whom he thought unsuitable for whatever reason.[30] The arrival of Tony Jacklin as Ryder Cup Captain for the remainder of the 1980s soon streamlined procedures and instituted the 'Captain's pick'. Jacklin demanded that he alone choose the final three players after the initial nine had been taken direct from the European prize money list, enabling those who plied their trade on the more lucrative American circuit to be part of the team. The influence of the Ryder Cup Captain on selection policy has been maintained ever since, although the number of wild cards has been reduced to two since 1995. Although the selectors now use a combination of world and European rankings, the major dilemma, however, has remained the same as that identified in the pre-war era: the fairest selection policy did not necessarily produce the strongest team. Should the team represent the best European players or the best players on the European Tour? The answer has sometimes depended on who held the captaincy.[31]

In spite of ongoing efforts to establish fair and reasonable selection methods, transparency has been difficult to achieve and anomalies have occurred. Seven meetings were held by the Ryder Cup selection committee of 1931. Four trial matches, comprising 24 players and 36 holes of golf, took place between February and May. Yet as a result of an 'informal meeting' of part of the committee and a subsequent phone call to the Chairman, a selected member of the team was asked to withdraw because of his lack of form. He had already spent the £50 allocated to him for the purchase of kit![32] In a reverse scenario, the official history of the Ryder Cup indicates that Sandy Lyle, a likely 'captain's pick' for the 1989 team, de-selected himself shortly before the selection deadline because of his poor form.[33] In 1959, when seven selected team members met with the tournament sub-committee to pick the remaining three from a short list of eight, a player whose name had not originally been included because he was unfit was unanimously chosen by his seven prospective team mates. Although a ballot took place among the selectors, as agreed in the rules, the addition of a new name caused another to be ousted. Unsurprisingly, the newly fit player was selected. And in a more recent controversy, Miguel Angel Martin, an automatic qualifier for the Ryder Cup team in 1997, was asked to take a late fitness test following injury. His failure to agree to this led to de-selection, allowing team captain Seve Ballesteros to pick the next man on the points table, who happened to be his long standing Ryder Cup playing partner Jose Maria Olazabal, as well as his two preferred wild cards. This sleight of hand enabled Ballesteros to field his 'dream team' and Europe retained the trophy.

This incident further highlights the power that can be wielded by a captain, the selection of whom has also proved to be controversial at times during the past eighty years. Until 1963, most captains were also team players; since then they have been non-playing. Sometimes the captain was chosen by a PGA Executive Committee months ahead of the players and became a selector himself; on other occasions the captain was only selected once the team was known, with the opinions of team members taken into account. In 1955 two dozen leading professionals threatened to boycott any international match sponsored by the PGA unless they were satisfied with the selection committee and captain. Overtly this was a demand from these tournament professionals that Henry Cotton be chosen as captain, an appointment viewed with apprehension by some within the PGA executive. The opposition to Cotton reflected the second, initially more covert, motivation of the tournament players for greater representation on the executive. To Cotton and his colleagues the PGA was too much concerned with the club professional to the neglect of the tournament player who was attempting to make a living from competitive golf rather than from giving lessons and selling equipment. They demanded a majority on the tournament sub-committee and that the Ryder Cup captain be chosen by the team rather than the PGA executive. However, once greater representation was conceded they agreed that they need only be consulted about the captaincy.[34] In 1961 it was agreed that the captain should be nominated by the team yet by 1963 the decision was firmly back in the hands of a tournament committee. As the European tour strengthened so the selection system increasingly moved away from the PGA and to the tour professionals. Now it is the European Tour Tournament Committee that chooses the Ryder Cup captain, though this has to be formally ratified by the Ryder Cup Policy Board comprising six players on the European tour, two representatives of the PGA and two others from the PGAs of Europe.[35]

Selection does not end with the establishment of a team: players have still to be chosen to play. Unlike the Americans who used all team members from the outset, on the grounds that if you were picked you were good enough, their British counterparts have frequently left men out in order to play those in form. Two of the ten British golfers in 1929 were forced to sit out the contest; the same number in 1959. In more recent times, controversy has surrounded Captain mark James' decision to omit players from the fourballs and foursomes at Brookline, only allowing them to compete in the singles on the final day.

Identity

Until the advent of the Ryder Cup, golf at the professional level had been essentially an individual affair. Apart from some pre-war home internationals and the occasional professional foursomes competition, team golf was the province of the amateur club or county player not the professional out to make a living.[36]

Once professionals began to represent) their country, the issue arose of what) nation were they playing for. The concept of 'Britishness' had emerged during the (eighteenth century as inhabitants of England, Scotland, Ireland and Wales, the latter trio possibly due to covert pressure from England, began to regard themselves as British, though not necessarily to the exclusion of more localised nationalisms.[37] This dual identity has caused tensions and many from Ireland, Scotland, Wales and even England, whose nationals are most likely to use British interchangeably for their own nomenclature, now prefer to see themselves less as British and more as a member of one of the home countries.[38] In sport such narrower allegiances have generally dominated. Great Britain has rarely featured as a team in international elite sport. The home nations refused to combine to play football in the Olympics; they did so in track and field but athletes were also offered the Empire, (later Commonwealth) Games where separatism was the rule; cricket was played under the banner of the MCC whilst commonly being called England even with players from the Celtic nations. There was, however, a precedent for a combined team in rugby union where a British Isles side has toured the southern hemisphere intermittently from 1888, though not always including players from all four home Unions.[39] There is recent evidence of British-wide loyalties in sport: significantly more home nationals would support a member of another home country against 'foreign' opposition than would not offer such backing.[40] If these contemporary surveys have any historical merit, the gelling of golfers from all over Britain into a British team should not have been a major problem. That said, most captains played safe by selecting the foursomes partnerships from golfers of the same nationality.

From the beginning the Ryder Cup team was labelled as being from Great Britain which excluded non-Ulster Irishmen as the Republic had separated politically in 1922 and its residents were considered as foreign players. But when a combined Irish PGA division was created in the early 1950s players from Eire became eligible for the Cup. The first golfer from the Republic to play in the Cup was Harry Bradshaw who was paired with Ulsterman Fred Daly in an unbeaten partnership in the 1953 tournament. Although born either side of the border, the two were firm friends and had already represented the PGA in a four-man tour to South Africa in the winter of 1950–51.[41] Both men had won the Irish Professional Championship which had always been an all-Ireland affair. From then till 2006 a further 5 Ulstermen and 10 Irish Republicans have played with no hint of any political issues arising.

In most cases of international competition in sport, identification is fragmented within Europe by national affiliations. From 1979, however, golfers had to be brought together and identity constructed above the national level, what Albrecht Sonntag has termed a 'transfer of sympathies on a supranational level'.[42] The concept of a European team was not totally revolutionary. The Ryder Cup innovation had been preceded by the European athletics team at the IAAF World Cup in 1977. However, there are differences between the two, primarily that the athletics team is a 'rest of Europe' team as the leading nation at the European Cup enters the World Cup as an individual country and, if held in Europe, the host nation can also take part with its own team. Additionally the World Cup only takes place every four years and, apart from the relays, is concerned with individual performances whereas the biennial Ryder Cup devotes two of its three days to foursomes and four-ball matches. There does not appear to have been any serious opposition, however, to the idea of a European golf team. If British professionals had any qualms about playing for Europe, they were pragmatic enough to realise that without extending the basis of their team there would be no Ryder Cup to play for. Mainland European golfers, who had no chance to represent their own nations, saw a new opportunity for international golf.

But to what extent was this a European team rather than a collection of British, Irish and continental European players, some of whom resided much of the year outside Europe? In initial European teams there were too few mainland Europeans to cause any problem. By 1983 when five continental Europeans were chosen Jacklin's policy as captain was to disregard the European dimension and exploit national pride by pairing Spaniard with Spaniard and Scot with Scot.[43] Most succeeding captains have followed suit. Mark James, Captain of the European team in 1999, claimed that 'on the tour we regard ourselves as all being European.'[44] Contrast this with the view of) Randy Fox, an American who organised travel for players on the European tour in the early 1990s. He reckoned that there was a significant nationalistic divide:

The Swedes will not go out to dinner – with a few exceptions – with anyone else. They refuse to stay in a room unless it's with another Swede. The Spaniards have never made any attempt to communicate with anyone else. The Italians are the same way .... And even among the British players, the Welsh don't want to room with the Scottish and the Scottish don't want to room with the English.'[45]

Another travel organiser, David Grice, argued that the biggest clique on tour was the Scottish one.[46] Nevertheless Fox accepted that there was no caste system among players on the European tour compared to the American where stars would not mix with the journeymen players; and current American captain Paul Azinger has acknowledged that the Europeans have exhibited more in the way of camaraderie than his own compatriots.[47] Possibly Irishman Paidraig Harrington summed up the Ryder Cup situation when he maintained that what they were really representing was their tour rather than any country or collection of nations.[48] And who could blame him for that? The European tour provided most members of the team with their livelihoods; it had grown from a prize fund of £250,000 when it was formed in 1972 to one of over £73 million by 2004?

Any unity within the team is possibly more anti-American than pro-Europe, perhaps based on golf politics rather than global ones. Although the press at different times may have utilised stereotypes of American arrogance, militant nationalism and lack of etiquette to promote an anti-Americanism in their readership, for the European players the issue may have been more one of resentment. Americans have attempted to dominate the professional game by holding three of the four major tournaments within the United States. There are also objections to the insularity of most American professionals who will not travel the world to play so content are they with the level of prize-money offered within the United States.

The blue European Union flag seems to have been adopted as the banner under which the team plays, possibly as a response to the American Stars and Stripes.[49] Yet it is a flag of convenience rather than one of unity. The official post-match photograph of the victorious European team shows two of the players holding European flags (Spaniard Jose Maria Olazabal and

Englishman Paul Casey) while Irishmen Paul McGinley and Padraig Harrington wore tricolour scarves and Scotsman Colin Montgomerie had a saltire draped over his shoulder. Clearly for the European players unity has not eclipsed more local nationalisms. In this they were merely representing Europe in a different sense. Although a 2005 survey showed that over 60% of Europeans felt 'proud' to be Europeans, it also revealed that they showed greater pride in their individual nations.[50] Hence Europatriotism can be regarded as a weak sentiment that supplements national pride rather than replacing it. The Ryder Cup players exhibit weak political identity but a strong team ethic.

The Ryder Cup has had a limited impact on 'Europeanness'. The fact that political and economic eurosceptics do not seem to denigrate the idea of a European golf team might suggest that it is not really viewed as a symbol of European integration, or, more likely, that sport is too trivial to concern them.[51] As sports journalist Simon Kuper has put it: 'the contest [would be] an ideal candidate for boosting European identity, except for the fact that most Europeans have never heard of it.'[52] Golf is still not a major pan-European sport. Britain has more courses than Germany, Italy, France, Spain, Switzerland and the Nordic countries combined.[53]

The lack of a European fan base has been reflected in the decisions to allocate venues in which continental Europe has scarcely featured. European players began to play on the Ryder Cup team in 1979 but not till 1997 was a non-English or Scottish site selected when the event was hosted by the Valderrama club in Spain. The next home match was back at the Belfry, thus reverting to the status quo. The decisions to hold the Ryder Cup in Ireland (2006), Wales (2010) and Scotland (2014) and at a yet to be determined mainland European course in 2018 owe less to Celtic and European integration and more to the economics of the PGA Tour. Once the Ryder Cup was reignited as a truly competitive event clubs vied to host it and were willing to pay for the privilege. The K Club in Ireland promised a ten-year deal to host the European Open; Celtic Manor in Wales offered a long-term hosting of the Wales Open; and Gleneagles in Scotland agreed to a permanent Johnnie Walker Championship. Even the earlier hosting of the Ryder Cup at Valderrama in 1997 was only partly a belated recognition of the Spanish contribution to the European team; it also necessitated the Spanish PGA and the Valderrama club holding almost forty tournaments for the European Tour and its various satellites.[54]

Conclusion

Selection policies for the Ryder Cup have been subject to complaint and criticism but never legal challenge. As an autonomous, self-governing organisation the PGA (and later the European Tournament Players Association) has the power to make rules and regulations affecting its members, including those dealing with Ryder Cup selection.[55] As 'monopoly' organisations the PGA and ETPA are in a position to insist that membership itself is a requirement for selection. A golf professional need not be a member of the PGA or the European Tour but, unless he is, he cannot play in the Ryder Cup as this is a competition between the two players' associations not between golfers from Britain and the United States. However legal cases in other sports have demonstrated that actual selection decisions can be challenged on several grounds including incorrectly interpreting the rules of selection, not following stated procedures, changing the regulations after they had been announced to obtain an 'acceptable' result, and bias (as distinct from reasonably held opinion) on the part of a selector. As shown above, all of these have occurred at times in the process of choosing the Ryder Cup team. Yet, unlike in other sports, neither the law courts nor even the Court of Arbitration for Sport has seen the process or procedures contested. Golf has not followed where other sports have led the way.

In contrast, where *European* teams are concerned, golf has been the pioneer but other sports have been reluctant to tag along. Indeed, except in golf, the Ryder Cup has not led to further integrated European sports teams. Perhaps this has been because the Ryder Cup itself was in a unique position: it needed European players in order to survive as an international competition. Their introduction ultimately led to boom rather than just survival. Other spin-offs in golf have followed including the Seve Ballesteros Trophy, in which a team from Great Britain and Ireland plays against one from continental Europe, and the Solheim Cup for female professionals from Europe and the

United States. However, other sports have not felt the necessity to follow suit, either because club and national followings are considered satisfactory or there is no obvious opponent at such a supra-national level.

References
1. The authors are grateful to the Leverhulme Trust and the British Academy for financial assistance towards the research costs of this paper.
2. Recent works include Lee McGinnis, Julia McQuillan and Constance L. Chapple, 'I Just Want to Play: Women, Sexism and Persistence in Golf', *Journal of Sport and Social Issues* 29,3 (August 2005), 313–337; David Nyland, 'Taking a Slice at Sexism: The Controversy over Excluding Membership Practices at the Augusta National Golf Club', *Journal of Sport and Social Issues* 27 (May 2003), 195–202; Marnie Haig-Muir, 'Many a Slip 'twixt Cup and the Lip: Equal Opportunity and Victorian Golf Clubs', *Sporting Traditions* 17,1 (November 2000), 19–38; Jane George, Joyce Kay and Wray Vamplew, 'Women to the Fore: Gender Accommodation and Resistance at the British Golf Club Before 1914', *Sporting Traditions* (forthcoming 2007).
3. Ray Physick and Richard Holt, '"Big Money": The Tournament Player and the PGA, 1945–75', *Contemporary British History* 14, 2 (2000), 60–80.
4. Kit Wheeler and John Nauright, 'A Global Perspective on the Environmental Impact of Golf', *Sport in Society* 9,3 (2006), 427–443.
5. Stephen Morrow and Graeme Wheatley, 'The Ryder Cup 2014: Golf's Homecoming?', *Scottish Affairs* 43, (Spring 2003), 108–126.
6. For a bibliography on this see Robert Chappell, 'Race, Gender and Sport in Post-Apartheid South Africa', *Sport Journal* 8,4 (2004) accessed online at www.thesportjournal.org
7. Hilary A. Findlay and Rachel Corbett, 'Principles Underlying the Adjudication of Selection Disputes Preceding the Salt Lake City Winter Olympic Games: Notes for Adjudicators', *Entertainment Law* 1,1 (2002), 109–120; Ross Thompson, 'The Form for Selection', *The Journal: The Journal of the Law Society of Scotland* (March 2006), 45.
8. www.britishorienteering.org.uk; accessed 19 April 2006.
9. Adrian Smith and Dilwyn Porter (eds.), *Sport and National Identity in the Post-War World* (Routledge, London 2004).
10. Albrecht Sonntag, 'Tears, Sweat and … Fun! Self-reflexive Irony as a Feature of European Identity', paper presented at CESH Conference

on Sport and the Construction of Identities, Vienna 2006.
11. Peter Fry, *Samuel Ryder: The Man Behind the Ryder Cup* (Wright: Dorset, 2000), 66–75.
12. Ibid, 95. Mitchell received a three-year contract giving him £500 and £250 in expenses per annum.
13. Ibid, 81.
14. Ibid, 100–101.
15. Ibid, 84–89.
16. Geoffrey Cousins, 'Golf' in John Rivers, *The Sports Book* (Macdonald, London 1948), 85.
17. *Daily Mail,* 22 September 1975.
18. Richard Holt, Peter N. Lewis and Wray Vamplew, *The Professional Golfers' Association 1901–2001* (Grant, Worcestershire, 2002), 148.
19. Physick and Holt, 71.
20. Quoted in Holt, Lewis and Vamplew, 211.
21. Findlay and Corbett, 115.
22. The discussion which follows is based on material in the Minute Books of the PGA held at the Belfry, Sutton Coldfield. The authors are grateful for access.
23. The team was expected to travel to and from America as a group. Cotton asked if he could remain there after the Ryder Cup as he wanted to play some tournaments but permission was refused. Peter Dobereiner, *Maestro: The Life of Henry Cotton* (Hodder & Stoughton, London, 1992), 32.
24. Ibid.
25. *Golf World,* May 1983.
26. *Golf World,* September 1985.
27. PGA Minutes, 12 January 1953.
28. PGA Minutes, 14 July 1975.
29. PGA Minutes, 5 January 1971.
30. Peter Alliss in *Golf World,* December 1981.
31. The only other example of a playing captain having a say in the selection of a national team was in cricket where from 1898 when the establishment of a Board of Control led to a selection committee of three who chose a captain who was then co-opted to the committee itself. In 1938 the committee was increased to four plus the captain who now had the casting vote.(Maurice Golesworthy, *The Encyclopedia of Cricket* (Sportsman's Book Club: London, 1964). However, it should be noted that those were the days when amateur captains, with associated class connotations, were the norm.

32. PGA Minutes, 15 May 1931.
33. Michael Williams, *The Official History of the Ryder Cup 1927–1989* (Stanley Paul, London, 1989),174.
34. Physick and Holt, 64–66.
35. In the late 1980s there was conflict between the PGA and the European Tour over who 'owned' the Ryder Cup. The trophy had been donated in perpetuity to the [British] PGA but now the players who represented Europe were no longer so aligned with the club professional as in the early days of the Cup. A compromise was agreed which distinguished between the PGA as a Founding Partner and the European Tour as the Managing Partner.
36. Wray Vamplew, 'Exploited labour or successful workingmen: golf professionals and professional golfers in Britain before 1914', *Economic History Review* (forthcoming 2007).
37. Linda Colley, *Britons: Forging the Nation 1707–1837* (Vintage, London, 1992); Norman Davies, *The Isles* (Macmillan, Basingstoke, 1999).
38. National Centre for Social Research, *British Social Attitudes* 17th Report (ed. Jowell et al) 2000/01, 156–158; 18th Report (ed. Park et al) 2001/02, 242; The Institute for Public Policy Research, *Who Are We? Identities in Britain* (2007).
39. Historically the team used the title British Isles, adopting the nickname British Lions in 1950, though in 2001 the more politically correct British and Irish Lions was agreed by the Unions involved.
40. National Centre for Social Research 2000/01, 161.
41. www.rydercup2000.ie
42. Sonntag, loc. cit.
43. *Golf World*, October 1983, 44–45.
44. *Scotland on Sunday*, 19 May 2002, p. 11.
45. Lauren St John, *Shooting at Clouds: Inside the European PGA Tour* (Mainstream, Edinburgh, 1991), 51
46. Lauren St John, *Out of Bounds: Inside Professional Golf* (Partridge, London, 1995), 198.
47. *Daily Telegraph*, Sport, 7 Nov 2006 S17.
48. *Financial Times*, 16 September 2006, p.12.
49. This was probably without formal permission as this is unlikely to be granted 'in a commercial context' which is undoubtedly what the Ryder Cup is now involved in.
50. *Financial Times*, 16 September 2006, p.12.
51. Despite the European Year of Sport in 2004 sport does not figure

high in European political discussion and commentary.
52. *Financial Times*, 16 September 2006, p.12.
53. *Financial Times*, 16 September 2006, p.12.
54. David David, 'The Greatest Sporting Contest of Them All', *Sunday Telegraph*, 17 September 2006, S3. See also Morrow and Wheatley.
55. Findlay and Corbett, 109–113.

Child Work or Child Labour? The Caddie Question in Edwardian Golf

What is child labour? We're conditioned to think in a particular way when we hear those words: children weaving Turkish or Persian carpets until they go blind, children making overpriced Nike trainers for a pittance, in short, children all over the Third World being exploited by global corporations for low cost production of consumer goods for the prosperous populations of the Western world. When these images first appeared in Western media in the early 1990s, many were upset and wanted to free the children from the low-wage slavery. But as it turned out, it's more complicated than that. Children have always worked; they have contributed to the provision of their families according to their ability. With increasing prosperity and degree of civilization, the Western world has managed to relieve the children of the need to work and provide them with a safe and secure childhood, as well as education for future security. But in large parts of the world, children still play a vital role in the family economy, and the alternative to work is more likely deteriorating material circumstances rather than orderly and regular school attendance. The more reasonable reactions to the revelations of children at work is found in ILO's convention 182 about eliminating the worst forms of child labour, and in the UN Convention on the Rights of the Child, which explicitly prohibits economic exploitation and "any work that is likely to be hazardous or to interfere with the child's education, or to be harmful to the child's health or physical, mental, spiritual, moral or social development".

What is child labour in sports? Is there such a thing? Well, it's not that easy to find children actually working in contemporary sports, at least not in ways that would represent a breach of the ILO and UN conventions. Wray Vamplew mentions the production of sporting goods, but also the girl gymnasts of the communist bloc and teenage African footballers that are imported to Europe and discarded when failing to meet the competition. Instead he turns to the history of sports, and observes that there were boy jockeys in horseracing and boy caddies in golf around the turn of the nineteenth century. It's the latter form of child labour that is the object of Vamplew's groundbreaking research. He has studied the labour market for caddies in the decades immediately prior to and following the year 1900, and he has found that the vast majority of the British golf club caddies were children, mainly boys between twelve and sixteen years old. Employing contemporary documents as well as secondary sources, such as golf club centennial jubilee books, Vamplew chronicles the situation for the young golf workers in terms of working conditions, remuneration, general welfare and education. His article forms itself into an important piece of social history of times and lives we knew very little about.

Introduction

Child labour in sport is often regarded as a relatively modern phenomenon, usually with exploitative implications, involving third-world workers producing sporting goods, the abused bodies of communist bloc girl gymnasts, and teenage African footballers discarded when they failed to make the grade in Europe.[2] Although historical examples are generally absent from the academic literature, there are late nineteenth and early twentieth-century instances in Britain in the use of boy jockeys in horseracing and, the subject of this chapter, the child caddie in golf.[3] For the purposes of this chapter children are considered to be young persons under the age of sixteen, the line generally taken by golf clubs. Hence the discussion of child caddies is not confined to those still at school but also includes school leavers, many of whom could be as young as twelve.[4]

The perceived problems of such caddies were part of a wider issue in Britain. At the turn of the twentieth century there was concern that a growing demand for child labour in occupations such as errand boys, machine minders and industrial packers was creating a pool of young workers, trained for nothing else and destined to swell the ranks of casual labourers as they became older and lost their jobs to younger and cheaper boys who in turn faced the same fate.[5] The list of jobs put forward by commentators as part of the 'boy labour' issue did not include the golf caddie, yet within golf the situation of the boy caddie had became recognised. In 1909 Garden Smith, editor of Golf Illustrated, estimated that there were 20,000 boys so employed. He believed that the mass of these boy caddies were living a 'casual, irresponsible and purposeless life'.[6] Three years later the Agenda Club – 'an organisation of men in all parts of the country who realise that "all is not well with England"'[7] – actually undertook a survey on the caddie question which emphasised the blind alley' nature of the job.[8]

Modern observers distinguish between 'child work' and 'child labour'. The former is regarded as normal social practice and is often seen as making a positive contribution to children's development by having them take responsibility and gain a pride in their activities.[9] Generally, however, such work refers to time-limited, small tasks around the home or family business. In contrast child labour, often coercive, is considered harmful or hazardous with children 'being exploited, or overworked, or deprived of their rights to health and education'.[10] Although examining a historical rather than a contemporary labour market, this chapter will draw on these concepts and assess where boy caddies were situated on the spectrum between work and labour.

The Caddie Labour Market

The actual number of caddies is difficult to determine. Garden Smith reckoned on at least 20,000 in 1909 while the Caddies Aid Association, set up by a group of golf club secretaries in 1911, estimated that 12,000 were 'employed regularly'.[11] Surprisingly the Agenda Club made no aggregate estimate but noted that 29 London clubs retained the service of 827 caddies in the summer months.[12] Admittedly these were among the larger clubs in Britain, but, in 1914 there were over 2,800 other clubs so, even though not all clubs had courses of their own, the number of caddies may have been higher than Garden Smith's estimate.[13]

Whatever figure is taken there is no doubt that caddying was a niche child labour market that expanded significantly in the four decades before 1914. At many golf clubs playing without a caddy was socially unacceptable, even when not specifically regulated against. Before the invention of the golf bag in the 1890s[14] it was impractical, but generally there was the implication that the manual labour associated with a round of golf should be done by someone other than the player. Others felt that 'golf was a very difficult science which required extreme mental concentration and the labour of being one's own caddie was an objectionable and serious distraction'.[15]

The majority of caddies were boys or young men with a leavening of adults and, at weekends, a staple of schoolboys to meet the peak demand.[16] Most caddies were labelled second-class whose duties essentially were to carry clubs, make sand tees, replace divots, and clean clubs after the round. Below them were the forecaddies, a hangover from the era when balls were expensive and terrain was hilly and rough. These were boys sent ahead with a flag to indicate when the fairway was clear and where balls had landed: both duties became of reduced importance as courses began to be laid out without hills as natural obstacles and balls became mass-produced with their loss less of a financial cost. Above them were the more experienced first-class caddies, who knew the intricacies of the local course. They did much the same as their second-class counterparts but also offered counsel to their employer of the day.

The rise in demand was in specific local labour markets, often in areas where there had been no club before, and there is no evidence that the caddie fee was driven up. The new clubs tapped fresh supplies from a reserve army of boy labour rather than competing against existing clubs in a limited market, so that generally clubs experienced 'no difficulty in keeping up the supply of regular caddies'.[17] Nevertheless, although some descriptions portray a horde of youngsters clamouring for work, the situation was probably not one of an oversupply of labour.[18] Pairs, trios and quartets of golfers setting out at regular intervals over a 18 hole course demanded a large supply of bag carriers. This appears to be reflected in the pay rates, rates set by the club, not the golfer or the caddie. At large clubs it was possible for caddies to earn 15 shillings a week though 10 shillings (exclusive of Sunday work) was more normal. Tips and food allowances could raise this by three shillings.[19] Such earnings provided a much needed injection of money into many local households.

Welfare Issues

Caddies were relatively well paid for what they did. A school leaver in Dorset could earn almost as much as his agricultural labouring father for significantly less effort and time.[20] However, critics considered such earnings demoralising as they encouraged youths to have false expectations of future income whilst at the same time the nature of caddying, with few transferable skills, offered little gateway to other gainful skilled employment. For some, albeit a minority, there was a future in golf. Of the 19 leading British professional golfers between 1890 and 1914, at least 13 began their golfing careers as caddies.[21] Golfing folklore also suggests that many, if not most, club professionals were also introduced to the sport in this way. There is sufficient logic in this view to render it more than an invented tradition. They could absorb the skills of the game by watching practitioners; they were often given old clubs by their employers; and there was the possibility of patronage from members impressed by their ability in the caddie competitions organised by some clubs. Nevertheless, even under the most optimistic estimations, less than two per cent of caddies became club professionals. Others might secure apprenticeships as club-makers or, as at Mid-Surrey where the best caddies were also employed as greenmen, they might progress to green-keeping posts elsewhere.[22] For most, however, caddying proved to be a dead end job. Once given notice by the clubs at age 16, as was often the practice especially after the coming of compulsory national insurance in 1912 for over 15s, they drifted into the ranks of unskilled labour or the unemployed.[23]

The work itself was not arduous but it had to be undertaken in whatever weather golfers opted to play in and their costume may have been more suited to the elements than that of the caddies. Some clubs provided a shelter for caddies to wait in prior to beginning a round, but out on the course there was no protection from the wind or rain. Garden Smith argued that 'round London … the average caddy is quite insufficiently clad and shod to stand the cold and wet of our metropolitan courses in winter'.[24] On wet days at Aldeburgh caddies were loaned capes, though this was designed to keep the clubs dry as well as those carrying them.[25]

The survey carried out by the Agenda Club demonstrated that most clubs provided little in the way of comfortable shelter. Indeed shelters for caddies when supplied often had no form of heating, sanitation and were in the words of Owen Seaman, chair of the Agenda Club committee of enquiry, 'little better than a cattle shed'.[26] Even shelters could have an ulterior motive as at Cathkin Braes where one was erected in 1911 to stop the caddies hanging round the veranda of the clubhouse.[27]

There was also a major moral issue. Whereas the boy labour issue was a work problem, the boy caddie issue was one of leisure. The caddie operated in a casual labour market where the demand for his services was dependent on the number of players on a particular day. Hence bad weather, transport disruptions and the change in seasons meant that there was no guarantee of employment.[28] Moreover, golfers tee off at intervals, so potential caddies could wait around for a while before picking up a bag. The Agenda Club estimated that up to two-thirds of their time at a club could be spent not involved in caddying activities leading to a situation where 'the regular caddie .... has about five hours' leisure five days a week, but nothing to do to fill them except idling or gambling'.[29] The adult caddies, with whom the boys spent waiting time, were not seen as a leavening influence. J Stuart Paton, secretary at Woking, believed 'the man loafer is unfortunately the standard type at so many clubs'; H.S. Colt, secretary at Sunningdale, concurred that 'the vast majority of men who act as caddies are inclined to belong to the loafing class'.[30]

Some members may have felt that working on a Sunday was also a moral issue. Indeed the whole debate on playing golf on the Sabbath exercised golf clubs throughout the late Victorian and Edwardian period. Although gradually the prohibitions were withdrawn, many clubs hedged their first ventures in Sunday play with a proscription on the employment of paid caddies, either absolutely or under certain ages, 18 was suggested at Copthorne.[31]

Solutions?

At the micro level, individual clubs attempted to ameliorate the situation of their caddies via benevolent patronage, discipline, inculcating the habit of thrift and encouraging them to obtain education or training.

An annual treat was not uncommon. The West Lancashire Club put on a 'Caddies' Supper' in 1909, with hot pot, bun loaf and entertainment for 140 caddies, while in the same year Hesketh Golf Club entertained 70 caddies in a similar fashion.[32] A few clubs built club houses for the caddies. At Mid-Surrey the caddie-master himself set one up in 1900, originally on a very small scale and housed at the caddies' own expense. Eight years later the Mid-Surrey members replaced it with a large clubhouse costing £600. It opened all day and three nights a week with books and games provided, food available at a coffee bar, the occasional concert and, less popular, the odd lecture. Unusually this was managed by a committee of caddies.[33] Thrift clubs were rarer. Sunning Park organised a penny bank under the Post Office Savings Bank (but only found eight depositors) and at Sheringham and Fulwell caddies were 'allowed' to bank a penny from the fee of each round.[34]

Disciplining young caddies was regarded as a way of increasing moral fibre. Most, if not all, clubs appointed a caddie master – sometimes yet another role for the professional – to organise and regulate the use of caddies by taking bookings from members and allocating caddies to players. This served to control the mass of casual labour seeking work but also allowed the clubs to ensure that the caddies did their job correctly, both in terms of due diligence and due respect. Fines were levied for bad behaviour and for losing balls. At some clubs the money was collected and given as prizes in caddie golf competitions, as Christmas boxes or to those junior caddies who had the best school attendance. Some clubs insisted that caddies worked on the course or undertook gardening around the club house to fill in their waiting time, for which at Woking and Pyecombe they received an additional small payment.[35] This inculcated habits of discipline and industry and, as the club secretary acknowledged, the club benefited from this cheap on-course labour.[36] Bramall Park was not untypical in warning caddies that they risked downgrading or suspension if they broke the working rules. The ultimate sanction was dismissal which could occur as at Axe Cliff for 'continued bad and obscene language'.[37] Caddies at the Stirling Golf Club were unusual in that they had to seek an annual licence from the local magistrates but were not untypical in being required to be 'decently clothed and strictly sober' and to conduct themselves 'at all times in a proper, civil, and decorous manner'.[38] If they misbehaved at the course or appeared in court for any offences, they could forfeit their licence; elsewhere summary dismissal was always an option.

Education and training were seen in some quarters as the way forward for the caddie. Sunningdale, with the indefatigable H.S. Colt at the helm, developed a two-pronged strategy. First they organised their own evening classes, initially in carpentry and clubmaking, but later, in conjunction with the local authority who had responsibility for the provision of public education in the county, also in 'rural science' which covered the basics of horticulture. The boys had to attend for a couple of hours at least twice a week for 20 weeks in the winter months. Attendance was aided by the inducement of a 'good tea'. Secondly, via a register of caddy interests, they encouraged members to find employment for the boys in jobs such as gardening, stable work and even driving.[39] Princes (Mitcham) was one of the first to insist that its caddies received some form of education and from 1890 it required them to attend evening school at least two nights a week. Several other clubs either encouraged or made such attendance compulsory.[40] At Purley Downs when caddies became 14, they had to select a trade and attend relevant evening classes three times a week from September to April (thereafter they were too busy caddying on the lighter nights). This was financed by a levy of a penny a round on members.[41] Education authorities in Eastbourne, Croydon and Folkstone among others made arrangements with local golf clubs.[42] Certainly in latter case boys were also expected to contribute financially. Some classes were those open to the general public; more useful were those specially planned for the caddies of a particular club. One problem was that many opted to be trained in club-making, thus leading to an oversupply of labour in what was, thanks to increasing mechanisation, a declining sector of employment.[43]

An exemplar among clubs was Royal Birkdale which set up an advanced welfare scheme for caddies in 1908 with the aim of providing material and spiritual welfare for the boys and to find employment for them where possible. The Birkdale Club Caddie Boys' Association did not allow the boys to gamble or smoke in the clubhouse, but the building did include a games' room, a gymnasium and facilities for the boys to have a bath. The club was also given clothes, games and books by Birkdale members, and the boys had singing and bootmaking lessons. The boys paid a penny per week and could have a bath for a further penny. The club leased premises for the scheme, employing the caddie-master as resident caretaker as it 'secured more control over the boys'.[44]

Caddies at Sunningdale, Birkdale and the like were fortunate as these clubs were rich with large memberships. At Sunningdale the members raised £1000 to provide a building for the evening classes and a recreational room for the caddies.[45] Moreover, they had energetic individuals such as H.S. Colt who were prepared to devote themselves to the cause of caddie improvement. Other clubs might have similarly zealous secretaries but their resources were limited and much less could be offered to the caddies. Some found their effectiveness diminished by being tolerated by the general committee of the club rather than actively supported.[46]

At the macro level, the first documented instance of collective concern for caddies, as distinct from that by particular clubs or individuals, came when an article about forming a caddies association appeared in The Times in 1906. The initiative appears to have come from Sherard Cowper-Coles, the inventor of a process to coat the heads of clubs, who had received a large number of letters from golf club secretaries. Each registered caddie was to pay an annual subscription of 2s 6d (about a quarter of a normal week's wages); help would be given to deserving cases and, where possible, employment found for those abandoning caddying. The executive committee was to consist of six or more secretaries of golf clubs: it is important to note that golf clubs were attempting to regulate the caddies, not help caddies organise themselves.

This organisation did not get off the ground, but eventually the Caddies Aid Society (CAS) was formed in the summer of 1911 and was supported by the Agenda Club which gave it free use of office space.[47] Among the patrons were politicians Bonar Law and Balfour, both avid golfers. The originator was Mark Allerton, editor of the World of Golf, and the driving force came from the secretaries of Sunningdale, Walton Heath and Mid Surrey, all of whom had already made their own attempts to ameliorate the problem.[48] Early meetings included representatives from the

Central Bureau of the Labour Exchange, the Board of Trade and the Apprenticeships and Skilled Labour Association. No caddies were invited to speak: indeed it is not apparent that caddies ever attended the meetings.

The Caddies Aid Committee (CAC), a joint offspring of the CAS and the Agenda Club, set up regional committees to produce reports on working conditions, post-caddying prospects, and ways of improving both.[49] Meetings discussed best practice and members suggested petitions to the Development Fund of the Board of Agriculture and the establishment of 'Care Committees' at each golf club.[50] All to little avail. Although by 1913 it was claimed that 25 'well-known' clubs had adopted schemes in the interests of caddies as recommended by the CAC, this was not a high proportion of all clubs and not even half of the limited number 60 [of 560 who had been appealed to] that had subscribed five shillings towards the publication debts of the Committee.[51]

Government Legislation

An aggravating factor in the caddy labour market was the introduction of compulsory national insurance in 1912 as part of the Liberal Government's social welfare policy. All workers aged 16 or over and their employers had to make contributions to funds which were to provide unemployment and medical benefits. Legally the clubs, not individual players, were the employers of caddies, and thus all liabilities and responsibilities in connection with the Act devolved upon them. Clubs responded by either adding a penny per round to the usual booking fee or not employing caddies once they reached the age of 16 and became subject to the legislation. Both the Atherstone and Northumberland clubs decided not to issue badges to caddies over 16 and Royal Eastbourne discharged all its caddies above 16.[52] At Cathkin Braes such a decision led to the unintended consequence of increased truancy from schoolboy caddies and an angry rebuke from the School Board.[53]

The last three decades of the nineteenth century were a period in which childhood was progressively lengthened as compulsory full-time schooling, introduced in 1870, replaced wage-earning as the accepted activity for many children.[54] The age to which a child had to attend school had been first set at 10, raised to 11 in

1893 and to 12 in 1899 though the latter was disregarded in many rural areas as recalcitrant employers and needy parents conspired to thwart enforcement.⁵⁵ The demand for boy bag carriers by members of golf clubs was 'a great temptation to poor parents' looking to supplement the family income;⁵⁶ so much so that in 1902 Chief Inspector Willis of the school inspectorate reported on 'children of nine, eight and even seven years old having been employed to drag clubs round the links'.⁵⁷ Eventually, however, particularly following the 1902 Education Act, school boards increasingly intervened and clubs had to employ boy caddies outside school hours; some clubs opted only to employ school children at weekends and school holidays.⁵⁸ Yet the prohibition was far from absolute. Even though their head teachers were golf enthusiasts, Gullane and Dirleton schools in East Lothian were probably not unusual in either allowing students leave to carry bags at the local club or simply closing the school at times of major competitions. However, this ceased in 1910 after visits from the school attendance officer.⁵⁹ Nevertheless, in the immediate pre-war years about half the children in elementary schools left between the ages of 12 and 14.⁶⁰ Those near a golf club did not have to look far for immediate employment. Almost 4% of all boys leaving elementary schools in Southport became golf caddies and at Churchtown School, close to Hesketh Golf Club, the figure was 28% of the 25 leavers.⁶¹

Gender

The extent of female involvement is unknown but was probably insignificant relative to males. Women as cooks or cleaners raised no issues at golf clubs, not so females carrying golf bags for members. Some clubs, such as Reigate Heath in 1902, specifically banned their employment.⁶² Others operated an unwritten discriminatory policy. Yet there were exceptions. The first mention of regular girl caddies seems to have been at Guernsey in 1890, though one golf historian claims that girls replaced striking male caddies for six weeks at Gullane in Scotland around 1870. From about 1890 too, four years after the club was founded, Lytham and St Annes employed girls, though they had to be over 14 and could carry only for lady members. By 1897, however, they could caddy for men and at the Autumn meeting that year girl caddies outnumbered boys.⁶³ Girls were also caddying at

Newquay in 1901 and at Huntercombe in Oxfordshire and several Yorkshire courses prior to the First World War. Nevertheless they were uncommon enough for comments to be made in Golf Illustrated about the fashion for girl caddies at some continental clubs.[64] Moreover, girl cadddies were not mentioned in the Agenda Club report. Possibly carrying a bag of clubs around the course was seen as being too heavy work for girls, but many members of clubs had no hesitation in employing young children for hard domestic work in their households. It might be that girls were supposed to do work indoors or around the house not in the fields or elsewhere outside. Possibly too it had something to do with the perceived disreputable nature of those who caddied, particularly adult males, and a desire to keep females protected from their influence.[65]

Conclusion

Unlike today, where social concern over child employment is a matter both of protecting children and also of acknowledging their rights, in Edwardian Britain the emphasis was on protection. However, child welfare in golf remained a voluntary rather than a legislative commitment, dependent on the individual club. Thus provision was sporadic and certainly not comprehensive. Some individual clubs took action to ameliorate the position of their caddies, hoping to avoid short-term idleness and longer-term unemployment. The boy's club was a success at Mid-Surrey; the value of discipline in obtaining later employment was proved at Woking; the provision of land on the course for the boys to grow and sell produce worked at Hanger Hill; evening classes were attended even when not compulsory at Sunningdale; the boys' spare time was used in a workshop at Fulwell; and the boys benefited from a clothing club at Birkdale. The problem was not only to persuade others to emulate these pioneers but for all clubs to develop the strands into a remedial package. As the Agenda Club enquiry put it: 'the parts having been successfully demonstrated, the whole should not be an impossibility'.[66] Unfortunately that proved to be the case.

Appeals to clubs and their members to act on the caddie issue were made by calling on their 'sense of duty' towards the boys and towards the nation and Empire, but these did not stir many to action.[67] Even in the progressive clubs it was a minority of members who voluntarily gave financial aid and an even smaller number who actually did anything practical.[68] Perhaps many members felt their social conscience had been salved by the tips they gave the boys, amounts 'often excessive and out of all proportion to the work done to obtain them'.[69]

Two caveats should be made. First, no attention seems to have been given to girl caddies, either because of their relative insignificance or because, unlike some of the boys, they had no future in golf. Second, there is the question of geography. A distinction may have to be made between 'those clubs near great centres of population' and those in the provinces where there was a dominant local industry such as in mining or seafaring areas where caddying was a stop gap until proper age and strength had been attained. Elsewhere, Garden Smith also accepted that in rural areas 'caddying offers a start in life to a poor lad'.[70] Whatever their gender or location, all caddies lacked power in the master-servant relationship of golf club employment, but additionally child caddies also experienced the impotence of the age relationship. Others, always older people, made decisions for them.

Clearly the child caddie suffered if the Convention on the Rights of the Child drafted by the United Nations in 1989 is applied retrospectively. There was no way in which the golf clubs or members followed the principle that the best interests of the child should be of primary concern.[71] Yet by contemporary standards caddies were not exploited economically. Although they were often competing with adults in the caddie labour market, pay differentials and job opportunities generally reflected knowledge and experience, not age. The introduction of National Insurance actually led to positive discrimination in favour of younger caddies but the increased enforcement of education legislation limited its impact on those still at school. Annual earnings were more than in most 'blind alley' jobs and the amount of time actually spent working much less. For boys the earnings were good but there was concern that this gave them a false view of life and led many not to prepare for the years after caddying. Non-wage rewards were less generous with generally inadequate provision of food, shelter and sanitary arrangements. Some commentators saw possible health and moral problems in that the boys were often hanging round the club in all weathers waiting for employment, but, worse than this, was it might be done in the company of adult males who, except at long-established clubs, were regarded as men of dubious character. 'Loafing habits' could be acquired while waiting for employment 'under insufficient supervision and in an uncivilised environment.'[72]

If Edwardian caddying is assessed using the International Labour Organisation's seven major characteristics of child labour, on virtually no count can it be classed as child labour in the pejorative sense.[73] They were certainly not working for very little pay nor working excessively long hours. Despite the temperament of some golfers and the severe strictures of some caddie-masters, generally the caddy could not be categorised as either working under physical, social or psychological strain or being subject to intimidation. Nor did the job lack stimulation (except possibly at times when waiting for a bag) or carry too much responsibility. Although the conditions out on the course could be climatically uncomfortable, even unhealthy at times, they were not working on the streets in generally unwholesome and dangerous conditions. Whether they were working too young is a subjective judgement, though ultimately school-age children were restricted in their hours and days of employment. Hence caddying in Edwardian Britain seems much closer to child work than to child labour. Perhaps an appropriate way to regard child caddying is to utilise Hedenborg's dichotomy between work activities that are socialising and those that are instrumental.[74] The goal of the former is to educate the child in some way: for some caddies this occurred in that they acquired golf-specific skills which helped them progress to become clubmakers or club professionals. For the majority of caddies, however, their work clearly sat in the instrumental category being *undertaken out of an economic need to enhance the family income.*

References

Adams, J. (1984) *Huntercombe Golf Club 1900–1983*, Henley-on-Thames, Higgs.

Agenda Club (1912) *The Rough or the Fairway: An Enquiry by the Agenda Club into the Problem of the Golf Caddie*, London: Heinemann.

Clark, Tim (1991) *Copthorne Golf Club Centenary 1892–1992*, Copthorne: The Club.

Cox, Michael (ed.) (1996) *Golfing Times Past to Present in Gullane and Dirleton*, Gullane: Gullane and Dirleton History Society.

Crampsey, Robert A. (1988) *The History of Cathkin Braes Golf Club 1888–1988*, Glasgow: The Club.

Darby, Paul (2000) 'The New Scramble for Africa: African Football Labour Migration to Europe', *European Sports History Review* 3, 217–244.

David, Paulo (2005) *Human Rights in Youth Sport*, London: Routledge.

Davies, John V. (1991) *Wallasey Golf Club 1891–1991*, Droitwich: Grant.

Donnelly, Peter M. & Petherick LeAnne (2004), 'Workers' Playtime? Child Labour at the Extremes of the Sporting Spectrum', *Sport in Society* 7.3, 301–321.

Foster, Harry (1996) *Links Along the Line: The Story of the Development of Golf between Liverpool and Southport*, Stroud: Sutton.

Hedenborg, Susanna (2007) 'Stable Chores: When Leisure Becomes Work' in Engwell, Kristina & Söderlind, Ingrid (eds.), *Children's Work in Everyday Life*, Stockholm: Institute for Futures Studies, 101–116.

Hendricks, Harry (1997) *Children, Childhood and English Society 1880–1990*, Cambridge: Cambridge University Press.

Hong, Fan (2004) 'Innocence Lost: Child Athletes in China', *Sport in Society* 7.3, 338–354.

Hopkins, Eric (1994) *Childhood Transformed: Working-Class Children in Nineteenth Century England*, Manchester: Manchester University Press.

Horn, Pamela (1978) *Education in Rural England 1800–1914*, London: Gill & Macmillan.

Hurt, J.S. (1979) *Elementary Schooling and the Working Classes 1860–1918*, London: Routledge & Kegan Paul.

Hutchinson, Horace G. (1892) *Golf*, London: Longmans Green.

International Labour Organisation (1992) *World Labour Report*, Geneva: ILO.

Johnson, A.J.D. (1988) *The History of Royal Birkdale Golf Club*, Stroud: Sutton.

Knowles, Freddie & Tait, Graham (1994) *The Bramall Park Golf Club Centenary 1894–1994*, Bramhall: The Club.

Lowerson, John (1984) 'Sport and the Victorian Sunday: The Beginnings of Middle-Class Apostasy', *British Journal for Sports History* 1.2, 202–220.

Mackenzie, Richard (1997) *A Wee Nip at the 19th Hole*, London: CollinsWillow.

Nickson, E. Anthony (1986) *The Lytham Century*, Lytham, Author.

O.F.T. (1982) *Aldeburgh Golf Club: The First Hundred Years 1884–1984*, Ipswich: The Club.

Pars Minima (1910) *An Open Letter to English Gentlemen: With a Note on the Agenda Club*, London: Williams & Norgate.

Rose, Lionel (1991) *The Erosion of Childhood: Child Oppression in Britain 1860–1918*, London: Routledge.

Sheldon, C (1982) *Reigate Heath and its Golf Club*, London: Straker.

Smith, Garen G., 'The Caddie question', *Golf Illustrated*, 23 july 1909, 125.

Stirk, David (1989) *'Carry Your Bag, Sir?'*, London: Witherby.

Tawney, R.H. (1909) 'The Economics of Boy Labour', *Economic Journal*, 517–537.

Thomas, Jack (1993) *Axe Hill Golf Club 1894–1994*, Seaton: The Club.

Vamplew, Wray (2008) 'Exploited labour or successful workingmen: golf professionals and professional golfers in Britain before 1914', *Economic History Review*, 54–79

Vamplew, Wray & Kay, Joyce (2005) *Encyclopedia of British Horseracing*, Abingdon: Routledge.

Walvin, James (1982) *A Child's World: A Social History of English Childhood 1800–1914*, London: Penguin.

Notes

1. This chapter stems from an on-going research project looking at the development of the golf club as a British social institution, one aspect of which is the labour and community relations of the clubs. The author is grateful to the Leverhulme and Carnegie Trusts for grant aid and to Jane George and Orla Gilmore for research assistance.

2. Donnelly & Petherick (2004), Hong (2004) and Darby (2000).

3. There is little significant historical literature on the caddie. Of the two books available, Mackenzie (1997) deals specifically with the caddies of St Andrews and Stirk (1989) with caddies more generally, but neither are serious scholarship. More useful are the histories of individual golf clubs which often refer to caddie conditions and earnings drawing on material from the club archives. A major source is a report by the Agenda Club (1912) which, although focusing on London clubs, has national relevance. On child jockeys see Vamplew & Kay (2005), 74.

4. See section below on government legislation.

5. Tawney (1909), 517–537, Hopkins (1994), 225–6; Rose (1991), 101; Walvin (1982), 69–70.

6. Smith (1909), 125.

7. *The Helper*, 6.4, April 1912, 49.
8. Those undertaking the survey opted 'to make personal and thorough investigation into 29 of the 56 'London clubs of importance' with additional references to 'provincial clubs' in England though information on these was 'insufficient to present an equally exhaustive survey of conditions in other parts of the country.' Agenda Club (1912), 19–21.
9. International Labour Organisation (1992), 14; Donnelly & Petherick (2004), 302–303; Hedenborg (2007), 107.
10. International Labour Organisation (1992), 14.
11. *Times*, 12 November 1912, 16.
12. Agenda Club (1912), 28.
13. Peter Lewis, Director of the British Golf Museum, has estimated the number of golf clubs in existence at 161 in 1885, 959 in 1895, 1939 in 1905 and 2844 in 1914. Cited in Vamplew (2008).
14. Mackenzie (1997), 64.
15. *Times*, 12 November 1912, 16.
16. Agenda Club (1912), 4–5.
17. Agenda Club (1912), 27.
18. Hutchinson, (1892), 304.
19. *Golf Illustrated*, 6 August 1909, 173; 13 August 1909, 197; Agenda Club (1912), 7.
20. *Times*, 27 July 1909, 19.
21. Vamplew (2008).
22. *Golf Illustrated*, 4 February 1910, 133.
23. *Times*, 17 March 1909. See also the section below on government legislation.
24. *Golf Illustrated*, 4 March 1910, 213.
25. O.F.T. (1982), 17.
26. *Times*, 12 November 1912, 16.
27. Crampsey (1988), 28.
28. Calculations based on three London clubs in 1910–11 show an average of 34.0% of rounds were played midweek, 29.9% on Saturdays and 36.1% on Sundays. Winter rounds accounted for around 20% of all rounds through the four seasons. Data from Agenda Club (1912), 22–23.
29. Agenda Club (1912), 129.
30. *Golf Illustrated*, 4 March 1910, 213; 30 July 1909, 149.
31. Lowerson (1984); Clark (1991), 13.
32. *Golf Illustrated*, 11 February 1910, 159.

33. Agenda Club (1912), 66, 106.
34. Agenda Club (1912), 68–69.
35. *Times*, 12 November 1912, 16; 30 December 1908, 17.
36. *Golf Illustrated*, 4 March 1910, 213.
37. Knowles & Tait (1994), 72; Thomas (1993), 9.
38. *Minutes of Magistrates of Royal Burgh of Stirling*, 29 December 1909, minute 321, Stirling Council Archives. I am grateful to Miss M Noble for this reference.
39. *Golf Illustrated*, 20 August 1909, 221; *Times*, 27 July 1909, 19.
40. Agenda Club (1912), 70–80.
41. *Golf Illustrated*, 30 April 1909, 184.
42. *Times*, 15 September 1909, 20; 18 December 1909, 7; 20 July 1910, 22; *Golf Illustrated*, 12 November 1909, 175.
43. *Golf Illustrated*, 4 February 1910, 133.
44. Agenda Club (1912), 119; Johnson (1988), 22–25.
45. *Times*, 16 December 1909, 6.
46. *Times*, 4 February 1914, 13.
47. *Golf Illustrated*, 21 March 1913, 17.
48. *Times*, 20 May 1911, 15.
49. *Times*, 4 February 1914, 13; 17 November 1911, 15; 28 November 1911, 11.
50. *Times*, 17 November 1911, 15; 28 November 1911, 11.
51. *Times*, 18 March 1913, 13; 9 December 1913, 15. *Golf Illustrated*, 21 March 1913, 17.
52. *Times*, 4 July 1912, 15; *Minutes of Atherstone Golf Club*, June 1912.
53. Crampsey (1988), 28.
54. Hendrick (1997), 63; Hopkins (1994), 231.
55. Hurt (1979), 188, 201; Horn (1978), 266.
56. *Golf Illustrated*, 23 July 1909, 125.
57. *General Reports of H.M. Inspectors of Elementary Schools for the Year 1902*, 106. Cited in Horn (1978), 268.
58. Davies (1991), 122.
59. Cox (1996), 13–15.
60. Hurt (1979), 188.
61. Foster (1996), 107
62. Sheldon (1982), 43.
63. Nickson (1986), 97–99.
64. Stirk, (1989), 112–113, 115; Adams (1984),19; *Golf Illustrated*, 25 July, 4 July, 24 October 1913; 13 March, 31 July 1914.
65. Agenda Club (1912), 9.

66. Agenda Club (1912), 144–145.
67. *Times*, 27 July 1909, 19; 12 November 1912, 16; Agenda Club (1912), 68, 89, 118; Pars Minima (1910), 21.
68. Agenda Club (1912),16.
69. Agenda club (1912), 9.
70. Agenda Club (1912), 38; *Golf Illustrated*, 27 August 1909, 245.
71. David (2005), 26–27.
72. Agenda Club (1912), 33.
73. ILO (1992), 14.
74. Hedenborg (2007), 107–108.

Facts and Artefacts: Sports Historians and Sports Museums[1]

1

Museums are containers of things. T. S. Eliot noted 50 years ago that "even the humblest material artefact, which is the product and symbol of a particular civilisation, is an emissary of the culture out of which it comes."[2] So it is with sports museums whose collections, if properly utilized, can tell us much about a nation's sporting culture and the social, economic, and political milieu in which it developed. Yet, generally speaking, sports historians have not made use of this potential resource. They visit as fans, but only a few enliven their teaching and enlighten their students by encouraging them to examine sporting artefacts and/or attend exhibitions. Fewer still conduct research in sports museums beyond the archive and library. Why have sport historians been so reluctant to analyze and interpret those remnants of the sporting heritage as preserved by museums curators?

We might commence our exploration of this by first considering the nature of the sports museum. There are, indeed, several types.[3] One possible set of classifications can be based on a combination of geography and collection policy. Few sports museums can claim to be truly international, though with its overarching mission "to make visitors aware of the breadth and the importance of the Olympic Movement," certainly the Olympic Museum in Lausanne, Switzerland, aspires to such lofty goals.[4] The proposed Scottish National Football Museum at Hampden Park in Glasgow intends to be international in scope but may have to concern itself with domestic priorities in the beginning.

By far the most popular sport museums are those that represent a nation's sporting development, the history of a club, or, more common still, those that consider a single sport. Two of the oldest museums that represent a nation's sporting development are in Prague and Helsinki, Finland, more recently museums have been developed in Paris and Basel. The Singapore Sports Council's museum, initiated by Desmond Don in the early 1980s, offers an introduction to the development of colonial sport in this part of the former British Empire,[5] and the Australian Gallery of Sport in Melbourne has a particular focus on Australia and the Olympics. Inevitably more numerous are the national museums devoted to a particular sport. The United Kingdom alone has institutions for rugby, rowing, horse-racing, golf, and tennis, with at least three for football. In Italy, despite a late start into sports museums, there are now three contenders vying to establish a major cycling museum.[6] However, the real leader in this field is the United States with its penchant for national halls of fame for every sport imaginable.

Although less popular and less visible, club museums exist partly because of a pride in the club's achievements and history. But more recently, club museums, especially in the case of the major professional organizations, have begun because of a growing commercial awareness that fans are prepared to pay homage to their heroes. In Britain, Manchester United's museum at Old Trafford attracts around 150,000 paying customers a year.[7] Most of the leading European soccer clubs have their own museums, but many of them function more as visitor centers, serving the public relations needs of the clubs, than as sports museums proper. The one-off exhibitions are displays by museums and galleries not normally associated with sport. At the elite level the British Museum took advantage of the Barcelona Olympics to look at sport in Ancient Greece; the Tate Gallery had an exhibition of early sporting paintings; and the Victoria and Albert Museum held a display of sporting trophies, although it had to close early because of a lack of interest. In Washington, D.C., the Holocaust Memorial Museum has developed an exhibition on the Nazi Olympics.

Museums around the world that are concerned with occupational history, ethnicity, or other specialities have held the occasional sports-related exhibition, such as the "Work

Hard, Play Hard" at Britain's National Coalmining Museum, which celebrated the age-old link between sport and mining communities. These have not been without their problems. Richard Cox, sports bibliographer par excellence, has postulated that some of the best collections of sports books are to be found within the massive general collections of major libraries.[8] Yet curiously most non-sports museums appear to have very few sporting artefacts on their accessions register, and even those are rarely documented in detail.[9]

Several local authority museums in Britain have used sporting exhibitions "to try and improve local community involvement in their museum,"[12] thus acknowledging that sport was part, often an important one, of life in the area. Local museums, such as the Museum of Liverpool Life and the Bourne Hall local authority museum dealing with the Epsom locality inevitably have had to integrate sport with local history because they are near the sites of the Grand National and Derby horseraces.[10] Other museums, however, have exploited an interest in sport specifically to attract visitors. In England the Old Grammar School Museum in Hull held a display of the history and significance of sport in Hull and Humberside; the Woodhorn Colliery Museum exploited the fame of nearby Ashington hero, "Jackie" Milburn, to examine the role of football in the region; and the Derby Museum's "Rams in Focus" had the dual objective of presenting the "local football scene, past and present" and "attracting a wide audience to the museum."[11] Local sports history can, however, have more than local relevance for, as sports historians develop their hypotheses about a nation's sports, the local level is surely the place to test their universality. And what could be more local than the club which, from the participant's point of view, is far more significant than elite level sport? Here we need less of the "Glory, Glory" genre and more on the club as a social institution, the site of much masculine voluntary work.

There are also many private collections of sporting memorabilia, usually at the small-scale, hobbyist level, though occasionally large enough to rival museum collections and become an investment rather than a consumption activity. Like art connoisseurs, some of these collectors are willing to loan artefacts to museums, but unfortunately others prefer to keep their collections solely for themselves. And, there is a miscellaneous category comprising such items as the taxidermy collections of hunting, shooting, and fishing enthusiasts, club trophy rooms, and the memorabilia put together by sports bars erupting throughout the world, whose proprietors often have little understanding of the significance of what they have collected and no idea how to conserve it apart from hanging it on the wall.

Overall, then, the artefactual representation of the sporting past is undertaken by a wide variety of institutions, some more reputable than others in the way that they approach sporting heritage. In the same way that there is no typical sports museum, there is a variety of sports historians. We have writers at the professional level who author books on such topics as the football grounds of Europe, the journalist who appreciates having his historical facts correct, the museum curator who displays sporting artefacts, and scholars who earn their living teaching and researching aspects of sports history. Then there are the amateurs who probably outweigh the professionals in number and often in factual knowledge—particularly their knowledge of their favorite sport's statistics and the detailed history of the club of which they are an enthusiastic fan. Almost as often though, amateurs do not have the broader historical knowledge to contextualize this information. There are also myriad memorabilia collectors. It follows that it is no use asking for a sports museum, however defined, to cater to the needs of the sports historian because there is no such animal.

2

There are several specific reasons why academic sports historians reject museum resources. For one, sports museums cater to the nostalgia market and have, almost without exception, institutionalized the concept of a "golden age" in virtually every sport. Errors of fact and interpretation persist and myths are perpetuated despite historical research to the contrary.[13] Indeed, the very location of the Baseball Hall of Fame in Cooperstown, N.Y., is based on the false historical premise that the game originated there.[14] In contrast, the Rugby Football Museum at Twickenham, England, takes the view that myths, as well as facts, must be addressed and acknowledges with skepticism that allegedly William Webb Ellis created the game of rugby, though the museum of rugby equipment attached to Gilbert's factory and Rugby School itself still refer to the 1890s as the time the rugby tradition began.[15]

One predominant complaint is that the presentation of information is too simplistic and fails to demonstrate the subtleties of historical argument. The major reason for this is the clientele of sports museums: the general public. Consequently, the display policy is likely to require that displays "keep it simple" and "keep it short."[17] It follows, both from the point of view of the academic sports historian who seeks more context and the amateur who seeks more detail, that there is an inadequate provision of information. There is also the danger that in minimizing the textual information, credence may be given to some of the myths that haunt sports history. Perhaps nonsports museums have more excuse for their ignorance. At the high art end of the cultural spectrum, for example, the Tate Gallery sporting paintings exhibition presented a particular view of rural England; sport basically consisted of killing animals or racing horses with no mention of folk football or even of cricket.[16] The only way to contextualize the information and to provide more detail is either to support paper publications or to develop the storage of information (e.g., statistical data) in accessible electronic form, as is being done by the International Rugby Hall of Fame, which has the world's largest electronic database of rugby on touchscreen computer.[18]

Artefacts are too often displayed without sufficient explanation. Too frequently the academic historian is tempted to ask "so what?" or "why did this happen?" A display of helmets and other equipment at the Pro Football Hall of Fame provided little guidance on the time frame of innovation or its effectiveness.[19] Baseball ephemera were displayed at Cooperstown with "nothing analytical in the way of how and why music, cards and stamps are tied into American culture."[20] By concentrating on the exhibition of cups, medals, uniforms, and equipment and treating their artefacts solely in archeological terms, curators run the danger of fetishizing sports history.[21] Moreover, as John Schleppi has pointed out in relation to those museums that are merely extended trophy cabinets, "trophies have a great similarity."[22] Even within the sport that they commemorate, a collection of equipment and apparatus can fail to "evoke the cultural heritage of techniques of the body"; they do not show how the objects were played with.[23]

The failure to present the sporting artefact in a wider context often stems from a lack of curatorial skills. Many of the smaller museums are, in fact, one person affairs, the result of a lifetime's devotion to a particular sport and the hoarding of associated memorabilia. These are collections, not museums run by curators. They know the minutiae of their sport but cannot set it into any nonsporting context, be it political, economic, or social. Many such curators are too far in the sporting woods to see beyond the trees; they list achievements but provide little supporting or contextual historical or cultural information. The Olympic Museum, in contrast, missed a golden opportunity to enlarge upon the political symbolism of the size and design of medals. It preferred, instead, merely to display them en masse. Several curators felt unable to challenge the conservative views of the trustees, sporting bodies, or clubs that employed them and who often saw sport solely in terms of competitive, adult, male-dominated activity.

Fortunately some sports museums have gone beyond the conventional boundaries of their sport. The National Museum of Racing and Hall of Fame at Saratoga Springs, N.Y., has a Civil War gallery; the Kentucky Derby Museum devotes a special section to the Afro-American contribution to thoroughbred racing; and both the National Italian American Sports Hall of Fame and the San Diego Hall of Champions takes the role of disabled athletes seriously. The curator of the Pierre Gildesgame Maccabi Sports Museum in Israel is adamant that the real worth of his artefacts is the "light they shed on the Jewish contribution to physical culture,"[24] and the inaugural director of France's National Sports Museum has stated his conviction that sports museums must be intellectually honest and present sport "with sympathy but not bias, without obscuring any facet of a subject, without amputation."[25] Yet, many major museums continue to focus solely on the artefacts, as with the New Zealand Rugby Museum where, according to the curator, "basically we accept anything we are offered that relates to rugby."[26] Here are highlighted the achievements of the sport that has become that nation's icon of masculinity, but no attempt is made to come to grips with the important sociocultural theme of gender fixing.[27] Similarly, a recent exhibition at the Pump House People's History Museum in Manchester associated with the European '96 Football Championships celebrated the game and its fans but "stopped short of attempting any critical exploration of the cultural phenomenon of football support."[28]

The nonsports museum may have an advantage where context is concerned, for example, the recent exhibition on the Nazi Olympics developed by the United States Holocaust Memorial Museum.[29] Although the presentation of material was very traditional (flat panels that featured reproductions of photographs, posters, and newspaper articles), it was powerful and successful because it was set within the context of the Holocaust itself. Nevertheless there is still a danger when the *raison d'étre* of a particular museum leads it to present a picture from a specific political stance. In Adelaide, Australia, the Museum of Ethnicity put on an excellent exhibition on "Fair Play," which demonstrated conclusively that aborigines, European ethnic groups, and women had not had a "fair go" in Australian sport. However, it was essentially a qualitative account that highlighted the few who had made it to the top despite the formidable barriers which they had to overcome. It did not point out or explain why, for example, aborigines were overrepresented in Australian Rules football, the rugby league, and, above all, in boxing where, although only comprising about 1% of the Australian population, they have produced 15% of Australian boxing champions.[30]

Whereas much recent work of sports historians has examined both participation and exclusion, sports museums in general and halls of fame in particular join the part of the sporting world that is obsessed with winners and winning. Jingoism at national and club triumphs abounds,[31] and insufficient recognition is given to the more typical competitive sports experience: losing. More attention should be devoted to the "also rans," those who come in fourth place, the defunct clubs, and the apprentice jockeys who never had to give up their claiming allowance. It is noteworthy that a special exhibition at the Olympic Museum on the marathon began with a quote from Emil Zatopek that all marathon runners were winners but then conspicuously failed to list any Olympic marathon participant who failed to last the distance.

Commercialism and modern museums are bedfellows, much to the chagrin of some sports historians. Certainly, as Garth Paton has observed, the tourist appeal of halls of fame and club museums "can overshadow historical objectivity."[32] Writing of the Hockey Hall of Fame, Bruce Kidd noted that it is "unabashedly commercial—appropriating the past not only for legitimation, but aggressive commodification and consumption."[33] Academic visitors often cringe at the contents of the ubiquitous museum shop. Yet sports museums have to generate income and, for most of them, this means attracting customers who pay for entry or sponsors who, in turn, want to maximize attendances.[34] Funding is a perennial problem of most sports museums and in practice, the not-for-profit incorporation label often translates into operating losses. Indeed the director of the Swiss Sports Museum has claimed that he has never "come across a single sports museum capable of paying its own way"[35] A study of major specialized sports museums in Britain undertaken in the early 1990s revealed that they "either have been, or are continuing to be, heavily subsidised by outside fundholders such as sports governing bodies, prestigious independent sports clubs, local authorities and regional tourist boards."[36] No one ever got rich catering solely to the needs of historians.[37] Hence, we have to accept naming rights for galleries and displays, kitsch items in the shops, and the occasional hard sell or there will be fewer resources available to the curators.

The financial imperative is not the only reason for attracting the general public or at least the sports enthusiasts among them. Most museums have a mission to educate and this too encourages them to cater to a broad market.[38] Indeed, these customer groups are likely to become even more diverse and even less academic as new markets are sought both for commercial and educational reasons. Sport attracts many people who would react adversely to the concept of a museum, so how is this to be changed? The Hampden Park Football Museum, for one, intends to target males age 18 to 30 through the placement of suitable historical material in the Scottish tabloid press and by leaflet drops in public houses. The same museum at an exhibition associated with the European Football Championships piloted its replication of youth culture via the adoption of a magazine format. The contents display enables any section of the display to be dipped into without a need to take an overview. Many museums now understand that museum visitors should not always be expected to come to the museum and promote outreach programs with touring exhibitions to schools, libraries, and sports venues. It is, of course, in the interests of sports historians to encourage the enlargement of the client base of sports museums, for therein lies the possibility of a greater awareness of sports history.

Sports museum curators are in a powerful position to influence the general public's perception of sports history; they choose what to display and what not to exhibit. Their personal bias and knowledge may not reflect the perceived historical process and care ought to be taken to be more open about curatorial decisions.[39] This is particularly relevant where sports figures are concerned. Kidd has criticized the Hockey Hall of Fame for not making public its selection policy regarding the players and administrators it chose to honor, consequently presenting a situation in which they "are presented as if chosen by divine intervention."[40] The Olympic Museum in Lausanne similarly provides no rationale as to why certain athletes are depicted as stars of the Olympic Games. The National Hunt Hall of Fame in Cheltenham, England, deliberately has no voting procedures with the intention that choices will create controversy and, thus, publicity.[41]

The philosophy of many sports museums is to "educate through entertainment."[42] The director of Prague's Museum of Physical Training and Sports aimed his displays both at "ethical education and at the satisfaction of the emotions ... to instruct the visitor but also—and primarily—to *please* them."[43] Part of the mission of the National Museum of Racing and Hall of Fame in Saratoga is "to convey the excitement of thoroughbred racing to the broadest possible audience."[44] Hence, it has endeavored to recreate the racetrack at the tote board, in the paddock, and behind the scenes in the jockeys' rooms. A survey of British sports museum curators showed that they generally believe that the introduction of action into their galleries is vital to convey the fast-moving nature of sport, but how to achieve it is another matter.[45] Although some scholars believe that "the entertainment orientation rather than a stricter historical focus might be considered a shortcoming," entertainment, properly used as a resource, can be imaginative. The Hockey Hall of Fame's full-size, walk-in replica of the Montreal Canadiens' dressing room, for example, features an interactive video that enables visitors to experience a simulated training room, as does the International Tennis Hall of Fame, which gives visitors the opportunity to play against tennis stars. The Ski Museum in Lahti, Finland, has virtual reality devices that allow visitors to experience winter sports without the wind and cold. Entertainment can also be educational. In Saratoga, an electronic display illustrates the tracing of bloodlines, a practical tool for sports history! Such devices could stimulate an interest in sports history, though the link may at times appear tenuous. We should not dismiss too readily the entertainment aspect of sports museums, for this is surely also a function of sport.

A major complaint voiced by sports historians is that museums are too uncritical in their approach to sport. Many sports museums, even at the elite level, eschew the controversial; they are reluctant to give the whole picture and deliberately omit things from history. World champions are presented without blemish, and world championships are presented without political context. Halls of fame in particular are driven by "the ever present emphasis on finding heroes...[which]... overshadows the less showy need for historical accuracy."[46] The tendency of museums is to celebrate the rise of a player from rags to riches but rarely to dwell his or her slide into obscurity, alcoholism, poverty, or social dysfunction. Revelations that famous players were also physically abusive to spouses or were recreational drug abusers or rapists receive the response that this occurred off the field and was not related to their sporting performance. An example, but not an isolated one, is the National Italian Sports Hall of Fame's lack of response to the problems faced by Jennifer Capriati or Lyle Alzado. The failure to accept the dark side of sporting heroes further perpetuates the myth first started by the Muscular Christians that sport promotes good character. Instead of history, the museum visitor faces a "miasma of wooly [sic] commentary, mawkish sentiment, and cardboard portraits."[47] There are exceptions. The Arsenal Football Club Museum, like the players themselves, has faced up to Paul Merson's gambling and drug problems and Tony Adams' alcoholism. In acknowledging their existence, however, it has stressed the courage of the players in recognizing their problems and emphasized that the club had stood by them.[48] Other museums have ignored the poor social behavior of lesser personalities by adopting the Stalinist practice of never acknowledging their existence at the club. Manchester United's museum, like all others, glosses over the dismissals of unsuccessful managers.[49] Few clubs in British football seem prepared to face up to the collective disorder; some of their supporters are hooligans.[50]

Halls of fame are shrines where fans come to worship their heroes; no false prophets must be allowed to preach. Do fans really prefer the happy ending?[51] This is questionable. What newspaper would adopt that approach? Surely a scandalous story sells copies, and the development of fanzines in Britain certainly suggests that club-level fans prefer the true picture to a sanitized version. The rendition of bland official statements that pass for most match programs serve the public relations interests of the club board rather than keep fans aware of what is happening. Could it be that the same directors prefer their version of history to be bowdlerized? Presumably this also applies to the executives of halls of fame who care too much for the image of the sport that they serve to risk it being undermined by historical evaluation. Discussions at conferences and seminars suggest that this partial use of history has often been the result of a commercial decision brought on by the belief that the fans of the sport might be upset by the intervention of real history into the fantasy world of nostalgia. As Bruce Kidd notes, "halls of fame represent established interests presenting partial views within a closed discourse of Olympian truth."[52] The curator of the Museum of Western Australian Sport, however, despite her willingness to present material with "no idolatry of elite athletes," found that "there is no desire to even know about these people outside their sporting lives."[53]

It is not just the sports museums that fail to deal with controversial issues in sport. Whereas the Holocaust Memorial Museum exhibition dealt with both the boycott issue of 1936 and the possible friction between Jewish and black athletes, it shied away from any comparison with later boycotts or looking at what the International Olympic Committee president was doing in the 1930s.[54] But some museums have attempted to face up to reality. Political change has encouraged the South African Rugby Museum to come to terms with the history of segregated audiences.[55] The Sporting Life Exhibition in Hull, Canada, presented "the negative aspects of sport alongside the achievements and successes." The curator argued that even if the "debate is controversial and painful," riots, disasters, violence, drugs, and cruelty to animals have had an "historically important" role in sport.[56] In contrast to the Hockey Hall of Fame, which glamourizes the labor situation,[57] the International Tennis Hall of Fame notes the fine line between pushing young players to great achievements and creating burnout.[58]

3

Are we, then, at an impasse—sports historians cocooned in their literary sources and critical of the approach and performance of the museums, curators willing to add sports historians to their clientele but restricted by finance and philosophy to catering for a broader audience (perhaps to the detriment of sports history)? As we approach the millenium is there any way in which curators and historians could come closer together?

Perhaps we should simply accept that sports museums can serve fragmented markets[59] and that for the academic sports historian it is the conventional historical sources existing in libraries and museum archives that are important. There are some outstanding collections available. In Finland, the Sports Museum Foundation has brought together a museum, an archive with almost a "kilometre of documented information," and a library of more than 20,000 volumes.[60] The Berlin Sports Museum has a library of 40,000 books, many dealing with distance running, for which it was named the AIMS Museum of Running.[61] The Mystic Seaport Museum has 50,000 books and periodicals and more than 600,000 manuscripts.[62] The USGA Museum and Library at Golf House, New Jersey, features a library of over 10,000 volumes, the largest such collection in the world.

Sports museums could certainly assist their research efforts (and, of course, that of their own staff) if they combined their exhibition efforts with the preservation of such traditional historical primary and secondary sources. Many are doing so, including the Australian Gallery of Sport which adopted such a policy when it inherited the Melbourne Cricket Club's library. It must, however, be acknowledged that museums do not exist for

Facts and Artefacts: Sports Historians and Sports Museums [235

that minority of the population called "sports historians" and that somebody must foot the bill for collection and storage. It is doubtful that sports historians or their societies will be rushing to the head of the sponsorship line. Similar arguments apply to the development of oral history archives and videotape libraries. Most academic sports historians generally prefer text. Some are numerate, but few make adequate, if any, use of artefacts and the like. As professionals, sports historians certainly need education to broaden their methodology both in teaching and research. What is required for sports historians is that they step outside the archive room and into the exhibition galleries, to add another dimension to their work. Sports museums can help us change by complimenting our literary text approach by emphasizing the visual, a component often neglected in the world of sports history scholarship. Photographic elements, for example, showing changes in stadia design, playing costumes or crowd composition, could be used, as could works of art detailing impressions of sport from one person's view or artefacts in the form of costume, equipment, or technological developments. A starting point may be to encourage them to utilize the photographs in the archives—80,000 of them in the Berlin Sports Museum, at least 100,000 in Prague's Museum of Physical Training and Sport, and more than a million of maritime sport in the Rosenfield Collection at the Mystic Seaport Museum. Indeed, even the most minor of sports museums appears to have a collection of sports-related photographs.

The new generation of historians, trained to teach with multimedia aids, may be more receptive to the visual than the chalk and talk of the *ancien regime*. Leadership by example could also play a role. Many of the curators might also consider themselves to be sports historians, and as such, they should be making more use of their own resources to produce less textbound sports history. Two aspects of sport may also be better demonstrated in a museum exhibition than in a narrative form. Performance, the crux of sport, certainly can be better appreciated using the video archive,[63] the interactive simulation of tennis using computer-designed, old-fashioned equipment, or by actually participating in traditional games and sports.[64] Excepting the finest historical writers, the drama and uncertainty of sport possibly can be better captured by recorded commentary or telecast. No text, moreover, could possibly capture the passion associated with fans' chants and songs, the focus of the collection at the Hampden Park Museum.

If curators, particularly of nonsports museums, made more use of trained sports historians in developing their exhibitions, a positive link could be forged that might have beneficial effects for both parties. Sports historians clearly can help set straight both the sporting and historical record. They can also provide the relevant background to assist museums in determining their collection policy, whether it is simply a matter of suggesting that a particular sports trophy has historical significance or writing detailed reports on the history of sports or sporting events as museum consultants. They can also offer help in determining the authenticity of artefacts: did the Spanish basketball player Fernando Romey really wear size 22 shoes?[65] Sports historians can help fill the lacunae caused by curators, particularly in nonspecialist sports museums, who have been trained in museology rather than in sports history. This can lead to errors in fact and interpretation; sports history is not an immutable stock of knowledge, and what was accepted ten years ago may have changed by now.[66] Updating their stock of knowledge should be considered as important as regularly updating their exhibitions.

Sports historians could also be encouraged to particiate in the educational programs of the museums; most of us, after all, are educators as well as historians. Possibly we could assist curators in distinguishing between education and an audio-visual experience. A number of professional museum curators feel that the Olympic Museum, in an effort to "avoid an over static display,"[67] has gone overboard on passive and interactive videos to the extent that "the various screens counteracted one another and rather marginalized the few objects that were on display"[68]

Although sports historians can appreciate the contribution that sport museums make to the preservation of our sporting heritage, there is a question of the extent to which a museum should be a laboratory rather than a reservation. Roland Renson, the authority on Flemish folkgames, addressed this issue in the context of game demonstrations with authentic or replica equipment. He states that "the best way to preserve ... traditional games is to play them."[69] How should sports historians view places like the Mystic Seaport Museum, designed as "a living and working replica of the past,"[70] or Saratoga, which aims at the "recreation of the sights, sounds and drama of racing"?[71] Should we reject them as pseudo-history or get onboard and use our research to promote greater authenticity?

In an age of technological literacy, perhaps we should be concentrating on the development of virtual museums rather than real sporting museums. The Victorians used plaster casts and photographs to distribute artefacts internationally. Today we can use technology—CD-ROM collections of sporting icons and sites on the Internet-to give global access. Supercomputers are capable of massive data storage not just of statistical and bibliographical material but also of digitized photographs and videos of sports performances, all of which could be downloaded by users visiting the site.[72] Greater accessibility to a nation's sporting heritage could be brought about by the arrangement of virtual visits to other museums whose collections are stored in electronic form so that hands-on access would be gained without the dangers of handling the artefacts.[73] This idea possibly might be easier to sell than most to both curators and historians, for these professions are changing. The new generation of sports historians, perhaps like the new generation of any activity, are better trained and equipped for technology.[74] Many museums too have already accepted that technology can aid their educational objectives and use portable CD-ROM guides to supplement the usual labelling of exhibits and self-guided tours. It is also clearly acknowledged that technology can contribute to the entertainment side of the exhibits. Most leading museums now have websites, and the National Baseball Hall of Fame Library has begun to place archival search engines on the Internet.

Sports museums are the public face of sports history and, indeed, halls of fame are at "the intersection between history and nostalgia."[76] Steven Pope noted that "there continues to be a vast gap between what sports scholars do and what the larger public consumes and conceives of as sports history."[75] Many professional sports historians nevertheless are also sports fans. They accept that there is a place for nostalgia, for devotion to one's sporting heroes, and for celebratory history. Clearly sports museums are the venues where these elements can be presented. Yet, as historians, we want to see accuracy and context. To rephrase the comment of Richard Holt,[77] is there really any reason why sports history exhibitions cannot be good history? Celebration need not be without critique. There is a major challenge to be faced in bringing the tough social issues of class, age, gender, and ethnicity into the public history domain of sport. The transition from academic to public history is a difficult one, but opening the eyes of the public to a different view of sports history can only serve the interests of the profession. Criticism need not eschew celebration; sports history exhibitions could also be entertaining history, Sports museums are the best places to replicate the performance, drama, romance, passion, and emotion of sport, something many sports historians fail to do when they move from reality to the record.

References

1. In addition to reading journals devoted to museum activities and others concerning sports history, information for this paper was gathered by writing to and/or visiting about 200 sports museums throughout the world and contacting sports historians on the Internet, by personal communication, or at seminar presentations. The bibliographies of a random sample of sports history books on the shelves of the International Centre for Sports History and Culture at De Montfort University were examined to ascertain what use was being made of museum materials by the authors,

2. T. S. Eliot, Notes *Towards the Definition of Culture* (1947) as quoted in Asa Briggs, *Victorian Things* (London, 1996), p. 1.

3. One point reinforced by the responses of some curators is that sport has some culturally specific aspects. Alexander Prince Hohenlohe politely pointed out that he regarded "hunting or stalking more as a passion passed from ancestors to successors rather than a sport." Alexander Prince Hohenlohe to the author, April 30, 1997. Spanish museum administrator, Enriqueta Sim-Fort noted that contemporary bullfighting is "more an art than a sport." Enriqueta Sim-Fort to the author, April 1, 1997.

4. *Discovering the Olympic Museum: Visitor's Guide* (Lausanne, 1994), p. 6.

5. John Saunders to the author, October 8, 1996.

6. Riccardo Grozio and Sergio Giuntini, "Sports Museums," *Panathlon International* (January/February 1997), p. I.

7. Michael Wright, "Glory, Glory, Man United," *Museums Journal*

(June 1996), p. 22.

8. Richard Cox, "Sports Archives, Libraries and Museums in the UK—What Should be the Policy?" *Sports Historian* 16 (1996), p.157.

9. Among the very few football items in Glasgow Museum is a donation from an old player documented as "5 international FC shirts from the 1930s." On the same page of the accessions register three-quarters of the space was devoted to a description of wallpaper saved from a tenement flat! Richard Williams, "Capturing the Hampden Roar: Creating a Scottish National Museum of Football," North West Federation of Museums and Art Galleries Conference, October 18, 1996.

10. Robert Mason, "A Load of Old Balls," *Museums Journal* June 1996, p. 24.

11. Richard Halliwell, "More Than a Game," *Museums Journal* May 1991, p.18. Ged O'Brien, Director of the Hampden Park Football Museum, believes that "every football exhibition put on in a museum has been a resounding success and broken all records for the respective institution." Letter, January 31, 1995.

12. P A. C. McCormack, *A Consideration of the Development of British Sports Museums* M.Soc.Sci. (Ironbridge Institute, 1993), p.133.

13. There is, however, no excuse for sloppiness in presentation, as in one temporary exhibition at the Lausanne Olympic Museum where adjacent panels on Olympic marathons contained conflicting information on the number of runners in the Paris and St. Louis races, or at the National Maritime Museum in Sydney where an exhibit purportedly dealing with the Second World War included a magazine from 1946.

14. Dean A. Sullivan, *Early Innings: A Documentary History of Baseball 1825–1908*.

15. William Baker, "William Webb Ellis and the Origins of Rugby Football: The Life and Death of a Victorian Myth," *Albion* 13 (1981).

16. *British Sporting Art*, April 11–July 2, 1995.

17. The Director of the British Golf Museum argues that a text panel should be only 250 words at a maximum, though he does allow that several text panels could be alongside each other. Peter Lewis in a lecture to MA Sport and Recreation: Historical and Cultural Appraisal students at De Montfort University, September 24, 1996.

18. Scott A.G.M. Crawford, "New Zealand Rugby Museum," *Journal of Sport History*, vol. 23, no. 3 (1996), p. 339.

19. John Neville, "The Pro Football Hall of Fame," *Journal of Sport History*, vol. 18, no. 2 (1991), p. 206.

20. Marc Onigman, "The National Baseball Hall of Fame and Museum," *Journal of Sport History*, vol. 17, no. 1 (1990), p. 113.
21. I owe the phrase to Richard Williams, a curator at the Hampden Park Football Museum.
22. John R. Schleppi, "The Kentucky Derby Museum," *Journal Sport History*, vol. 20, no. 2 (1993), p. 317. Yet the work of John Burnett at the National Museums of Scotland in Edinburgh shows what can be done to set trophies into context. See, for example his publications on "The Marchmont or St Ronan's Arrow" and "A medal of the Newtongrange Lothian Cricket Club, 1887" in *Proceedings of the Society of Antiquaries of Scotland* 125 (1995), p. 1175–1191.
23. Roland Renson, "The Comeback of Traditional Sports and Games," *Museum* vol. 170, no. 2 (1991), p. 81.
24. Joseph Hoffman, "Recalling Judaism of Muscles," *Museum* vol. 170, no. 1 (1991), p. 73.
25. Jean Durry, "Sports in a Museum?," *Museum* vol. 170, no. 2 (1991), p. 64.
26. Letter from Bob Luxford, April 2, 1997.
27. Crawford, p. 339.
28. John Davis, "The Beautiful Game Show," *Social History Curators Group News* 40 (Autumn 1996), p. 15.
29. Roy Rosenzweig, "The Nazi Olympics: Berlin 1936," *Journal of Sport History* vol. 24, no. 1 (1997), pp. 77–80.
30. Richard Broome, "Professional Aboriginal Boxers in Eastern Australia 1930–1979," *Aboriginal History*, vol. 4, no. 1 (1980), p. 50.
31. P. Honkannen, "The Sports Museum of Finland," *Museum* 160 (1988), pp. 222–223.
32. Paton, p. 89.
33. Bruce Kidd, "The Making of a Hockey Artifact: A Review of the Hockey Hall of Fame," *Journal of Sport History* vol. 23, no. 3 (1996), p. 329.
34. There are some exceptions. The Cheltenham National Hunt Hall of Fame offers free entry because they regard the exhibition as a useful add-on for attracting wedding receptions, conferences, etc. Interview with Edward Gillespie, Cheltenham's managing director, August 21, 1996.
35. Maximilian Triet, "A Sports Museum is also a Business," *Museum* 170.1 (1991), p. 83. In his research towards his brief for establishing the National Hunt Hall of Fame, Edward Gillespie says he quickly realised that a museum was not a money-making concern. Interview,

Facts and Artefacts: Sports Historians and Sports Museums [241

August 21, 1996. See also McCormack, p. 48.
36. McCormack, p. 89.
37. In Britain the national lottery has opened up the chance of funding from the nation's gambling, but these are usually subject to public accessibility being given priority. Both the Football Museum at Preston and the Hampden Park enterprise have received several million pounds from this source. There is also the possibility that new sports museums may be funded, including those for country sports, as heritage money convinces the landed gentry that their family history is also the nation's history. I owe this point to Professor Grant Jarvie.
38. Already 25% of the visitors to the Olympic Museum in Lausanne are either children or youngsters. Grozio & Giuntini, p. IV.
39. A point raised by Dr. Joyce Kay.
40. Kidd, p. 331.
41. Interview with Edward Gillespie, August 21, 1996.
42. *National Museum of Racing and Hall of Fame Catalogue* (1989), p. 4.
43. Tomas Grulich, "Prague: Sport as History," *Museum* vol. 170, no. 2 (1991), p. 69.
44. Garth Paton, "The National Museum of Racing and Hall of Fame," *Journal of Sport History* vol. 24, no. 1 (1997), p. 87.
45. McCormack, p. 61.
46. E. John B. Allen in *Journal of Sport History* vol. 21, no. 3 (1994), p. 306.
47. Nicholas Dawidoff, "Fields of Kitsch," New *Republic* August 17–24, 1992. Cited in S.W. Pope, "Sports Films, Halls of Fame Museums: An Editorial Introduction," *Journal of Sport History* 23 (1996), p. 311.
48. Interview with Iain Cook, Arsenal EC. Museum Curator, 11 August 1997.
49. Mark S. Wylie, Curator Museum &Tour Centre, Manchester United F.C. Letter 14 August 1997.
50. Athough the Manchester United Museum has covered aspects of this in temporary exhibitions there is no mention of it in the permanent displays. Wright, p. 22.
51. Barbara Melosh in Warren Leon & Roy Rosenzweig, *History Museums in the United States: A Critical Appraisal* (Urbana: 1989), cited in Pope, p. 311.
52. Kidd, p. 332.
53. Letter from Sarah Murphy, January 9, 1997.
54. Rosenzweig, p. 79.
55. Tom Graham, Project Manager, South African Rugby Museum.

Letter, April 1, 1997.
56. Jayne Tyler, "Displaying the Game," *Museums Journal* June 1996, p. 27.
57. Kidd, p. 332.
58. Nancy E. Spencer, "International Tennis Hall of Fame," *Journal of Sport History* vol. 23, no. 3 (1996), p. 337.
59. The mission statement of the International Tennis Hall of Fame Museum is to make "the gallery experience multigenerational by appealing to children, adults, families, athletes, spectators, those from urban, suburban and rural backgrounds, as well as those from foreign lands" and its library and archives collection is to "serve grassroots tennis fans, officials of the sport, social historians, print media journalists, radio and television journalists, the entertainment industry, students of all ages, faculties of educational institutions, authors, publishers genealogy researchers, museums and libraries."
60. Information supplied by Kenth Sjoblom, Sports Archives of Finland.
61. "The Berlin Sports Museum." *Sporting Heritage* 1 (1995), pp. 117–118.
62. Scott A.G.M. Crawford, "Mystic Seaport Museum," *Journal of Sport History* vol. 24, no. 1 (1997), p. 84.
63. Mark Wylie, the curator at Manchester United, has lamented that as late as mid 1996 "for a sport that's about movement we have nothing moving to show anyone" and the introduction of films are part of his development program. Wright, p. 22.
64. I am grateful to Roland Renson for information on such are-creation at the Sportsmuseum Vlaanderen in Belgium.
65. Actually he did, as a visit to the Adidas Sports Shoe Museum will show.
66. This is often a problem with volunteer guides who have an idea that history is fixed in a time warp. Letter from Bernard Whimpress, Curator Adelaide Oval Museum, January 8, 1997.
67. *L'Oeil. Lausanne Musée Olympique: Art, Sport et Culture* (1994), p. 8.
68. McCormack, p. 79.
69. Renson, pp. 79–81.
70. Crawford, "Mystic Seaport...," p. 84.
71. Paton, p. 87.
72. The author is currently involved in the Higher Education Library Image Exchange project in which compilations of images will be made available online over SuperJANET, the British universities' computer

network. Although the HELIX project is concerned with social and political history generally, about 1,000 images relating to sports history will be utilised in the pilot scheme.

73. The Canadian National Research Council has developed a high resolution, three dimensional, four colour scanner which, it is claimed, will allow the inspection of 3D reconstructions of objects more closely than they could be examined in a museum. *Daily Telegraph*, 7 May 1996. Such technology if affordable, would be welcomed by curators in, for example, sub Saharan Africa where "the display and handling of an object exposes it to...serious and numerous...dangers which include often torrid heat, omnipresent humidity, pervading dust, rodents, and insects of all shapes and sizes." Julien V. Minavoa, "The Olympic Museum of Benin: What it can do with what it has," *Museum* 170.2 (1991), p. 90.

74. On this see Jan Tolleneer, "Electronic Information Techniques for Sports History Research and Teaching," *IV Congress of the International Society for the History of Physical Education and Sport*, Lyon, July 1997.

75. Stephen W. Pope, *The New American Sports History* (Urbana: 1997), p. 21.

76. Pope, "Sports Films," p. 310.

77. Richard Holt, "Sport and History: The State of the Subject in Britain," *Stadion* vol. XVIII, no. 2 (1992), p. 288. There are, of course, some high-quality publications asociated with exhibitions with illustrations based on the collections displayed, though these are essentially two-dimensional.

At the Start: Note the flag used by the starter to indicate a false start of which there were many as jockeys sought to gain an advantage.

COURTESY OF MR. J. FAIRFAX-BLAKEBOROUGH.

Taking a Gamble or a Racing Certainty: Sports Museums and Public Sports History

Sports history is all around us. This can be demonstrated easily, even if we restrict ourselves solely to examples from the turf. In Newmarket, generally acknowledged as the headquarters of British racing, there are streets named after famous jockeys (Fred Archer Way, Fordham Road), trainers (George Lambton Avenue, Noel Murless Drive), owners (Howard De Walden Way) and administrators (Rous Road).[1] Other places have statues of famous horses: ex-jockey Philip Blacker has been responsible for many of the racecourse sculptures on display in Britain, including Red Rum at Aintree, Desert Orchid at Kempton Park and Generous at Epsom. Racing has contributed to our language in "first past the post" and "on one's tod," the latter an acknowledgment of the dominance of Tod Sloan, one of the American jockeys who invaded the British turf at the end of the nineteenth century. Then there is the ubiquitous pub quiz, often asking about past Derby and Grand National winners and occasionally delving into the arcane with questions such as "When did Good Friday last fall on Boxing Day?"[2] Additionally, almost everyone who bets makes use of sports history in a complex antiquarianism in which the formbook features extensively. Hence the *Racing Calendar* can perhaps be viewed as a sports history text!

Yet getting the message over to the general public is not easy. Much sports history is concerned with a specific life experience of ordinary people, that of men or women who play and watch games: it is part of the historical reconstruction of the social life of communities, classes and populations. However, this group appears to have little contact with the academic version of sport history, save for being its subject matter a generation or so later. The public does not consult articles in sport history journals, which generally have a small and (self)-selective readership.

Therefore when Hilary Bracegirdle, Director of the National Horseracing Museum at Newmarket, asked me to assist in the development of a new gallery dealing with the history of betting, I jumped at the chance. Not only would it assist my department in the forthcoming Research Assessment Exercise (a measure of research quality that the government utilizes to distribute funds to universities) by raising some external grant money and disseminating research findings to an audience wider than peer academics, it was also an opportunity to venture into an area where I had criticized practitioners on several counts as presenting an inadequate public face of sports history. These included their involvement with nostalgia, the inadequate provision of information, and a general lack of critical appraisal.[3]

Almost without exception my 1990s survey of sports museums worldwide showed that they catered for the nostalgia market, thus often institutionalizing the "good old days" and allowing misplaced views of a "golden age" to breed myth and misconception.[4] Searching historical evaluation was not allowed to impinge on the fantasy world of the nostalgic visitor. Too many museums adopted an uncritical approach that eschewed controversy, emphasized ludic performance, and downplayed or ignored any unwelcome social or political aspects. The rise of celebrities was featured but rarely any subsequent slide into obscurity, alcoholism, poverty and social dysfunction. Moreover, the subtleties of historical nuance were nowhere to be found as the intricacies of history became lost in a mission statement of "keep it simple" and "keep it short" so that visitors were not overwhelmed with information. Artifacts were often exhibited without proper context so that the visitor was unaware of the significance of the piece on display or, even worse, without any indication of how it was used.

Now there was a chance for the critic to go to the other side of the display cabinet and do something better: or, would I be sucked up into the culture of sports museums? The working brief was to agree and research display themes, review the existing collection (including the library) of items relating to the history of betting and identify gaps, liaise within the industry in an attempt to acquire relevant items, identify potential loans, source images for the display, and draft the wording of the information panels. The overarching challenge was to be informative without being boring and to be brief without losing authority, in other words, to simplify but not dumb down too much: a task perhaps increasingly facing many academics in the classroom these days.

Old-Time Jockey: Note the upright riding style reminiscent of the hunting field. COURTESY OF MR. J. FAIRFAX-BLAKEBOROUGH.

The background to the development of the gallery was a donation of £30,000 from the trustees of the Bookmakers' Benevolent Society. It was being wound up because quite literally they could not find sufficient impoverished bookmakers (some punters might think this an oxymoron!) requiring assistance. So they gave triple their normal amount to the few unfortunate souls still on their list (no doubt men who forgot the basic principles of turf accountancy and failed to round their books), £10,000 to the charity Riding for the Disabled and the rest to the museum. This led to a substantial delay as it involved serious argument with the Charity Commissioners as to whether the donation was allowable under the deeds of trust. The idea was to commemorate Charles Layfield, who was instrumental in the formation of the Bookmakers' Afternoon Greyhound Service in 1967 and remained a director of it till 1989, subsequently acting as a consultant. A former director of William Hill, one of the elite bookmaking firms, he was a leading figure in the National Sporting League, a major organization of off-course bookmakers, being both its president and chairman. He was also a member of Tattersall's Committee, the group that arbitrates in gambling disputes. He died in 1999, aged eighty-eight.

Opened by the Queen in 1983, the National Horseracing Museum at Newmarket is the major repository for racing memorabilia accessible to the public in Britain. It is located in the former Subscription Rooms on High Street next to the Jockey Club, the ruling body of British racing. At one end of the display spectrum it houses the British Sporting Art Trust collection of paintings; at the other it offers hands-on education through entertainment. In the "Practical Gallery," one that is staffed by retired trainers and jockeys, visitors can tack up a model horse, find out about the daily routine in a training stable, dress up in silks, weigh out and ride a horse simulator. Special exhibitions are held regularly and have included ones on royalty and racing, the development of racing in Yorkshire, and the work of jockey turned thriller writer, Dick Francis. There is also a library that racing researchers can consult. Although limited in its range of books, it has excellent runs of periodicals such as the *General Stud Book* and a complete series of the *Racing Calendar* since its initial publication by the Weatherby family in 1773.

In these days of soaring prices for all forms of sporting memorabilia, the museum has a difficult task in developing its collection. The racing industry itself, whilst appreciative of history in the guise of the formbook and studbook, is generally focused on the here-andnow and the production of winners for tomorrow. Fortunately, there are generous individuals and fund-raising "friends of the museum." Without these the curators would find it difficult to convey the excitement of thoroughbred racing to the general public and make their displays more than merely glorified trophy rooms. Nevertheless, funds are tight and hence the offer from the bookmakers provided an irresistible opportunity to advance the cause of racing history.

A preliminary list of possible themes for the gallery—shown in the left-hand column of the table on the opposite page—was dispatched to the trustees, and I was invited to a meeting with the group overseeing the project. Basically, I think this was to assess if I knew what I was talking about. It also provided a useful reminder not to jump to conclusions, by having my stereotyped image of bookmakers shattered when a representative of their profession noted that a particular incident had occurred while he was reading chemistry at Cambridge. The meeting also included a tour of the Jockey Club premises that proved to be virtually an art gallery with accommodation and dining facilities. To the horror of the museum director, an art historian by training, valuable paintings by Stubbs and Reynolds hung above open fires. Yet there were also some artifacts that could be borrowed for the exhibition, in particular a wheel from a van used in 1836 to transport Elis north from Goodwood to win the St. Leger at Doncaster. Only a week before the race Elis, a fancied runner, was still at his Goodwood training quarters. In those days horses were walked to meetings and, as it would take two weeks for Elis to reach Doncaster this way, the bookmakers, certain that the horse would be a non-runner, widened the odds offered. The owner of Elis, Lord George Bentinck, placed his bets and had the horse transported north in a van drawn by a series of posthorses. Elis went on to victory by two lengths, and Bentinck won a fortune.[5]

Any exhibition is limited by the artifacts that can be put on display. Even before the new gallery had been proposed some items relating to gambling were already on view. These included the multi-colored jackets of "Prince" Ras Monolulu, a tipster made famous from the 1930s to the 1950s by his catchphrase, "I gotta horse," and a Bookmakers Protection Association badge worn by its members at racecourses. However, neither of these was contextualized. There was no mention of racism, even although Monolulu was one of the few black men involved in British racing, and no mention of the racetrack gangs that forced bookmakers to unite for defense.[6]

Proposed Exhibition Themes		
Initial Thoughts	Revised Scheme	Final Selection
Time Line		
Betting and Racing	Betting and Racing	Betting and Racing
On-course Betting	Early History of Betting	
Off-course Betting	Bookmaking and Bookmakers	Bookmakers
Government and Betting	From Street Betting to Betting Shops	
Touts and Tipsters	Seeking Information	Communication and Information
Betting Communications	Shouting the Odds	
Coups and Scandals	Coups and Corruption	Coups and Corruption
	State Intervention	The Tote
	Punters Large and Small	Punters Large and Small
Other Types of Betting	Back to the Future: Betting Exchanges	
Opposition to Betting		
Judging Form and Making a Bet		
	Problem Gambling	Problem Gambling

A venture into the storerooms of the museum revealed a plethora of artifacts that may never see the light of day in any exhibition. Several of these were anatomical including many fetuses and hooves of famous horses. Yet there were a few items that were relevant to the gambling gallery that had not yet been displayed. These included whole sheets of bookmakers' tickets, race bills and a couple of clock bags. When customers placed a bet on the racecourse, the bookmaker's clerk wrote details into a ledger and a numbered ticket would be given as a receipt. These were often individualized with photographs and mottoes. Off the course most illegal bookmakers employed "runners" who received commission on the bets that they collected from pubs, factories and small shops, especially tobacconists. These were picked up in clock bags, leather purses which when closed set the time on the clock to confirm that the bets had been placed before the race started. Racebills were early versions of racecards. The ones at the museum showed that jockeys were named and racing colors of owners indicated much earlier than the literature states.

Nevertheless, there was insufficient readily available material to mount an exhibition, and artifacts had to be sought elsewhere. Letters were sent to all British racecourses, more in hope than expectation, but three bore fruit. Both Yarmouth and York had a bookmaker's joint (large umbrella, stand, bag and betting book). Goodwood offered to supply photographs and also put me in touch with Jon Franklin, a British photographer living in Sweden, whose website contained several striking images.[7] He later supplied several photographs for use on the text panels.

Within the racing industry, a previous contact, Dr. Paull Khan, Director of Finance and Racing at Weatherbys (essentially the civil service of the racing industry) put me on to Adrian McGlynn, secretary of the company. He pointed out that Weatherbys had nothing to do with betting but had a few documents relating to the Running Rein scandal of 1844 in which a disguised four-year-old horse won the Derby at Epsom, the classic race for three-year-olds.[8] What a find! There in a glass case next to the staff dining room was a multi-page affidavit from Charles Weatherby stating that he had received the entry of the horse in July of 1842, a letter from Lord George Bentinck (at that time chief Jockey Club Steward) objecting to Running Rein's participation in the forthcoming race, and a letter from Baron de Tessier to Charles Weatherby declining to release to the Jockey Club statements made to him as an Epsom Steward at the time of the race. This and other material donated by Weatherbys provided much more detail on the incident than had been known to historians and made it clear that the racing rumor mill had been grinding long before the race took place. It also showed that the Jockey Club did not yet control British racing.[9] What was worrying as an historian was that the material was handed over to me without any request for identification. Unfortunately, space limitations meant that the museum missed an opportunity to retell and revise a famous racing story. Only one page of the material is displayed whereas an audio-visual presentation could have delivered a fascinating detective tale on how the plot was discovered and the perpetrators tracked down. In fairness this might have given undue prominence to just one aspect of gambling history.

Several bookmaking firms offered assistance, and in particular Stanley Racing and Ladbrokes proved useful. Stanley provided an old till and security camera from one of their betting shops, and Ladbrokes came up with a "no limit" credit card issued to the Duke of Windsor, the emblem from their first betting shop, and a mechanical time stamp used by telephonists at credit bookmakers.

The Tote (racing parlance for the organization running the totalisator form of betting) was also very helpful but did not even know its own history. I had to tell its publicity director when it first came into operation![10] In tote betting, stakes on a race are pooled, deductions made to cover costs and a contribution to racing, and the remainder is divided amongst winning punters, according to their stakes. In effect, tote customers bet against each other rather than a bookmaker. The dividend declared is determined by the volume of betting at the "off," unlike betting with the bookmakers who declare odds at the time of the bet. For the exhibition the tote offered old machinery used to calculate the dividend and uniforms from the "ladies in red," as their female operatives have become known.

Following the initial research and identification of relevant artifacts, as shown in the central column of the table, some themes were dropped or modified. To my surprise, the museum curators rejected the time line that I had prepared as a means of giving historical context to the exhibition as being too old-fashioned a device.

Then came a double bombshell. At a later meeting the tote representative offered to set up a model totalisator betting office, which would take at least a quarter of the available gallery space.

The Judge's Box: The judge decided who was first past the post and hence whose were the winning bets. COURTESY OF MR. J. FAIRFAX-BLAKEBOROUGH.

Then the museum director received the welcome news that a bid for new premises was likely to succeed. The trustees decided that the betting gallery should not display all the artifacts collected nor cover all the themes envisaged so that a revised, larger exhibition could be put on when the new institution opened its doors. The right-hand column in the table shows the effect on my plans.

Given that a text panel was limited to between 250 and 300 words, this decision meant that the whole, albeit selective, history of betting had to be summarized in about 1,500 words. Although the labels on the artifacts allow more to be said, much of this had to do with the provenance of the exhibits. An example of what I was able to achieve is shown in the Appendix dealing with one of the sub-themes. As a researcher I felt that the proposed display missed much of the argument that can be found in the academic literature on gambling, though those interested in knowing more about the history of betting can be directed to the museum library, which used some of the Benevolent Fund bequest to expand its holdings on gambling.

My experience at the National Horseracing Museum tempted me to retrace my steps from the mid 1990s and revisit several other British sports museums.[11] Although I now have considerably more sympathy for curators and the problems that they face, some museums certainly could be improved, particularly in their organizational operation. Except at the national level (where it is required for registration) only a minority of museums appear to have thought-out (and documented) acquisitions policies by which they check legal validity to title, offer full and secure documentation in retrievable form, decide when to conserve and when to restore, cover details of storage, handling and disposal, and possess a risk management strategy. Frankly at most of the smaller museums (especially club museums) the situation is a shambles. This can be explained—in terms of time and financial resources—but not excused.

Resources are a major problem for most museums. As any academic can testify, resource scarcity is not a problem unique to sports museums, but at least British universities have some government backing unlike any sports museum in the country. Indeed, no major sports museum has flourished without significant subsidy or patronage: certainly there would be no British Golf Museum without the financial backing of the Royal & Ancient Golf Club or a Museum of Rugby without help from the Rugby Football Union. The National Horseracing Museum itself receives no overt support from the racing industry and constantly has to seek funds to purchase artifacts, the cost of which is rising in a market place that has realized the value of sporting memorabilia. Only recently one (not even a pair) of batting gloves worn by the legendary Australian cricketer, Don Bradman fetched £5,000 at a London auction. Works of art are even more expensive. On my first research visit to the National Horseracing Museum the director was on the phone trying to raise half a million pounds at short notice for a painting by Stubbs of a thoroughbred owned by Duke of Marlborough. As the Duke had only had one winner on the turf this could have been a rare piece. Fortunately for the museum's coffers, an expert on Stubbs ruled that the painting was done ten years before that particular horse raced. Nor do some organizations make it easy for their associated museum to raise revenue. The Scottish Football Museum is located at Hampden Park, the ground where Scotland plays its home internationals. However, it is also the home of Queen's Park Football Club, an amateur team in the lower echelons of the Scottish League, and on match days, when custom might be expected, the museum is not allowed to open as two of the main display rooms are used for hospitality purposes.

It is ironic that institutions that concentrate on the past have no guarantee of their future. Few sports museums know if they will be in existence twelve months hence. York Racing Museum was closed two years ago when a new stand was built which needed hospitality space. The Scottish Rugby Union Museum suffered the same fate when Murrayfield Stadium was redeveloped in 1996. What has replaced the museum at Murrayfield (and is increasingly becoming common in other stadia) is the tour. The library services post there has been combined with that of tour manager, and electronic mails contain the addendum: "Feel the passion of Scottish Rugby for your self [*sic*] by taking a behind the scenes tour of Murrayfield Stadium. Follow in the footsteps of legends as you visit the dressing rooms, players tunnel, Royal Box, hospitality suites and the world famous pitch." Poor punctuation and nostalgia reign! Nor have museum staff any guarantees. As this paper was being prepared for publication, negotiations were underway with the director of the Scottish Football Museum regarding future cooperation between his organization and researchers and teachers at Stirling University. Only two days after a suggestion that we work jointly on the early history of Scottish football came another email informing us of his impending redundancy. The museum is left with one keen but unqualified curator.

One point that should be acknowledged is that, despite the simplicity of text panels, certainly at those museums with official registration substantial research is undertaken on the topics and on the establishment of provenance for artifacts. There may be simplification out front, but it can all be backed up with real scholarship. Indeed, some of the researchers involved are fine scholars in their own right. To mention but two: Christopher Dodds, consultant to the River and Rowing Museum, is an acknowledged international expert on the history of rowing; and Peter Lewis, Director of the British Golf Museum, was awarded the Murdoch medal for his work on the history of golf. At the Scottish Football Museum detailed ongoing work promises a fresh interpretation of the origins of the world game, naturally with Scotland at the forefront, but there on the basis of

A Stylized Georgian Race Meeting: Note the beer tent and grandstand on the left and the musicians, pugilists, and hawkers in the foreground, though, at this time no obvious bookmakers. COURTESY OF MR. J. FAIRFAX-BLAKEBOROUGH.

solid research not Celtic mythology.

It is the conveying of the results of the research that is the real issue. A few museums do attempt to offer sports history to the younger generation both on educational and financial grounds. Not unfortunately the National Horseracing Museum or the Scottish Football Museum, despite a desire to do so, as they have no money for education officers. In 1997 the National Horseracing Museum employed a teacher to develop educational resource packs, but much of the racing information in them is now obsolete and the museum cannot afford to update them. The Scottish Football Museum director had planned to integrate two classrooms into the museum complex, but the Scottish Football Association, proprietors of Hampden Park, overrode this to change them in to a 250–seat lecture theatre used primarily to host press conferences. The British Golf Museum is only just moving into education over a decade-and-a-half after opening. At Twickenham the Rugby Football Museum offers free "educational" packs, but by far the most pro-active in the sports history educational field is the Wimbledon Lawn Tennis museum, which organizes workshops with packages for key stages in the national curriculum for history, geography, art and science. At

£7.50 a pupil, this also makes an appreciated contribution to the museum's funds, especially with the museum shop stocking a wide range of "pocket money" tennis gifts!

However, Wimbledon is less impressive when it comes to presenting critical sports history. Nowhere, for example, does it discuss shamateurism, one of the banes of tennis until the sport went open in 1968. Similarly, Lords does not examine the downside of W.G. Grace, one of England's most successful all-round cricketers but a cheat and shamateur *par excellence*. In contrast the Scottish Football Museum has looked at trouble on the terraces and is actively soliciting academic help for a major display (subject to Scottish Football Association approval) on football and sectarianism. The director at the time believed he must be doing a reasonable job as everyone thought he was biased against them. At Newmarket an exhibition has been held on "Racing Scandals," and the new betting gallery may eventually consider problem and addictive gambling.

Whether sports museums should attempt to bring in such issues as gender and racial discrimination is a major concern of curators. On the one hand some feel a responsibility to try to educate the public, especially children, on these matters, but offsetting this is a fear that they might lose or alienate their audience if they try to impose ideologies on them. Aggravating the situation is the question of whether those who practice discrimination—as with sectarianism in Scottish football—should have the opportunity to air their views. Academic freedom warrants that space should be given to those whose views differ from ours, but political propaganda is not the same as rigorously researched scholarship. Or, are we being too patronizing to the non-academic public in assuming that they can be taken in too easily?

If I may be permitted a sweeping generalization, it is that most sports fans prefer positive memories of their sport. Much academic history, however, is more interested in demythologizing the public's romantic perception of sport and thus often runs counter to "the happy face of sport."[12] Admittedly, sports museums catering solely for the downside of sport would be a disaster commercially and, to be fair, would be unrepresentative of the true history of sport. Yet one of the problems of sport, unlike business, is that one team's triumph is always another club's loss. I am not sure that sports historians or even museum curators can adequately deal with a subject in which there has to be more losers than winners. As an economic historian I constantly remind my students that all teams can make profits but only a few can win trophies. Even a list of winners by implication infers that there were losers.

One possible other "problem" is that of compromising our academic history to suit the needs of the museum curators. I do not think that this is really a major issue. Many of us are prepared to give first-year students in an introductory course less-nuanced lectures and tutorials than we would to a final year honors class. Perhaps we have to accept curators are the scholars that many of them undoubtedly are, provide them with our contribution to the store of historical knowledge, and allow them to be the judges of their marketplace and its consumers. The end result—as with the occasional noviate student—may not always be what we would ideally like, but at least we are making a contribution to sports history output and possibly pointing someone towards a new way of thinking about an historical situation.

Apart from those few academics gifted enough to write for many audiences, possibly most of us should concentrate on providing the rigorous scholarship on which the museum curators can base their exhibitions. Whether they can be trusted with the material is another matter. Museum curators do not deliberately seek to mislead their visitors. Indeed in my experience they are certainly keen to correct factual errors when they are pointed out and authenticated. Certainly from my own dealings and observations I would place more confidence in curators not to abuse our specialist knowledge when they use it to popularize issues than I would with television producers, journalists and filmmakers.

However, at least in Britain there may be less scholarship for curators to consider. There is a growing concern that in an academic world where financial decisions are increasingly dominated by a science model of research, British academics may become less free to pursue research that does not cover its full economic costs (including overheads) even if some contribution is provided by sponsors be they government institutions, charitable trusts or the universities themselves.[13] Ultimately, the rigor of research in sport history may well become that of rigor mortis.

Or, more likely, given the nature of those who move into the academic world, sport history might become a voluntary spare-time function financed by the academics themselves outside their "professional hours."

When I started work on sports museums in the mid 1990s I believed that they were likely to advance the popularity of sport history. They offered "infotainment," the fun of sport and the results of research. I am now less certain that sports museums are the way forward for sport history, not because of the curators and researchers who strive hard to present new facts to new audiences but because of the environment in which they operate. A major difficulty is the formal and informal pressure that sponsoring bodies can exert on nominally independent institutions. While the museums at Twickenham and Wimbledon seem financially soundly based, thanks to the generosity of the Rugby Football Union and The All-England Club, neither seem too willing to deal with (really) controversial issues. Even at the National Horseracing Museum, which has appeared to be more open in examining the seamier sides of the sport, politics intervened when one of the trustees insisted that a bust of George Wigg be removed from display. Wigg, a life-long socialist, was appointed Head of the Horserace Betting Levy Board and used the position to challenge the racing establishment.

To return to a query that I raised in my previous survey: is there really any reason why sports history exhibitions cannot be good history? There is a place in museums for nostalgia, for devotion to one's sporting heroes, but it need not be devoid of historical accuracy and context. Celebration need not exist without critique. There is a major challenge to be faced in bringing the non-heroic aspects of such social issues of class, age, gender, and ethnicity into the public history domain of sport, one traditionally focused almost exclusively on triumphant ludic personalities and generally referring only to social issues as part of a romantic success story. The transition from academic to public history is a difficult one, but to open the eyes of the public to a different view of sport history can only serve the interests of the profession. As Martin Johnes and Rhiannon Mason point out, museums have the advantage of providing "a multi-sensory context through the combination of material culture, sound, film, photography, oral testimonies and stories told through spatial arrangements." This is more likely to grab the attention of ordinary people than the pages of this journal. More than this, however, museums offer the opportunity for social interaction between visitors and an "exchange of memories and histories between individuals."[14] Surely this is a form of public history that should be nurtured and stimulated. Conversely limiting ourselves to writing solely for our academic peers is an abrogation of our public responsibility as historians.

Epilogue

When redrafting this paper following the comments of the reviewers, I traveled to Newmarket to view the gallery for the first time. Academic commitments had prevented my attendance at the official opening. I was both surprised and disappointed. Within a generally well-laid out and reasonably documented display, I found that several suggested photographs had not been utilized (for cost reasons), that the totalisator contribution had not materialized on the promised scale, and that the sub-theme of problem gambling had been dropped, hopefully only temporarily. The director of the museum and her curator are continuing to collect material for a future enlarged display, but the move to the new premises is now unlikely to take place until 2008.

I had hoped to advance the academic cause of racing history by getting away from lists of winning horses and champion jockeys, the very items on which halls of fame thrive. In this I had some success and managed to introduce issues on the downside of gambling including the gullibility of the public and the relative role of the bookmaker and the totalisator in assisting the fortunes of the sport. Where I joined the ranks of the "also rans" was in failing to avoid the cult of the personality. Each section of the exhibition mentioned particular individuals be they Helen Vernet, the first generally recognized female bookmaker; Phil Bull, the math teacher turned tipster and large-scale bettor; or John McCririck, the television personality who demonstrates the mysteries of "tic tac," the non-verbal betting language.

All that said, in July I also visited the new Australian Racing Museum and Hall of Fame situated on three floors of the upmarket Federation Square area of Melbourne.[15] Financed by unclaimed Totalisator Agency Board winnings and the fractions from rounded-down dividends, it has less financial worries that the Newmarket operation. It also has fewer artifacts. One floor is devoted to the ubiquitous museum shop; another—the penthouse site—to corporate hospitality; and just one to the museum proper: and most of that to infotainment rather than racing history. Need I say which museum I prefer.

Appendix
Punters Large and Small

Panel Text

Punters come in all shapes and sizesy For most betting is a hobby, occasionally profitable; for a few it is a profession; for all it is excitingy Although betting books are very private property and much information is anecdotal, some gamblers have achieved fame through the size of their bettingy During his gambling career, Phil Bull, originator of the Timeform system of rating racehorses, won the present-day equivalent of over £5 milliony Credit betting has always been the province of the more well-to-do (such as Bull became), yet the overwhelming amount of betting on racing takes place in small-scale cash wagers in local betting shopsy

For over a century from 1853 most punters were criminalsy Cash betting away from the racecourse was illegaly This did not stop gamblingy ilkmen, bar staff, shopkeepers and other "bookies' runners" collected bets and passed them on to illegal bookmakers, often with a blind eye being turned by the local policey Eventually, in 1961, the government acknowledged the demand for off-course betting facilities and legalized betting shopsy Initially, they were not allowed television, comfortable seating, refreshments or even a toilet!

Racing has become dependent on the punter in the betting shopy For most of the late twentieth century a major proportion of the industry's income came through the betting levy, paid by the bookmakers usually in proportion to betting turnovery The fixture list became organized so as to provide regular betting for the puntersy In turn the levy kept midweek racing viabley Even though a commercially negotiated agreement between bookmakers and the British

Horseracing Board has now replaced the levy, it is still the money spent in betting shops that determines how much the bookies are prepared to pay.

Panel Illustrations
- Punters with large stomachs and rolls of banknotes (Franklin)
  - Old man on Trundle Hill, Goodwood (Franklin)
  - Small boy with binoculars and racing paper (Franklin)
  - Old lady at Tote (Riddington)
  - Cartoon of punter from Daily Express 16 September 1966 (Ullyett)

Artifacts
Till and security camera (Stanley Leisure)
  The famous Glasgow bookmaker, John Banks, described betting shops as "a license to print moneyy" The tills rang up the profits and the camera protected them.
Ladbroke Shield emblemy (Ladbrokes)
  Labrokes, like other major bookmakers, did not open betting shops immediately when the law allowed but waited to evaluate their potential profitabilityy This emblem came from their first shop, opened in 1964. By 2003 Ladbrokes operated 1,865 licensed betting shops.
1930s mechanical time stamp (Ladbrokes)
  To protect themselves from fraud by gamblers placing their bets after a race had started—even more so after it had finished—credit bookmakers installed mechanical time stamps that their telephonists used to identify when a bet had been madey
Photographs of Duke of Windsor and rsy Simpson and their "no limit" credit account cards (Ladbrokes)
  Bookmakers normally set a limit to the amount of credit that a client could have but in rare cases no such cap was imposedy Such was the case in 1963 when Ladbrokes gave the Duke and Duchess of Windsor "no limit" credit accountsy This may have been for publicity, but the Duke used to bet regularly with the firm when he was Prince of Wales.
Copes Racing Encyclopedias, Rule Books, Diary and Adverts

(National Horseracing Museum)
> Credit Office bookmakers made sure that clients were reminded of their rules and regulations.

Runner's Purse/Clock Bag (Ladbrokes)
> Most illegal bookmakers employed "runners" who received commission on the bets that they collected from pubs, factories and small shops, especially tobacconistsy They were picked up in clock bags, leather purses which when closed set the time on the clock to confirm that the bets had been placed before the race started.

Bookmakers Board with Odds Displayed (National Horseracing Museum)
> Odds declared such as 11–10, 5–4, 13–8 are hangovers from the pre-decimal currency days when eight half-crowns or ten florins (two-shilling pieces) made up a pound and represent the odds to certain proportions of the old currency.

References

✝. This paper was given as a personal position statement to the *State of Play* Conference and has been written up for publication as such. Those who wish a panoply of references are directed to Wray Vamplew, "Facts and Artefacts: Sport Historians and Sports Museums," *Journal of Sport History* 24 (1998): 268282, and a recent study by Martin Johnes and Rhiannon Mason, "Soccer, Public History and the National Football Museum," *Sport in History* 23 (2003): 115–131. The author is grateful for comments from participants at the conference, an anonymous referee of this journal, and Mel Adelman.

1. For information on these persons and other aspects of British racing, readers should consult Wray Vamplew and Joyce Kay, *Encyclopedia of British Horseracing* (London: Routledge, 2005).

2. The answer is "in 1899," Good Friday being the name of a horse that failed to get round the track at Wolverhampton in the post-Christmas Thorneycroft Steeplechase.

3. See Wray Vamplew, "Facts and Artefacts: Sport Historians and Sports Museums," *Journal of Sport History* 24 (1998): 268–282.

4. For a view of nostalgia and sports history see John Nauright, "Nostalgia, Culture and Modern Sport," in *The Essence of Sport*, eds. Verner Møller and John Nauright (Odense: University Press of

Southern Denmark, 2003), 35–50.

5. For a discussion of vanning, see John Tolson and Wray Vamplew, "Facilitation Not Revolution: Railways and British Flat Racing 1830–1914," *Sport in History* 23 (2003): 89–106.

6. Although racism has featured in scholarship on other major British sports such as cricket and football, it has not yet been studied extensively within horseracing. In his recent book, *Horseracing and the British 1919–39* (Manchester, U.K.: Manchester University Press, 2003), Mike Huggins, an academic authority on racing, does remark that in the period he studied gypsies were perceived as a problem, that a number of tipsters were black, and that many leading bookmakers from the East End of London were Jewish. Further he argues that "racing provided employment opportunities for ethnic minorities often marginalized in wider society" (p. 144). On the downside he notes that several of the racetrack gangs that demanded protection money from on-course bookmakers were Italian or Jewish in origin (p. 147). The Bookmakers and Backers Racecourse Protection Association (later known simply as the BPA and with an emphasis on the bookmakers rather than the bettors) was founded as a defensive organisation in 1921 though the protection rackets continued well into the 1930s. Carl Chinn, *Better Betting with a Decent Feller: Bookmakers, Betting and the British Working Class 1750–1990* (London: Harvester Wheatsheaf, 1991), 201–203.

7. Striking though not always accurate. When examined closely, one picture labelled "old man studying the race form" actually showed him reading the football pages in a tabloid newspaper. Another example where perception of illustrative material does not always fit reality was a picture, allegedly of a bookmaker, in John Tyrell's book *Running Racing* (London: Quiller, 1997). Researchers at the London Transport Museum traced the poster to 1920s and offered an original copy. It was called "The Racegoer" but clearly depicted a bookie. It can only be conjectured that the sensitivities of the time allowed London Transport to advertise the racing but not the associated gambling.

8. Mike Huggins, "Lord Bentinck, the Jockey Club and Racing Morality in Nineteenth-Century England," *International Journal of the History of Sport* 13 (1996): 432–444.

9. Wray Vamplew, "Reduced Horse Power: The Jockey Club and the Regulation of British Horseracing," *Entertainment Law* 2 (2003): 94–111.

10. For centuries punters backed their fancies and bookmakers took

their bets, but neither contributed a penny to racing itself. The tote, first used for flat racing at Newmarket and Carlisle on July 2, 1929, was introduced to British racing so that gambling would begin to help finance the sport.

11. Much of the information below comes from interviews (personal and by electronic mail) with the relevant directors and curators. Most of these practise public history, but their qualifications are in museum studies, heritage management or art history. Public history as such is not yet firmly rooted in British universities. Currently, there are five academic courses, all at post-graduate level, available at Bristol, Leicester, Newcastle, Nottingham Trent and Ruskin College, Oxford.

12. I am grateful to Mel Adelman for this apt phrase.

13. For more detail see Higher Education Funding Council, *Transparent Approach to Costing*, 3 vols. (Bristol, U.K.: HEFCE, 2004), volume 3.

14. Martin Johnes and Rhiannon Mason, "Soccer, Public History and the National Football Museum," *Sport in History* 23 (2003): 120–121.

15. For a detailed "description" see the special twelve-page advertising feature "Champions: Australian Racing Museum and Hall of Fame," *Herald Sun* [Melbourne], 1 July 2004.

www.ingramcontent.com/pod-product-compliance
Lightning Source LLC
Chambersburg PA
CBHW061437300426
44114CB00014B/1717